REGNUM STUDIES IN MISSION

Where Is Our God?
African Christianity and Responses to Pandemics

Series Preface

Regnum Studies in Mission are born from the lived experience of Christians and Christian communities in mission, especially but not solely in the fast-growing churches among the poor of the world. These churches have more to tell than stories of growth. They are making significant impacts on their cultures in the cause of Christ. They are producing 'cultural products' which express the reality of Christian faith, hope and love in their societies.

Regnum Studies in Mission are the fruit often of rigorous research to the highest international standards and always of authentic Christian engagement in the transformation of people and societies. And these are for the world. The formation of Christian theology, missiology and practice in the 21st century will depend to a great extent on the active participation of growing churches contributing biblical and culturally appropriate expressions of Christian practice to inform World Christianity.

Where Is Our God? African Christianity and Responses to Pandemics

Edited by

J. Kwabena Asamoah-Gyadu

Mark S. Aidoo

&

Esther E. Acolatse

First published 2024 by Regnum Books International

Regnum is an imprint of the Oxford Centre for Mission Studies
St. Philip and St. James Church
Woodstock Road
Oxford, OX2 6HR, UK
www.regnumbooks.net

British Library Cataloguing in Publication Data
A catalogue record for this book is available from the British Library

ISBN: 979-8-8898-3873-9
eBook ISBN: 979-8-8898-3874-6

Typeset by Words by Design

Cover photo by Tai's Captures on unsplash.com

Distributed by Fortress Press in the US, Canada, India, and Brazil

Contents

Contributors

J. Kwabena Asamoah-Gyadu is the Baëta-Grau Professor of African Christianity and Pentecostal Theology and President, Trinity Theological Seminary, Legon, Ghana. Prof. Asamoah-Gyadu is also the Director of the Seminary's Centre for the Study of Christianity in Africa (CESCA).
Email: kwabena.asamoahgyadu@trinity.edu.gh

Esther E. Acolatse is a professor of Pastoral Theology and World Christianity at Knox College, Toronto School of Theology, University of Toronto, Canada.
Email: esther.acolatse@utoronto.ca

Nimi Wariboko is the Walter G. Muelder Professor of Social Ethics at the School of Theology, Boston University, USA. Email: nimiwari@bu.edu

E. Okelloh Ogera is a senior lecturer at St Paul's University, Kenya.
Email: revokellohogera@gmail.com

Charles Amarkwei is a lecturer in Systematic Theology at the Trinity Theological Seminary, Legon, Ghana. Email: c.amarkwei@trinity.edu.gh

Elizabeth Olufunmilayo Akinbobola is a senior lecturer in Systematic Theology at the Nigerian Baptist Theological Seminary, Ogbomoso, Oyo State, Nigeria. Email: bethjoe2015@gmail.com

Kwaku Boamah is a senior lecturer in Church History at the Department for the study of Religions at the University of Ghana, Legon, Ghana.
Email: kboamahgh2000@yahoo.com

Daniel Nii Aboagye Aryeh is the Rector of Perez University College, Ghana and a senior lecturer in New Testament Studies.
Email: danielniiaboagyearyeh@gmail.com

Mark S. Aidoo is an Associate Professor of Old Testament Studies at Trinity Theological Seminary, Legon, Ghana. Email: ms.aidoo@trinity.edu.gh

Patrick Kofi Amissah is an ordained minister of the Methodist Church Ghana, an adjunct lecturer at Trinity Theological Seminary Legon, and a visiting lecturer in Old Testament Studies at Cardiff University, United Kingdom.
Email: samanpa2010@gmail.com

Abbreviations

5G	Fifth Generation
AICs	African Independent/Initiated/Indigenous Churches
ANE	Ancient Near East
AP	African Pentecostalism
ATR	African Traditional Religions
ATS	African Theological Studies
CESCA	Centre for the Study of Christianity in Africa
ESV	English Standard Version
GTV	Ghana Broadcasting Television
IEC	Independent Evangelical Charismatic
IOT	Internet of Things
LHB/OTS	Library of Hebrew Bible/Old Testament Studies
MRH	Ministry of Repentance and Holiness, Kenya
NDMA	National Drought Management Authority, Kenya
NKJV	New King James Version
NIV	New International Version
NPM	Neo-Prophetic Movements
NRSV	New Revised Standard Version
NT	New Testament
OT	Old Testament
PPE	Personal Protective Equipment
PCCs	Pentecostal/Charismatic Churches
ST	Systematic Theology
TANAK JPS	Hebrew–English Bible
WBC	Word Bible Commentary
Gen.	Genesis
Ex.	Exodus
Lev.	Leviticus
Num.	Numbers
Deut.	Deuteronomy
Judg.	Judges
II Sam.	II Samuel
II Kgs.	II Kings
II Chron.	II Chronicles
Ps.	Psalms
Prov.	Proverbs
Eccl.	Ecclesiastes
Is.	Isaiah
Jer.	Jeremiah
Lam.	Lamentations

Ezek.	Ezekiel
Dan.	Daniel
Hos.	Hosea
Mic.	Micah
Zep.	Zephaniah
Matt.	Matthew
Lk.	Luke
Jn.	John
Rom.	Romans
I Cor.	I Corinthians
II Cor.	II Corinthians
Gal.	Galatians
Eph.	Ephesians
Phil.	Philippians
I Thes.	I Thessalonians
I Tim.	I Timothy
Heb.	Hebrews
Jas.	James
I Pt.	I Peter
Rev.	Revelation

Acknowledgements

The papers in this volume were first delivered – some in person and others virtually – at a conference hosted by the Trinity Theological Seminary, Legon, Ghana, in 2021. This was a year after the outbreak of the COVID-19 pandemic. We thank the Seminary's President and Director of its Centre for the Study of Christianity in Africa (CESCA), Prof. J. Kwabena Asamoah-Gyadu, for providing the opportunity, space, and resources, for the conference and subsequent publication.

Prof. Abimbola A. Adelakun and Seth Akintoye provided extensive editorial and copy-editing support respectively, to bring the publication up to the required standard. The editorial team is grateful to Regnum for accepting to publish the manuscript. We thank them for their patience and meticulousness in the processes towards publication. Any mishaps found in the manuscript are solely the responsibility of the editors.

Preface

This book is a collection of essays focusing on African perspectives of God, Pentecostal Christianity, and approaches to pandemics. African Christians who typically emphasise God's ability to heal all diseases have been greatly challenged in finding answers to pandemics such as COVID-19, HIV/AIDS, yellow fever, Ebola, and polio. Preparing for and responding adequately to the dynamics of pandemics and epidemics in the lives of Africans is crucial due to the severity of an outbreak and how the problem of underdevelopment can exacerbate its effects. Since the majority of Africans believe in God, they approach all issues and problems first from a religious perspective. How God is understood shapes all thinking about religious responses.

The uniqueness of this publication is how it addresses the absence or veiled nature of God in times of such crises. It also looks at how some Christian leaders approached pandemics throughout history, thus adding great insights to the study of African Christianity. The collection presents a balanced theology of God and offers a critique of the overemphasis on God's transcendent nature and omnipotence in African Christianity. The essays help construct an African Christian theological understanding of health and healing as well as a conceptual basis for ministry in times of suffering and evil. They also provide a practical ministry and views from church history that can offer lessons for contemporary African Christianity.

Part one focuses on African Christianity. J. Kwabena Asamoah-Gyadu discusses how pandemics shape science and faith mindsets and how African prophetic Christianity can adapt meaning-making or interpretative frameworks for making sense of the pandemics. He looks at the way the prophetic wave of the Pentecostal/Charismatic streams of Christianity in Africa have responded to COVID-19 as evil, and how the responses sometimes do not make sense, whether in the worlds of religion or science. Nevertheless, the mobilisation of prayer in response to the pandemic ought not to be dismissed as nonsensical as it goes right to the heart of faith in God and how it is articulated for the resistance to evil. Esther E. Acolatse points out that the interpretations from churches and church leaders show a misunderstanding of providence within new African Charismatic Evangelical Christianity, but there are religious-cultural concepts of destiny and free will that are consistent with biblical theological understandings of providence and free will. Her resources to help hone biblical theological ideas may be utilised in tandem with pastoral practice in this pandemic.

Part two focuses on African Pentecostalism and interpretations of pandemics. Nimi Wariboko reflects on the effects of pandemics upon society and how African Pentecostal Christianity likely responds to the incidence of such terrors. He uses three major responses in Christian theological thought: eschatological attitude, apocalyptic attitude, and "closed predicament" to show how the pandemic has demonstrated that Pentecostals are powerless – or their pastors' knowledge to explain, predict, and control events is hollow – because they are trapped in apocalyptic thinking. E. Okelloh Ogera argues that in order to make meaning of COVID-19, many prophets within the Neo-Prophetism in African Christianity, especially in Kenya, have been propagating an apocalyptic theology as a way to encourage their adherents to sustain spiritual exercises. Charles Amarkwei also interrogates how a philosophical understanding of the relationship between science and eschatology could go a long way to dispel the spread of conspiracy theories undercutting the proper management of the COVID-19 pandemic. Elizabeth Olufunmilayo Akinbobola highlights human suffering in the African context and provides a pastoral response to understanding this suffering from God's omnipotence.

Part three reflects on some of the approaches used in addressing pandemics. Kwaku Boamah draws on case studies from the Early Church during the outbreak of smallpox or the Plague of Galen in 165 AD and measles in 251 AD in the early Roman Empire. The early Christian reaction to these pandemics suggests possibilities for innovation and theological reframing in times of pandemics. Daniel Nii Aboagye Aryeh focuses on the need for African Pentecostals to adapt/adopt private means of mediating the divine during pandemics using online and media space to propound a theory of "space and divine" in the Ghanaian Christian context.

Part four focuses on the Bible, pandemics, and healing. Mark S. Aidoo critically reflects on Psalm 102 from an African perspective and explores God's faithfulness amid the sufferings of the righteous. Patrick Kofi Amissah's chapter evaluates the extent to which biblical examples of hygiene, social distancing, and quarantine as preventive measures against infectious diseases offer hope during a pandemic. In all, a theologically relevant approach to interpreting pandemics is needed to make Christianity relevant in the African context.

A renewed perspective of God will shape Christianity on the path of healing and reconciliation and affirm the relevance of Christianity in Africa. With these wide-ranging perspectives, the book will be useful for students in higher education and the Christian church.

The world would seem to be moving on very quickly, with some even now speaking of a post-pandemic world. However, the last century has had a lot to teach humanity about how the world and all the happenings within it might not necessarily be within human control as the worlds of medical science and technology would have us believe. The outbreak of COVID-19 shook the socio-economic and political worlds, medical science, and technology to their foundations. It also pushed religious faith, especially the gospel of prosperity propagated by certain waves of Christianity, to its limits, with many of its ardent proponents asking, "Where is our God?" In the face of evil of any kind, Africans have found religious faith and believe a source of "explanation, prediction, and control," and it is hoped that this volume would help us articulate a religious understanding of health, wealth, and evil, and the impact they have on our common existence and humanity against the backdrop of faith in the sovereignty of God.

Where Is Our God? African Christianity, Coronavirus, and Prophetism in Times of Panic

J. Kwabena Asamoah-Gyadu

Introduction

In this chapter, we offer some thoughts regarding where God has been in what has been going on during the outbreak of the coronavirus pandemic and how African Christians have responded to it. This chapter gives disproportionate attention to the prophetic wave of the Pentecostal/Charismatic streams of Christianity in Africa and their responses to COVID-19. In other words, we explore African Christian responses to a pandemic whose effects overwhelmed both the worlds of religion and science. In *Powerful Devices*, Abimbola Adelakun (writing under COVID-19 lockdown conditions), talks about how many of the discussions and news reports pervading the social space, which were made by people equally stuck at home during the pandemic, betrayed the fears and insecurities "about the spectral forces and modernity that threaten collective survival."[1]

In dealing with the COVID-19 pandemic, medical scientists explained it to be the result of the spread of coronavirus and prescribed vaccination and non-medical observances such as wearing masks and washing hands. Despite these remedies, the public responses ranged from deploying conspiracy theories to using performance prayers, fasting, and prophetic declarations to deal with this perplexing public health issue. Since the beginning of March 2020 when the world started taking the outbreak of COVID-19 more seriously, prayers and sermons in churches have been directed at dealing with it. Pentecostal/Charismatic-style warfare prayers were quickly deployed, based on the discourses of supernatural evil that accompanied the public explanations of the sources of the pandemic. The tendency of spiritual warriors to "vigorously use social media to organise prayer assemblies against the kingdom of darkness" has been on full display during these pandemic times.[2]

Studies on religion and society in Africa underscore that Africans search for God in crises. The sensational nature of the COVID-19 pandemic, Adelakun avers, offered the opportunity for spiritual warriors, whose stock-in-trade consists of verbally violent assaults on supernatural evil, to "enact their impulse

---

[1] Abimbola A. Adelakun, *Powerful Devices: Prayer and the Political Praxis of Spiritual Warfare* (New Brunswick: Rutgers University Press, 2023), p. xi.

[2] Adelakun, *Powerful Devices*, p. x.

to disestablish on a grand global scale by tackling science-based and global political institutions."[3] For example, some of those who adopted religious responses during the pandemic resorted to 2 Chronicles 7:14 in which God promises healing for the land, if "those who are called by my name" repent of their sins and call upon him. There were prayer rallies across Africa, with some sponsored by governments, that used this text from the book of 2 Chronicles as the rallying call.

Except for some cases, such as with Pastor Chris Oyakhilome of the Christ Embassy Church and Bishop David Oyedepo of Winners' Chapel, who resorted to conspiracy theories, African religious leaders did not generally discount the importance of science in explaining and dealing with the outbreak of COVID-19. Bishop Oyedepo, for example, saw the pandemic as "a conspiratorial scheme targeted against the church" to prevent it from carrying out its divinely ordained mission.[4] There were powerful politicians, such as Tanzania's late leader, John Magufuli, who, following President Donald J. Trump of the USA, joined the conspiratorial discourses on COVID-19. However, on the African Christian front, the consensus was that this public health tragedy called for prayer and fasting at all levels of society. Ghana, from where most of my case studies are drawn, for example, is a largely religious country. With an official figure of a little over 70 per cent claiming a Christian heritage, faith has been at the forefront of the religious fight against coronavirus.

In Africa, the historic mission churches are much older and doctrinally much more well-defined. However, when it comes to spiritual responses to public crises, it is the more Pentecostal/Charismatic streams of Christianity that usually speak the language of the supernatural and call for prayerful interventions. This stems from their stronger religious belief in spiritual causality regarding the sources of misfortune, calamity, and evil. At the height of the pandemic, virtually all the churches were involved in the search for solutions from the supernatural realm, and the Pentecostal/Charismatic leaders with their better media networks and ministries proved more effective in that wise. The one word that perhaps captured the reality of the outbreak of this terrible disease is "evil" and it has been used worldwide by both religious and secular sources to characterise the reality of the effects of the coronavirus pandemic.

From a Christian viewpoint, "evil" is any phenomenon – whether natural or supernatural, physical, or spiritual – that negatively disrupts the normal/ideal order of creation and the flow of human life as God intends. In the absence of evil, life goes well, feels well, and does well, and that is the definition of human flourishing.[5] Christopher J.H. Wright explains evil as "the total negation of all that God is and wishes, hostile to the life, blessing, and goodness that God

---

[3] Adelakun, *Powerful Devices*, p. xii.

[4] Adelakun, *Powerful Devices*, p. 81.

[5] Andrew Briggs and Michael J. Reiss, *Human Flourishing: Scientific Insight and Spiritual Wisdom in Uncertain Times* (Oxford: Oxford University Press, 2021), p. 24.

creates."[6] Evil is a setback to human flourishing and negates the abundance of life that Jesus promises to those who believe in Him: evil comes to steal, kill, and destroy.

In contrast, Jesus grants fullness of life (Jn. 10:10). The characterisation of the COVID-19 pandemic in terms of supernatural evil could be understood against the backdrop of Pentecostal/Charismatic discourses on prosperity in which the will of God for the believer is nothing short of full health and wealth. Thus, any phenomenon that eviscerates the spirit of prosperity in human life is considered an evil that must be exterminated in the name and through the power of Jesus Christ. It is therefore not surprising that, at the heart of the pandemic, "power in the blood of Jesus" was constantly invoked to curse an evil virus that was considered akin to some of the diseases that broke out among the Ancient Israelites in the Hebrew scriptures.

A Spiritual Virus

Bishop David Oyedepo adopted biblical language in referring to the outbreak of COVID-19 as "noisome pestilence" that would be spiritually crushed.[7] Another of the African Christian Charismatic figures who framed the COVID-19 pandemic with biblical idioms is the Archbishop Nicholas Duncan-Williams of Action Chapel International. He defined the virus in spiritual terms as follows:

> The coronavirus is a name, a person without body and in the name of Jesus, as we bow our knees and we pray, this plague, pestilence and virus will bow the knee and stand down and go back to where it came from.[8]

With that, the Charismatic archbishop set the tone for a spiritual onslaught against a virus akin to an evil spirit in the Pentecostal/Charismatic worldview. In Charismatic religious thought, to borrow Wright's terms, "evil is uncompromisingly rejected and denounced, and categorically doomed to ultimate destruction and eradication."[9] In the African context, where the reality of evil is part of the general worldview of life, much energy and spiritual resources are dedicated to fighting and resisting evil. The ritual contexts created for the denunciation of evil include performance prayers such as hooting at, rejecting, cancelling, and verbally assaulting and resisting the presence of evil in society and human life.

---

[6] Christopher J.H. Wright, *The God I Don't Understand: Reflections on Tough Questions of Faith* (Grand Rapids, MI: Zondervan, 2008), p. 58.
[7] Adelakun, *Powerful Devices*, p. 79.
[8] Nasiba Yakubu, "Duncan-Williams Declares Thirty-Days Fasting, Prayers Against Coronavirus," *My Joy Online*, 16th March 2020 [Available at: https://myjoyonline.com/coronavirus-duncan-williams-declares-30-days-fasting-prayers-against-coronavirus/], [Last accessed: 19th July 2023].
[9] Wright, *The God I Don't Understand*, p. 58.

In the context of the Genesis story of the Fall, the onset of evil is depicted as alienation from the Creator, God. Thus, from a biblical viewpoint, the serpent serves as a source of evil by deceiving Adam and Eve into disobeying God, unleashing evil in the world. Jesus picks up the same theme when he says in John 10:10 that the devil does not come but to steal, kill, and destroy and that he, Jesus, comes to give life and give it in abundance. That which is in the world to "steal, kill and destroy" is that which causes evil. Evil dehumanises and impoverishes and, within the context of this chapter, evil would be a counterpoint to Pentecostal/Charismatic prosperity preaching on health and wholeness. The COVID-19 pandemic stretched the prosperity discourse by putting its central claims under great strain. In many cases, it simply did not make sense that the producers and consumers of prosperity teachings were confused. The coronavirus presented to prosperity thinkers a major pastoral problem because its worldview simply came unstuck and that is why the virus has become, for many, the face of evil.

We do not have just one source of evil. Evil intrudes into human life in many ways or through a combination of factors and behaviours. Evil could come through natural disasters, wrongful personal and communal choices, the wickedness and carelessness of others, and sometimes, from a biblical viewpoint, by hostile spiritual powers such as what Paul refers to as "principalities and powers" in Ephesians 6:12. Evil comes through human participation in "unfruitful works of darkness" and Paul warns the recipients of his letter not to participate in them, but instead to "expose them" (Eph. 5:11). In the African Pentecostal/Charismatic worldview, dealing with the coronavirus as Archbishop Duncan-Williams did is problematising the disease as a spiritual entity that ought to be approached; a supernatural evil that needed to be dealt with decisively through invocations of the name of Jesus and the power of the Holy Spirit.

The Sovereignty of God and the Persistence of Evil

What makes evil a problem relates to why it comes, in spite of our faith in the sovereignty of God. It is that belief that underlies the theology of the Book of Job. The book responds to the question: "Where is our God in whom we trust?" Obviously, it is precisely because God Himself was aware of this human need for Him in times of distress that He inspired Isaiah to write:

> When you pass through the waters, I will be with you;
> And through the rivers, they
> Shall not overwhelm you;
> when you walk through the fire
> you shall not be burned,
> and the flame shall not consume you.
> (Is. 43:2)

Where is our God? The word of God in Isaiah quoted here might be precisely the sort of assurance that nations and people need at a time when even the most powerful and wealthy of nations are struggling to cope with the devastating effects of a virus that has been described as *novel* because its nature and behaviour patterns are unknown.

Religion and Social Media

When the coronavirus broke out at the beginning of 2020, the world initially did not know much about this novel virus. Leaders of powerful nations like President Donald J. Trump of the USA downplayed and racialised the disease while some religious leaders turned it into a chance to be frivolous (or even creative). On the Christian front, Pastor Chris Oyakhilome, an influential Charismatic leader in global Pentecostalism, was adamant that the outbreak of COVID-19 was fake. Western powers, he claimed, were using the lockdown periods to clandestinely install a 5G intrusive media technological network for whatever evil purposes they had against Africa, thus incorporating conspiracy theories circulating on social media into liturgy. Across the continent, some Christians and pastors who publicly claimed that their Pentecostal faith insulated them against the effects of the virus succumbed to it and died. To that end, African readings of the Bible at the height of the pandemic changed from mere defiance to focusing on those parts that promise divine protection, health, and vitality such as Psalm 91:1-3:

> You who live in the shelter of the Most High, who abide in the shadow of the Almighty, will say to the Lord, "My refuge and my fortress; my God in whom I trust." For he will deliver you from the snare of the fowler and from the deadly pestilence.

The mention of deliverance from the "deadly pestilence" struck the right chord among many Africans because a virus that had seen the powerful nations of the North, with all their sophisticated medical systems, unable to help ought not to be underestimated, supernaturally speaking. In the African context, when life is threatened or weakened, prayer is most abundant as a means of restoring wholeness and balance in life.[10]

The public discourses on the virus were that it could have resulted from an ambitious scientific experiment gone awry, a deliberate attempt by someone to disrupt the joyful flow of human life, or the unintended consequence of our abuse of the environment and lack of attention to creation care. At the bottom, however, it shows that evil is part of the reality of our world, and we must deal with it using a powerful counterforce. The world over, many are desperate to see God's intervention and it is in such times of desperation that humanity also becomes most vulnerable. Humans clutch at straws in times of distress without much thought because we lose the capacity for sound judgement. At such times, even straws become sources of hope.

---

[10] Laurenti Magesa, *African Religion: The Moral Traditions of Abundant Life* (New York: Orbis Books, 2014), p. 195.

Vulnerability brings exploitation and we see this in both the economic sphere and sadly, in religious spaces too, with all kinds of prophetic claims being made about the source and meaning of the dreadful situation on our hands. In online marketplaces, an interminable number of books and resources were published overnight to account for the root of the disease. For African preachers who had already made online marketplaces their ministry, a global sensation like the pandemic was the chance to aggressively market prophesies and prayers to combat the disease. Even those unopposed to scientific methods thought they needed something more. Most people of faith turned to God. In Pentecostal/Charismatic preaching, the reason for the outbreak of COVID-19 was even overstretched to include the promotion of alternative sexual lifestyles in contravention of the teachings of the scripture. In other words, for many who were so inclined, the outbreak of COVID-19 amounted to God's chastisement on a world that had rejected His Word.

The Prophetic in Times of Crisis

Several religious messages and short videos of a religious nature circulated on social media platforms at the onset of the COVID-19 pandemic. Many of these videos and pictorial images were meant to be educative or informative, or, in most cases when they targeted Christians, to reassure of God's ability to deliver His people in times of crisis. One of such images combined the Old Testament story of the blood of the Passover lamb and the New Testament idea of the blood of Jesus as protective of God's people. We see in that picture an image of a compliant Hebrew man painting the blood of his Passover lamb on the lintels of a closed door. The words accompanying the image are: "The blood of Jesus protects our family against COVID-19."

In African Christianity, invoking the blood of Jesus in times of crisis is quite common because it fits the biblical narrative and the traditional narrative of blood as a potent means of cleansing evil. People invoke the blood of Christ all the time in the process of cursing evil. It is thus striking that among the divine instruments which have been invoked in the spiritual fight against the coronavirus, passages from Exodus 12, the Epistle to the Hebrews, and Revelation, which point to the potency and therapeutic properties of the blood of the Lamb, feature extensively in the responses.

On the evening of Saturday 21st March 2020, I received one such video clip that, instead of finding solace in the prophetic as people are wont to do in times of crisis, challenged it instead. The clip came from a Ghanaian friend resident in the USA whom we shall call "Anaa." Anaa's video was a clip featuring a young woman chastising Ghana's prophets for their inability to foretell the outbreak of the coronavirus. "You are all false prophets," the young woman says in the video, "and the Lord has exposed the falsity of your prophetic predictions." The video continued to address the prophets directly:

> You see how you have all lost your prophetic voices in these times of crisis? Where is the God that you claim reveals to you the deaths of prominent citizens during Watchnight Services? It was only a few months ago that we celebrated Watchnight Services and God did not reveal to you that some two months after that a virus was going to wreak such havoc on Ghana and the world? You must be ashamed of yourselves, you false and dubious prophets…

To place this prophetic chastisement into some perspective, Ghana has in the last few years seen the rise of several Charismatic Christian figures claiming a prophetic call and mandate from God. For prophets who claim the ability to see into the future to have completely missed the pandemic, and be just as stumped by the disease as anyone, put the prophetic unction in a state of crisis.

The prophetic ministry has always been a key feature of Christian religious innovation in Africa. This has been so since the early 20th century with the rise of the Aladura movement and Spiritual churches. Indeed, the first set of these churches partly emerged as a response to the 1918 influenza pandemic that similarly killed so many people around the world. David K. Patterson, for instance, reports that during the 1918 influenza epidemic, some saw "the Hand of God at work in the epidemic" and "an open-air prayer meeting" was called to deal with its effects.[11] Lamin Sanneh wrote about how, in this worldwide influenza epidemic, an indigenous Christian prophet from Ijebu-Ode in Nigeria, Joseph B. Shadare, formed a prayer group that offered "spiritual help" against the plague.[12] The founder of the Aladura movement was Joseph Babalola and, as Sanneh notes, his role in the movement was an illustration of the crucial place that prophets occupied in the lives of the independent church movement. In his words: "The prophet channels the forces of healing into the community, presides over the awakening when it arrives, and sustains prayer as the essential supply-line of the struggle."[13]

The early 20th century African prophets engaged aggressively with the realities of the supernatural world. They contested the reality of traditional gods and their functionaries, likening them to the prophets of Baal in the Old Testament. In terms of crisis (such as drought) and for the influenza outbreak, they relied on the power of prayer and invoked the power of the Holy Spirit to deal with the situation. Prayer in this movement had a very existential focus because it was targeted at contemporary developments of evil in the lives of people and communities as Sanneh argues from his study of the Aladura:

> It is clear that the focal point of the life and practice of the group was prayer. Prayer was understood in two specific ways. First, it was the means whereby the individual received certain benefits, including the fulfilment of wishes and desires, and secondly, it was the obtaining of guidance. In this way personal need and control,

---

[11] K. David Patterson, "The Influenza Epidemic of 1918–19," *The Journal of African History*, 24(4), (1983), p. 489.

[12] Lamin Sanneh, *West African Christianity: The Religious Impact* (Maryknoll, NY: Orbis Books, 1983), p. 184.

[13] Sanneh, *West African Christianity*, p. 195.

which used to form a prominent part of traditional religious life and practice, acquired a new lease of life in a Christian setting.[14]

Scholars in contemporary expressions of African Christianity would not be surprised at the re-emergence of the prophetic in the closing decades of the 20th century. Prophetism is a perennial phenomenon of African life, wrote Christian G. Baëta, and whether in relation to or independently of events or developments in society, the individual endowed with Charismatic abilities is likely to have influence in such situations.[15] The powers traditionally accredited to such prophets, Baëta noted, include such endowments as the possession of a sense of divine vocation, healing, inner illumination, revealing hidden things, predicting the future, and cursing and blessing effectually.[16]

The prophetic was a perennial phenomenon of African religious life because parts of it resonate with African religious sensibilities. When epidemics strike or people find their vitality waning and they lack any natural explanations for those situations, supernatural evil is suspected. Africa's prophets compete with traditional diviners and priests for clients looking for supernatural interventions. The constant search for supernatural powers of protection and for dealing with evil has been cited as a critical reason for the popularity of new religious movements in Africa that "promise original solutions to contemporary problems" and the prophetic phenomenon belongs to this category.[17] In Pentecostal/Charismatic theology, the prophetic is highly regarded as one of the key gifts of the Spirit and Paul, in I Corinthians 14, isolates prophecy as a "greater gift" of the Spirit as compared to the many others that the Holy Spirit inspires in God's people.

In both popular and academic discourses today, the activities of such prophets have been discussed with the general feeling being that most of them engage in these prophetic acts for the pecuniary advantages they bring. On many media platforms, the whole culture of the prophetic has, in Africa, become the subject of coarse joking and suspicion due to the abuses to which it has been subjected by those who claim to possess the gift. The prophetic ministry is quite popular within the contemporary African religious space not simply because of its resonances with the Old Testament prophetic ministry in particular, but also because it seems to respond well to the African worldview, in which calamitous events and misfortunes are usually explained in terms of the works of evil spirits, witches, and demons. To that end, the coronavirus has been imagined in sermons as an evil spirit unleashed on the world by the devil and it is only in the power of the resurrection that it can be defeated.

---

[14] Sanneh, *West African Christianity*, p. 191.

[15] Christian G. Baëta, *Prophetism in Ghana: A Study of Some Spiritual Churches* (London: SCM, 1962), p. 6.

[16] Baëta, *Prophetism in Ghana*, p. 7.

[17] Stephen Ellis and Gerrie ter Haar, *Worlds of Power: Religious Thought and Political Practice in Africa* (London: Hurst and Company, 2004), p. 95.

Mystical Causality and the Reality of Evil

In this African supernatural worldview, things do not merely happen by chance. Virtually everything, especially misfortune, has a cause and is usually explained in terms of curses, the work of enemies such as envious relations or colleagues, etc. Generally, we live in a society of mistrust in Africa because of these beliefs. When the Bible is used selectively to justify them, as the prophets usually do, they are very persuasive and convincing. A large majority of clients who attend any of the many prayer vigils that abound in Ghana, or any of the prayer camps, do so because they believe their problems are spiritual and not natural. This is where the prophets fit into the puzzle. Claiming supernatural ability to diagnose spiritual problems and deploy the power of God in fixing them, they have become some of the most sought-after Christian functionaries within Ghana's very pluralistic religious marketplaces.

There is a very strong connection between the prophetic ministry and the deployment of Charismatic ability for financial gain. On a continent where the most stable businesses and personal economies could wobble with the slightest uncertainty or with changes in political terrains, there is a high level of vulnerability in domestic, private, public, socio-economic, and corporate affairs for which most people would like to depend on some supernatural power for support. There are market women, public servants, politicians, and businessmen and women who even, like some of the kings of Israel, engage personal prophets who visit their homes and offices to pray, prophesy, decree, and declare all kinds of blessings upon them. The idea is that, for prosperity and flourishing to occur, the activities of the agents of evil – forces of darkness – have to be spiritually tamed if not exterminated in the name and blood of Jesus.

Crisis and Vulnerability

In Ghana, the liminal hours between 10pm and midnight every 31st December offer prophets a window of opportunity to make all kinds of declarations and predictions for the ensuing year. The prophets have become notorious for predicting calamity for key public figures. People are at their most vulnerable selves within this period and, in the run-up to 31st December, large billboards appear in public places as pastors and prophets promise people nights in which all their problems and failures will end. On that "crossover" night, God goes into another gear as He descends at the command of prophets to deal with the enemies of prosperity and release powerful blessings meant to propel people into success in the following year.

Although the Watch Night Service is a Wesleyan legacy, the Charismatics – with their more empowering, dynamic, engaging, and spiritually charged services – have become more visible and attractive as a place of supernatural succour for the vulnerable of society in these times. It is popularly believed that these predictions, especially when they come on the eve of a new year, are a form of prophetic blackmail meant to instil fear and panic in important personalities and their loved ones. In their panic, some are tempted to run to these prophets to seek help overturning the evil that may be awaiting them in the ensuing year and of course, the consultations are not free, even if not explicitly stated as such. The material interests of the prophets play a significant role in these targeted prophetic revelations. Some have called the bluff of the prophets, but others have fallen victim to their claims.

The Watch Night or Crossover Service – also dubbed Exodus, Passover, and several other designations that allude to the Bible – is usually a night of resolutions and declarations. Most of these declarations may be of such general tone that anyone can identify with them:

> In the year […] I prophesy that you shall not die; I decree and declare that your business shall not fail; anyone looking for your downfall will be surprised; for the Lord will lift up your fortunes; you shall be the head and not the tail; money and wealth will chase you; you shall give birth to that baby; that business will not go down; anyone sitting on your international travel will die and you will receive your visa; promotion is coming; you will trample on your enemies and those who hate you will live to see your elevation; and so on and so forth.

Responses of "amen" and "I receive it" accompany the declarations and of course, they are in order. Who does not want to prosper and flourish in this life? A theological examination of "decreeing and declaring" in Charismatic Christianity is beyond the scope of this chapter. However, it is worth pointing out that these claims and appropriations of the "promises of God in Christ" constitute practical outworking of the notion of empowerment that comes with the experience of the Spirit of God in Charismatic Christianity.

In historic mission church spirituality, we come to God as "miserable offenders" or "unworthy sinners" looking for forgiveness and therefore one has to literally plead with God for His grace and abandon things to His will. It is not so with Charismatic Christianity, which theologically is founded on the belief that believers possess authority in Christ to defeat the powers of evil and forge ahead in life. In that context, prayer is expected to be powerful; that is, assertive and authoritative, and the believer has the right to claim things from God. In other words, whereas the Charismatic leader prays standing on the authority of God as a fundamental right in Christ, the historic mission pastor prays in tones that demonstrate that we are at the mercy of God. If the theology of Charismatic prayer is founded on a "name-it-and-claim-it" approach to God, prayer in the historic mission church tradition – which is often written to be read anyway – is based on "pleading with God for His mercy in time of need."

This categorisation of prayer is not absolute because there are variations in between. The religious terrain has changed. Now there are historic mission church pastors virtually mimicking the modus operandi of their more Charismatic compatriots. The Charismatic prayer culture is generally based on one's perceived authority in Christ, whereas the historic mission approach God as humble supplicants, sinners, in need of help. One way to understand the difference is that, normally in a typical Charismatic service, there is little room for the public confession of sin. In the others, prayers of adoration and thanksgiving would almost always be followed by prayers of repentance for sins of commission and omission. The Charismatic Christian comes to the throne of God as one who has authority in Christ, but the average historic mission church Christian comes as a sinner looking for forgiveness.

Evil and the Prophetic

We now return to the content of the video to which we referred earlier. The chastisement that the prophets of Ghana received from the woman in the video reminds me of some words spoken by Amos concerning prophetic revelations and messages:

> Is a trumpet blown in a city,
> and the people are not afraid?
> Does disaster befall a city,
> unless the Lord has done it?
> Surely the Lord does nothing,
> without revealing his secret
> to his servants the prophets.
> The lion has roared;
> who will not fear?
> The Lord has spoken;
> who can but prophesy?
> (Amos 3:6-8).

The trademark of the prophetic ministry of Amos was his preaching against social injustice. The prophet of social justice worked with a theological mindset in which calamity would come upon the nation because of sin; the pursuit of wealth and power at the expense of the weak and vulnerable of society. When the trumpet was blown in the city, it was usually a sign that the nation was being readied for battle. Here in Amos, the blowing of the trumpet was being used as an indication that something had gone horribly wrong, and God was ready to visit His judgement on those who were culpable. But God is also a God of love who does not like people to perish and so He gives sinners the chance to repent and return to Him (Lam. 3:40).

It is precisely because the Lord likes to reveal His mind and give His people the chance to repent that He reveals looming disasters to His prophets. The Book of Joel provides a classic example of this situation, where the nation is called to repent so that God may avert the looming disaster of the invasion of locusts that were decimating agricultural produce, with the consequence of drought and hunger. In Jeremiah 23, we know what the prophet must do to receive such insights from God. The prophets, that is, the genuine ones are those who have been in council with God:

> Thus says the Lord of hosts: Do not listen to the words of the prophets who prophesy to you; they are deluding you. They speak visions of their own minds, not from the mouth of the Lord [...] For who has stood in the council of the Lord so as

to see and to hear his word? Who has given heed to his word so as to proclaim it? (Jer. 23:16, 18).

These are rhetorical questions directed at those who claim to be prophesying the word of the Lord but who, in fact, have not received any word from Him. They have not been in "council" with God and therefore, these false prophets have no word of "counsel" from Him: "But if they had stood in my council, then they would have proclaimed my words to my people…" (Jer. 23:22). What the false prophets speak, therefore, are delusions of their own minds. In short, they are false prophets, as Jeremiah explains:

I did not send the prophets,
yet they ran;
I did not speak to them,
yet they prophesied.
(Jer. 23:21).

Genuine prophets wait upon God – presumably in prayer, fasting, and holiness of life – so that, as vessels separated from what may be considered ignoble and contaminating, God would speak to them and they – as His mouthpieces – would deliver that message to God's people. That is what Peter explains to us in II Peter 1:20-21:

First of all you must understand this, that no prophecy of scripture is a matter of one's own interpretation, because no prophecy ever came by human will, but men and women moved by the Holy Spirit spoke from God.

Amos 3:7 is critical of the issues that we are trying to interrogate here: "Surely the Lord does nothing, without revealing his secret to his servants the prophets."

The theology about the sovereignty of God is that there is nothing that happens outside of His knowledge in the universe. God is not just omnipotent, but He is also omnipresent and omniscient. Against this backdrop, it means God knew that early in the year 2020, the coronavirus accompanied by the disease COVID-19 would afflict His world and its effects would be felt everywhere, including Ghana. The effects of the outbreak of COVID-19 on lives, businesses, education, travel, politics, health institutions, social activities, and church life cannot be quantified. There is great consternation everywhere and, for most Christian preachers, Psalm 91 has offered the appropriate scriptural text around which to galvanise prayer and claim the promises of God. Psalm 91:3-4 in particular has proved useful:

For he will deliver you from the snare of the fowler
and from the deadly pestilence;
he will cover you with his pinions,
and under his wings you will find refuge;
his faithfulness is a shield and buckler.

In this psalm, the promises of God for His people in times of crisis is a place of refuge. What makes it attractive in times of disaster such as the outbreak of COVID-19 is the references to "snare of the fowler," "deadly pestilence," and the fact that those in trouble will find "refuge" under the wings of the Almighty God.

So clearly, the world had a disaster on its hands and if, as Amos prophesied, God does not do anything without revealing His secrets to his prophets, then how come the prophets had no foreknowledge? This question raises critical issues, as Anaa pointed out in her video. What has gone out in the name of the "prophetic" in contemporary Christianity has often been nothing but an exercise in the pursuit of religious fame, power, money, and celebrity status through the exploitation of the insecurities and vulnerabilities of a general public already trying to plumb their way through the quagmires of life. There are many genuine prophets around, but among the wheat we also have prophetic tares that may even be counted as sources of evil because, like the serpent of Eden, they deceive and mislead people. Persons who pursue Christian ministry for sordid gain, whether they use the tag prophet or not, belong to this category of false prophets who exploit the insecurities of others for selfish ends. In a sense, we go through the valley of the shadow of death daily and what we require are genuine men and women of God who will bring a word in season and out of season from Him.

What are Christians required to do at this time? First and foremost, we have to trust the sovereignty of God, which means to have the confidence to defer to His wisdom in our time of need and distress, as we read in Psalm 46:10: "Be still and know that I am God." Second, a crisis of any sort (as with persecutions recorded in the New Testament) calls for fervency in prayer and spirituality. Indeed, it is through faithful prayer that we demonstrate belief and confidence in God's sovereignty. That is because prayer symbolises dependence on a power beyond the human realm and in the Christian context, this is God and the Father of our Lord Jesus Christ. Third, we must be orderly and disciplined. Faith must be backed by wisdom. In Ghana, a pastor was fined for defying the authorities to hold church services, claiming that not holding meetings was a sign of lack of faith in God's salvation. Such a Christian leader simply fails to look at things from the viewpoint of others. "Our help comes from the Lord" (Ps. 121), yes, but he also grants us the wisdom to determine how to conduct ourselves in the face of evil, especially when it is one in which obeying authority would help to minimise the pain of other people.

Fourth, in the face of evil, we need to practise hospitality. The Samaritan committed resources to help a victim of armed robbery that he did not know. One of the standout stories of the COVID-19 outbreak is the Italian Catholic priest who donated his ventilator to a younger victim of the disease whom he did not know and passed on just days after this act of Christian charity. Father Giuseppe Berardelli, 72, died in a hospital in Lovere, Bergamo – one of the worst-hit cities in Italy. In times of evil, we look after each other's interests and, if one may apply this directly to the prophetic ministry under scrutiny, we need to avoid using deceptive declarations and revelations that put fear and panic into people. What we need is prophetic leadership that knows the Lord and not people who masquerade as God's prophets. Like the false prophets in Jeremiah 23, they only prophesy with their own material interests in mind. Finally, in the face of evil, we must constantly find out what lessons we learn for future guidance.

Conclusion: Where Is Our God?

This is a question that God Himself asked, when Jesus cried on the cross: "My God, my God, why has thou forsaken me?" We could consider that cry of desperation the equivalent of Job's question in his time of crisis. Evil is not of God and it does not have a place in God's creation. In the words of Wright, evil has no validity, no truth, no integrity. The Bible's general affirmation is that God is good, all-loving, and all-powerful, and yet it still does not deny the reality of evil. We find evil at the beginning of creation and we find it in the life of Christ. Evil is an intruder, He says, and it is there to be resisted and expelled.[18] God demonstrated that when He resisted evil and proved that it must never be allowed to have the last word.

When we understand certain types of evil, it helps us to deal with it. For example, the devil serially tried to use an insider to access Jesus. He first tried to use Peter to get Jesus not to travel to Jerusalem. When that failed after Jesus gave Peter a sharp rebuke, the devil turned to Judas. Judas was never able to deal with the "demons" of greed and covetousness in his life. The enemy pounced on those weaknesses and used him to reach Jesus. Consequently, Jesus was arrested, humiliated, and crucified, but the supremacy of God was to come to the fore shortly thereafter, when He rose again from the dead. Just when the devil thought he had been victorious, Jesus rose triumphantly from the tomb. In raising Jesus from the dead, "we have God's word and deed that he will be victorious in the struggle against all that frustrates his desire," as Wright quotes John Calvin.[19]

Similarly, the coronavirus, wherever it came from, can never have the last word. This world remains God's world. If the world has problems, they have come from the choices we have made, sometimes even arrogating to human achievements things that ought to be explained in terms of God's power and sovereignty. The mere fact that Jesus included a line in the Lord's Prayer that says "deliver us from evil" presupposed that God knew that, although He meant us to enjoy creation, we do not have to take our place in it for granted and live as if there is no tomorrow and as if we are not accountable to anyone. This is where I suppose the church in Africa may need to get its theology of the prophetic right. Paul outlines three main purposes for the gift of prophecy in the church. They are for the up-building, encouragement, and consolation of the community of faith (I Cor. 14:3). Those who speak in tongues, Paul says, "build up themselves," but those who prophesy, "build up the church" (I Cor. 13:4).

In other words, the prophetic is a Spirit-inspired word for God's people, but given its religious focus, it comes in quite relevantly in times of crisis when

---

[18] Wright, *The God I Don't Understand*, p. 42.

[19] Quoted in Wright, *The God I Don't Understand*, p. 55.

everyone may be asking, "Where is our God?" Getting the message to the congregation becomes so critical that Paul even warns that there may not be the need to utter the prophetic if it comes in tongues and there is no one to interpret it for their benefit (I Cor. 14:5). In responding to the question of "where is our God?" I would like to quote the words of Anaa, the Christian woman who has had to live with a difficult medical condition in recent years and who sent the video I referred to at the beginning:

> … I feel that this whole virus-scare has put the whole world in a position to feel a little bit of what I feel – where is our God when "none of this" is our doing, the constant fighting of a battle, yet waking daily to one, the fear of death yet the bravery of an effort to ward it off, the refraining from people because your immunity is low yet finding it difficult to explain without being standoffish, the constant prayer for a breakthrough in medicine to grant you freedom yet obviously stagnant, constantly all ears for good news yet bad news prevails, having done all, just standing and trusting God! The prayers are increasing and as we pray on for the sick, God will continue to come through for us all. This world will never be the same when this passes away. God loves me, no doubt now, if ever there was doubt.

So, here are the words of someone who walks daily in the valley of the shadow of death and yet, this fellow believes that in the middle of this valley, God is still sovereign. The one who neither slumbers nor sleeps will hear our cry and come through for us. The scars of coronavirus will remind us that we went through the waters and the fire, and that God also remained solidly behind His own. Finally, here is God Himself speaking: "Let the prophet who has a dream tell the dream but let the one who has my word speak my word faithfully" (Jer. 23:28).

African Pastoral Responses to Pandemics in a Digital Age: Between Providence, Prudence and Politics

Esther E. Acolatse

Introduction

The COVID-19 pandemic took the world by storm, and the figures of infected people worldwide were in millions. It seems no nation was untouched by this virus. According to the World Health Organization, even the remotest places on earth had a case or two. From the first moment of the pandemic and until now, fear-mongering and merchandising of local feel-good remedies and panaceas filled the airwaves. We witnessed pharmaceutical companies rally and cooperate to find a vaccine for the virus; health officials offer directives to curb the spread; and the religious, such as Christian leaders, offer theological explanations for the church and the world. While pandemics have been with humankind far longer in history, the internet and ubiquity of social media platforms have made immediate access to information abundant and simultaneous. If one chooses to indulge, the information flow can be ceaseless. This easy access to multiple sources of information magnified the perceptions around the pandemic, since it constantly offered an almost real-time account of the situation. Overstimulation of the senses and hyper-vigilance became the norm for many, if not all of us.[1] From those who were down with the virus, to the care providers who suffered additional (and undue) stress,[2] to the grieving families who sometimes had to grapple with multiple deaths occurring within days of each other: everyone experienced a kind of allostatic load. The overall effect on the health and wealth of nations was unquantifiable. The need for release from the allostatic load had people searching for and offering answers. Responses ranged from nonchalance

---

[1] Humanity has encountered such devastation in the art of living side by side in the common space inhabited by other created reality, seen or unseen. In recent history, we have had what has been known as the Spanish Flu about a century ago, and there are a few living people who came through that pandemic. The worst pandemic known to mankind is still the Black Death that ravaged Europe for about five years starting in 1347, with some estimated 20–50 million deaths. Following that was the bubonic plague in the seventeenth century known as the Black Death.

[2] The *New York Times* reported what it terms combat fatigue in many health care workers in this season under the onslaught of the COVID-19 pandemic. Many of the emotions expressed mimic post-traumatic stress. [See reported stories at https://www.nytimes.com/2020/11/25/health/doctors-nurses-covid-stress.html], [Last accessed: 27th June 2023].

to bravado, conspiracy theories, and the blame game that intensified xenophobia against Asians (who are assumed to be the cause and source of the pandemic). People in the religious world, especially Christians, were bombarded with myriad contradictory prophecies, many of which have eschatological undertones. The proliferation of these prophesies, more present among Independent Evangelical Charismatic Christians,[3] was a genuine attempt to read the moment through theological lenses. Yet, the attempts to theologically address the "why" among African Christians exacerbated the problem. The main problem was how African pastors and some Christians view the two interrelated concepts of divine providence and free will.

Some African Views of Providence, Free Will, and the COVID-19 Pandemic

African pastors, to whom many turn in this current crisis, also struggled to find answers for the devastation of the pandemic. Where was God in this suffering and death, and what did it mean to pray for healing for ailing people, yet many still died? Was the devastation evidence of the end times as prophesied in the Bible? If so, should the faithful not have been kept safe as promised in the scripture? If Christians are guaranteed protection, then adhering to lockdown rules and guidelines implies a lack of faith in God's ability to protect as promised. That God protected Israel from the plague that devastated Egypt is enough reason to believe He would do the same for the faithful during the pandemic. So the people of faith were encouraged to attend church services *sans* masks as an indication of true faith. As vaccine rollouts began in large cities that could become the epicentres of the spread of the virus, some pastors discouraged congregants from taking them and urged them to instead stand firm in the belief that God would protect them. To take the vaccine was thus a lack of faith. It was not uncommon to see slogans like "God is my PPE [personal protective equipment]" or hear people say, "The blood of Jesus is my vaccine." Not only was the pandemic and attempts to ameliorate it with a vaccine called into question by these pastors as indicative of a lack of faith, but the devastation produced by the pandemic was also read through an eschatological "end-time" motif. The approach of these pastors to the pandemic is not new, since physiological healing and prediction of the future as evidence of knowledge of the mind of God are key elements in Pentecostal/Charismatic belief. What was different in this instance was the access to communication tools via satellite that allowed them to reach vast audiences beyond the locals. In fact, many of these

---

[3] This is a broad term that describes many of the new independent churches which are the offshoot of classical Pentecostalism and thus fall under neo-Pentecostalism. These are the fastest-growing churches and are the focus of my reflections.

pastors have mega-churches in the West and would broadcast via various social media to their congregations across continents.[4]

The theological issues raised by the current attitude to the pandemic, the attempt at ameliorating it, and the attempt to address it from a scientific basis raise legitimate questions. Christian theology allows us free will in relation to divine providence, which, in theological terms, is the belief in the oversight of all created reality by a benevolent Creator God and which has usually been addressed regarding personal evil. With the pandemic, however, it is arguable that, regardless of the origin of the virus, its rapid spread is also in the realm of human causality (or free will), thus necessitating a conversation around providence and free will, or what I am calling prudence. Additionally, the political posture of national leaders was complicit in this moment, with a deleterious effect on how people exercised their free will. How the church has dealt with pandemics in the past, as well as how the scriptures understand and process disasters, are markedly different from what we observe in the COVID-19 pandemic. Even the witness of the church in Africa demonstrates that the attitude to this current pandemic is different than in times past.[5] Also different was the similar politicisation of the disease in both the US and in some parts of Africa due to their shared connection.[6] To some extent then, the conversation needs to include politics and indeed the body politic. While the scope of this paper does not allow for full engagement with the literature on public theology, we are to pay attention to what theology can (and should) say in the public sphere, even as we give priority in discussion to the pastoral theology that can engender hope in crisis. A public and pastoral theological statement might be as simple as: "Wear a mask; heed social distance guidelines." But I get ahead of

[4] A good example of such a church would be Christ Embassy International, whose home page includes access to numerous apps: https://christembassy.org/loveworld-apps/.

[5] Take the recent Ebola crisis and ongoing HIV/AIDs pandemics in Africa, for example. The prompt responses of the church in following WHO directives and numerous focus papers from conferences among African theologians is well known, notable among them are papers on the impact of globalisation and the church's response to the crises. Of course, there were the few who cared for their congregants in life-affirming and self-preserving ways. See Jean-Daniel Plüss, "Covid-19, the Church and the Challenge to Ecumenism," *Transformation: An International Journal of Holistic Mission Studies* (2020), pp. 1–11. Accessed at: journals.sagepub.com/home/tm https://doi.org/10.1177/0265378820961545. The benefits of the lockdown for churches to reflect on the faith is also noted. See J. Kwabena Asamoah-Gyadu, *Christianity and Faith in the Covid-19 Era: From Hosannah to Pentecost* (Accra, Ghana: Step Publishers, 2020).

[6] Here I am thinking of my native country, Ghana, where the count of infected people was low and the protocols to check the spread were so impressive it was touted by the WHO and offered as an example to other nations. At the time of writing this article, the numbers are inching up and the initial protocols, including social distancing crackdowns, are being ignored and the obvious reason is the impending elections in the first week of December. We wait to see if the protocols will be reinstated.

myself. I turn now to the Old Testament (OT) to see what we might glean about the theologically adequate stance on pandemics/natural disasters/inexplicable suffering.

Old Testament Antecedents in Thinking About Providence in a Pandemic

Stories abound about disasters that befell humanity in the OT. Many of the stories were about Israel's suffering, although they also include the calamities that befell Israel's neighbours. Israel viewed those calamities as punishment from Yahweh for how these nations treated Israel. How Israel records these calamities or pandemics gives us a clue as to how the OT understands pandemics – we are offered a view of how Israelites reacted to and processed what befell them, especially in exilic times. Even though the OT itself has no corresponding word for pandemic (*deber* – plague – is the nearest equivalent), how the OT describes Israel's attitude during plagues and other calamities offers insights into theologising modern pandemics.

First, it is insufficient to speak of such events as "judgement." While God is conceived as the originator of such happenings, mainly to avoid dualistic thinking and to underscore God's omniscience, there is no strict and all-time linear cause–effect relationship between wrongdoing and disasters. This is the case, since Israel does not have such a concept regarding calamities even in articulation of the origin of plagues or calamities or even sometimes individual ailments.[7] Even in the cases of God's purposeful acts when Israel has been disobedient, the imagery of God's dealing with them is not that of judgement as used in the Western judicial system (which is how modern humans frame it) but of chastisement, as in discipline, in this case an offspring.[8] Always, in the OT, Israel frames the processing of their chastisement in light of deliverance history across time. What is evident in various narratives is how nuanced and open-ended their understanding is of the chastisement. As Goldingay and Goldingay point out in reference to Solomon's prayer of dedication of the Temple (II Chron. 6:28-30), "Solomon leaves an intriguing space and ambiguity between epidemic and divine chastisement."[9] Thus, his entreaty invariably throws itself on the ultimate mercy and omniscient judgement of the God who sees all hearts and would thus deal with Israel according to God's overarching purposes. Since there is no tight link between epidemic and divine chastisement, he can pray, leaving all in God's hands because "Yahweh would know that they might need pardon,

---

[7] The quintessential story of Job is a case in point, where neither Job nor his friends nor the reader are offered any reasons for the calamities that befall him. See especially Job 38–42.

[8] John Goldingay and Kathleen Scott Goldingay, "Thinking with the Old Testament 20bout the Pandemic," *Theology* 123(3), (2020), p. 192.

[9] Goldingay and Goldingay, "Thinking with the Old Testament," p. 192.

but they might not; they might just need deliverance." We would encounter a moment captured in this prayer later in God's dealing with Israel under Jehoshaphat's reign (II Chron. 20:1-12).[10]

Moreover, as many times as Yahweh threatens Israel with one epidemic or other, a threat which Israel often prepares to avert, there is no record of Yahweh making good on those threats. It is safe to suggest that what is at play is the hyperbolic nature of ancient speech acts that Jeremiah and Ezekiel (the two noted prophets) employ. Yet even when pandemics (plagues) occur, as we note in the Exodus account, even when they, as they did, target the oppressors or enemies of Israel, the significance touches Israel too. This aspect of God's dealings with Israel among the nations is vital to underscore, especially given how the COVID-19 pandemic produced the tendency to blame, name call, and suggest that others may be more at fault and are thus due punishment.[11] With such judgement is born the idea that the originators of the pandemic are deserving of the horror and so others may distance themselves from the cause (and the course) of the pandemic by dismissing it as a hoax. The extreme effect of such inward-looking attitudes is demonstrated in how people flouted the protocols meant to curb the spread of the virus.

Reading Providence in the Pandemic

How are we then to read providence from a biblical point of view in the time of pandemics? The coincidence of free will and divine providence, termed compatibilism,[12] is at the heart of the general OT stance on how to read the providence of God. Examples abound from accounts of the lives of the patriarchs and the prophets. Consider the example of Joseph's reading of his misfortunes (Gen. 50:19-20). He reads his hardships in the larger scheme of God's overarching plan for him and Israel, while at the same time not absolving the brothers of the acts that led to his hardships. Some of the prophets and how they interpreted the circumstances of Israel's sufferings point to how divine providence and human free will coincide (see Is. 10). Neither one cancels out the other without undercutting God's sovereignty in the situation, for always human free will and sovereignty are held in tense unity while giving conceptual priority to the latter. No human action, or in a sense even nature, red in tooth and claw, which one can assign to an evil spiritual being, make God's actions in time and space contingent.

---

[10] As Goldingay and Goldingay note, both the Chronicles and Kings version of the prayer leave the possibility of Yahweh's mercy and punishment open.

[11] Jesus' pointy instruction is a NT corollary when he disavows the idea of the intrinsic connection between sin and sickness and sin and calamitous events.

[12] For a fuller exposition, see D.A. Carson, "Biblical-Theological Pillars Needed to Support Faithful Christian Reflection on Suffering and Evil," *Trinity Journal* 38(1), (2017), pp. 55–77.

The mystery behind providence is precisely the fact that these seemingly mutually incompatible propositions can be held in tension and rendered compatible. Even when human foibles seem to overrun divine providence and even when it looks like Yahweh is orchestrating events by His authority (as in the Exodus with the plagues in Egypt), the story, read providentially, is always from the rearview mirror. It is always thus, in perspective to God's overarching plan towards the unfolding of history, not just for Israel but the whole world. As much as Israel disobeyed and acted in unfaithful ways, what is equally clear is the incontrovertible fact enshrined in their history that God's faithfulness and providential care outrun their failures (Deut. 5:9-10). What we seem to have is a nuanced exploration of pandemics and how Israel reads them. The coincidence of divine providence and human freedom is portrayed in a way that defies any systematisation or even a straight-line cause–effect relationship.

The multifaceted viewing approach to pandemics in the Torah is replayed in the prophets, especially Jeremiah and Ezekiel as they pronounce woe and grace simultaneously from Yahweh. Their pronouncements echo both impending judgement and admonishment to avoid impending doom. As Goldingay and Goldingay point out, the aim of the Torah (which is taken over in the Prophets), is not to fact-check the explanations of pandemics but to help Israel reflect and repent.[13] This is a theme taken up by Jesus in Jesus' reference to the fall of the tower of Siloam (Lk. 13:1-5).

What, then, may we learn about appropriate responses to pandemics from these vignettes? First is how to read the situation and also how the situation was read by Israel – not the content of the stories but how the events which populate the history are refracted. Studies in the Ancient Near East (ANE) often show how some of these disasters are cast in relief and in tension with that of the surrounding nations. A good example is the story of the plagues in Egypt with the Exodus motif. From start to finish, when read in the context of Egypt's role in the formation of Israel, the focus is not so much the plagues but a contest of Yahweh seen as creator and de-creator and the Egyptian god of order and rule. What the OT, with its stories of pandemics/disasters, offers us is the various angles through which to read suffering. This forces us to think in different ways, listen to others, and think with them rather than do so alone and be bogged down (or undone) by the disaster.

Secondly, we learn of the prophetic in times of disaster. A key aspect of pandemics in the OT is how the prophetic element shrouds pandemics. It is therefore important to explore how the prophetic, tied with the political, expresses itself in OT pandemics. Since the prophetic element has been marching in step with both politics in general and the politicisation of the pandemic in the US and parts of Africa, we see similar moves being orchestrated in recent pandemics. Injustice in one form or another is a basis of pandemics suffered in the OT, and the scourge is assumed to be punishment from Yahweh. What stands

[13] Goldingay and Goldingay, "Thinking with the Old Testament," p. 192.

out is the timeline of the prophecies in the OT versus that of the current situation and generally how to understand time and space in the grand scheme of divine providence.

One more issue the pandemic raised for most religions, especially Christianity, is end time. The foreboding about end-time prophecies that have lingered in the social imaginary was combined with imaginatively fabricated conspiracy theories and carried in waves over numerous social media platforms. Suddenly, chronological time and how we acknowledge and factor it into day-to-day living shifted, forcing a rethinking of history. As already intimated, modernity's march, which we assume to be forward towards progress, should now be seen as more lateral than forward. With the pandemic, we are not only invited to hold lightly to presentism but to live in the fluidity of time – a concept that is not new to Africa. This concoction of time is what Koselleck describes in framing the hermeneutics of time as *Zeitschichten*. *Zeitschichten*, he says, is "several layers of time of differing durations and differential origin which are nonetheless present and effectual at the same time."[14] His conception of history based on this concept of layered time is the needed remedy for the current situation. This multilayered view is like the traditional African conception of time as one in which past, present, and future all interpenetrate. As such, real-time is tied to significant occurrence and noted as *real* only because it is linked to a certain common reality. It is conceivable and perhaps even helpful that humanity might require this African concept of time with its fluidity to accommodate our state in this pandemic. It is possible that framing and settling into this dimension of time (especially in the lockdown months when the days bled into each other) might situate individuals for flourishing during a pandemic. This concept of time is indispensable for navigating this moment of epochal changes. Perhaps this new perspective and attitude to time are needed to return humanity to the normal pace of life for which they were created. This is a pace with the right balance and rhythm of work/rest so we can be humans with zest rather than the automatons of the artificially created and industrialised world of capitalism. Humans now largely belong to the corporations as disembodied beings living with artificially created time bounds rather than within God's freedom and love punctuated by Sabbath rest.

The element of time is also crucial to what now fascinates Christians both in North America and Africa – the prophetic element in worship. M. Herrero, working with Koselleck's concept of time and history, invites us to see how the future (the realm of prophecy) interpenetrates past and present. The future lingers intrusively, and dogs both the past and the present. Koselleck names the two categories of temporality as "space of experience" and "horizon of expectations"

---

[14] Reinhart Koselleck and Hans-Georg Gadamer, *Zeitschichten: Studien zur Historik* (Frankfurt: Suhrkamp, 2000), in Montserrat Herrero, "Deconstructing Historical Expectation: Lessons from the Pandemic," *Political Theology* 21(70), (2020), pp. 571–73.

and suggests that these are not fixed categories. Space of experience and horizon of expectations orient us to time and space and allow us to make meaning of experience in time and space. Such meaning-making activity, where past, present, and future coalesce, is impossible without engaging theological imagination. Theological imagination aids us to first read history properly and rightly judge prophetic time. Herrero suggests that we need to understand prophetic time as "a kind of historic time that is made effective by means of a narrative in which a certain interpretation of the present as well as, crucially, the past with a future destiny."[15] He goes on to point to the "unimaginable, unforeseeable and incalculable character of such a future destiny which shows itself more in the form of a 'divine trace through the course of history'."[16] For the prophet is neither a diviner (which many these days have sought to be and even more seek out for various issues of life) nor even a theologian interpreting revelation. The prophet is instead "the voice of God" who is trying to "decipher the meaning of events of a particular people" in relation to the God they know in salvation history. With this perspective, we eschew probing and trying to feel out what God is doing (divining) and we avoid trying to cast a systematised theological lens over the occurrence. Following the true prophets of Israel, our stance would be what I see as a pastoral move, to indwell the situation churned up by the pandemic and lean into where the God of all the earth is ushering all creation to its ultimate destiny/destination through this circumstance.

This destiny/destination is not in any way what the so-called prophets, whether in the North American or African Evangelical scene, paint it to be with end-time apocalyptic motifs. It is instead a destination in the now and future. It is at once in God's promising future (which is yet present in the God who is still at work) in whom all creation finds its existence. The prophetic work in construing spaciotemporal horizons is to follow the work of the Spirit in the world. The splendour of that work is recorded in the testimonies of the acts of kindness, perseverance, and resistance witnessed across the board and across the globe. Talk of epiphanies!

The provocative question Herrero poses of history is one already anticipated in the scriptures. That is, the future direction towards which we are led, and by which we ought to read present circumstances, is paradoxically "the already and not yet of the kingdom." For, as he notes, prophetic time is the opening of time, "the idea of the *absolute future* as an ever-historically-displaced future that is always present in history."[17] Paradoxically, it is in this future-focused perspective that we read our lives, indeed, human history and its vicissitudes, from the rear-view mirror and affirm what we know tacitly about the future. This is the primary task of the church in hard and confusing times. The church has been here before, as I have indicated. Allowing geopolitics to read the situation

---

[15] Herrero, "Deconstructing Historical Expectation," p. 572.

[16] Herrero, "Deconstructing Historical Expectation," p. 572.

[17] Herrero, "Deconstructing Historical Expectation," p. 572. Emphasis is the author's.

and to allow it to determine appropriate responses unwittingly undercuts her witness in the world. The church needs this witness of and to God's providence to allay fears while it guides towards prudence. This way, providence and prudence can be more in consonance with compatibilism, a stance to which I subscribe, due to its biblical and credal direction in the conversation.

Altogether, to speak of providence in a biblical sense, then, is not so much about a grace-filled life and a life lived in gratitude under God's protection, but to speak almost in primordial mode of the very beginning as, "In the beginning, God [...]" (Gen. 1:1). It is to speak of the place under God's purview, the place of creation, recreation (playfulness and rest), and continual re-creation of God. It is where the first light of creation shines in its many prismatic forms and, in recasting this light as spiritual light of and in the Spirit, the full fruit of the Spirit is on display. In this light, humans are invited to engage life, especially when the darkness in all its multiple forms attempts to encroach and confound the light, and even more so when we witness inexplicable evil as a pandemic. A further theological exploration on providence is in order, and here I want to attend to how providence has been either misunderstood or misrepresented (sometimes too broadly, sometimes narrowly) in our approaches to delivering a theological scaffolding for the architecture of theodicy.

Human Freedom and Providence in Theological Perspective

Based on our explorations of approaches to pandemics/disasters/plagues in the OT, we can therefore make some theological pronouncements. But again, following the OT example, these pronouncements cannot be dogmatic, even if we speak them firmly and persuasively.

Much of the theology at the forefront of a majority African Christian diet these days is the thin gruel of the leftover prosperity gospel from North America making the rounds and being regurgitated. This kind of theology does not prepare us for the automatic suffering we will encounter if we live long enough (and these days we can take longevity for granted, thanks to medical science). Our moral architecture, for the most part, cannot support a genuine or thoroughgoing biblical account of suffering nor of providence and how it relates to human freedom. This problem of a theologically inadequate account of suffering, arising from the belief that believers should not suffer, is even more evident in African Independent Evangelical churches.[18] By and large, people are praying and expecting God to intervene in this pandemic, but they see the lockdowns and government closures of churches as an affront to God. There are many Christians

[18] These are the fastest-growing churches, which are also the ones propagating the prosperity gospel with its attendant prophetic utterances that encourage congregants and the general public to ignore directives from medical experts and to depend on faith in God to protect themselves from the virus. To wear masks or to receive the vaccine were indications of a lack of trust in God.

who see the call to wear masks or not to gather in worship as lack of faith in God's providential care rather than as prudence which comes with human freedom exercised under God's purview. The question at the heart of the confusion is the conflict between these contradictory statements framed in David Basinger's reflection on the issue:

1. God creates human agents such that they are free with respect to certain actions, and therefore, morally responsible for them.
2. God is an omniscient wholly good being who is omnipotent in the sense that he has (sovereign, providential) control over all existent states of affairs.[19]

Holding human freedom and divine providence in tension as both true despite the seeming conflict is a nearly impossible task. This is the view of Christian theists who hold that God creates humans as free beings to make choices within this limited freedom and are responsible for their actions. On the other hand, God the Creator is omniscient and omnipotent and has sovereign, providential oversight of all created reality. This is the position that is termed compatibilism. Christian theists have propounded various arguments on the compatibility of two opposing tenets. Often, these are based on an understanding of the extent of freedom or sovereignty. While the conflict is never quite resolved, Christian theology has held these seemingly incompatible statements as both valid and consistent with scriptures.

Compatibilism and Incompatibilism in Perspective

We begin by contrasting compatibilism and incompatibilism and their respective abilities to account for human freedom. In the theological realm, compatibilism states that human action may be freely chosen even if God determined that same act. What comes to mind immediately within the realm of a disaster/pandemic is Pharaoh's refusal to let Israel go while God was seen as simultaneously hardening Pharaoh's heart (Ex. 4–14). The accounts shuttle between Pharaoh hardening his heart on some occasions (Ex. 9:7) and on other occasions, the hardening is attributed to God (Ex. 9:12).[20]

In contrast, incompatibilism claims that free will is incompatible with determinism.[21] Incompatibilism assumes that genuine free will is not truly free

---

[19] David Basinger, "Human Freedom and Divine Providence: Some New Thoughts on an Old Problem," *Religious Studies* 15 (1979), p. 491.

[20] Biblical commentators often point to the difficulty of this passage by highlighting the deterministic relationship it casts between God and Pharaoh and thus humans. See an extended discussion by Robert R. Wilson, "The Hardening of Pharaoh's Heart," *The Catholic Biblical Quarterly* 41(1), (1979), pp. 18–36.

[21] See Kevin Timpe and Audra Jenson, "Free Will and the Stages of Theological Anthropology," *Philosophi Christi: Journal of the Evangelical Philosophical Society* [Available at: https://www.epsociety.org/articles/free-will-and-the-stages-of-theological-anthropology/], [Last accessed: 28th June 2023].

given God's providence. But how we are to understand the extent of free will considering what current neuroscience says about causal determinism (the brain structure constrains certain choices and actions) is yet to be explored theologically.[22] We can assert that the position of compatibilism connects with the scriptural narratives that describe how God relates with individuals and peoples within the bounds of God's own freedom and love. The history of the actions and reactions of the church in times of pandemics attests to this understanding of the coincidence of providence and free will.

The Church and Pandemics: Historical Precedence

The theological insights we have explored have not been in a vacuum because the church has entered conversation with pandemics and grappled with the issue of evil and the justice of God, while at the same time responding to the ravages of pandemics. The accounts portray that, in times of pandemics, the church has come alongside people in a manner that is credal and biblical. The church has cared for all regardless of race, creed, and political stance as enjoined in the Torah (Leviticus in particular), taught by Jesus (Matt. 5:44) and reiterated by Paul (Rom. 12:14). History bears witness to the role of the church in the Cyprian plague of the third century.[23] This plague started in Ethiopia around Easter of 205 and reached Rome a year later, spreading as far as Greece and Syria, lasting about 20 years and killing an estimated 5,000 people. The non-Christians attributed it to the anger of the gods (much as contemporary Christians attributed the current pandemic to sin and God's displeasure) while being unable to offer any real basis for the pandemic. It was an opportunity for the church to display Christian hospitality to the ailing and offer a hope of the afterlife to the dying. Holistic Christian practice of care for the dying and support for those ailing with the disease is considered to account for the growth of the religion following the plague. Rather than making pronouncements of the apocalyptic prophetic messages, often based on conspiracy theories via social media, the Independent Charismatic churches could learn a lesson first from the biblical and theological reflection on God's sovereignty and human freedom.

---

[22] I think here of some compulsive addictive behaviours such as gambling. See B. Mohammadi *et al.*, "Intertemporal Choice Behavior is Constrained by Brain Structure in Healthy Participants and Pathological Gamblers," *Brain Struct. Funct.* 221 (2016), pp. 3157–3170 [Available at: https://doi.org/10.1007/s00429-015-1093-9], [Last accessed: 28th June 2023].

[23] Named the Cyprian Plague for St Cyprian, the Bishop of Carthage whose first-hand observations preserved and offered the world access to the events. See a summarised history by John Horgan, "Plague of Cyprian, 250–270 CE," *World History Encyclopedia*, 13th December 2016. [Available at: https://www.ancient.eu/article/992/plague-of-cyprian-250-270-ce/], [Last accessed: 28th June 2023].

In addition, there are African religious-cultural resources existing for thinking about how these key theological ideas are indispensable to formulating a culturally relevant response to the present pandemic and even for providing a much surer footing in navigating natural as well as corporate evil.

African Understanding of Sovereignty and Free Will

In African understanding of the human being within the cosmos, an individual is a person only in community and never fully a person unless related to others. The blessing and bane of the gods are believed to be visited on whole clans (much like in all ancient cultures and in the OT), stressing the "we-ness" of existence. Unlikely as it may sound, African understanding of divine sovereignty and human freedom is closer to the theistic compatibilism model than a cursory glance shows. While there might be a sense of freewheeling with the concept of fatalism and a *que sera, sera* attitude among Africans generally, especially when it comes to the vicissitudes of life, this is not absolute. In pithy sayings, proverbs, stories, and sagas of the brave and in the annals of kings and queens continent-wide are stamped ideas of the conjoined relationship between what the gods and the Supreme Being wills and what humans will and do. Space precludes an extensive history and discussion, but these few examples from three people groups in West Africa suffice.

Among the Ewe-Fon of West Africa is the concept of *dzɔgbɛsɛ*. This word stands for destiny, broadly speaking, and literally means commandment for one's life or the guide/rule received on the day one is born. It is believed to be given randomly by the Creator, *Mawu-Lisa*, to everyone before they enter the world. It is thus one's destiny, which we might see in Christian theological parlance as providence and God's providential rule in one's life. It is believed that some are granted good destinies (*dzɔgbɛnyui*) and others are unfortunate and receive bad destinies (*dzɔgbɛvɔe*). What is clear (and often this is a hindsight view) is that even if one was born with either a good or bad destiny, by dint of hard work (free will) one can rewrite the bad *dzɔgbɛsɛ* through what is known as *agbagbadzɛdzɛ*, or one may squander one's good destiny and become a worthless person. In short, destiny, which translates as providence, always works with free will/human input. Moreover, child-rearing practices help mediate destinies for good and the judicial system offers punishment as a deterrent for transcending what might be the caprice of a bad destiny.

An example from the Akan follows the same idea and belief system as the Ewe-Fon. Among the Akan is the idea that everyone enters life with two life maps – the *nhebia* and *nkrabea* (the life command and parting words respectively) – and they frame the destiny that the human comes to earth to fulfil. At the same time, all humans possess *kra*, soul (different from the life-giving force from the Creator),[24] and this *kra* (perhaps the closest Western equivalent is the ego), can be heavy (*duro*) or light/weak (*hare*). Already, a weak or strong ego and how that allows for navigating or succumbing to the stresses on the psyche is at play here. Embedded in the concept of the weak or strong *kra* is the idea that individuals can outrun and outperform their destinies.

The Gã of Ghana speak of one's parting words (life command) as the newborn leaves the realm of the spirit life from whence all people come to the world of bodily existence as *osheemii*. This destiny is often entangled by *gbeshie* and can be experienced as good or bad. When a person is acting out of character because of an unruly *gbeshie*, rituals to ward off the powerful spirits are not uncommon. This action supports the belief that destiny can be transcended by dint of human free will.

We could go on with other examples, but perhaps one more from the Igbo of Nigeria, popularised by Chinua Achebe, helps to underscore the point. "When a man says yes, his *chi* (the spirit that drives destiny) says yes also."[25] It is very likely that this concept is part of the social imaginary continent-wide and I take it to mean a clear understanding of how the African lives with the tension of divine providence (destiny) and human freedom. It is in light of these considerations that a suggestion of the ways in which Biblical and African conceptions of human free will and divine providence relate to guide human life. I return to the Bible and its teachings on suffering to forge a viable approach to dealing with the pandemic in the African context because much of the pastoral practice in the main churches under consideration is bibliocentric and might be more likely to utilise approaches centred in scriptures.

Suffering in Biblical and African Perspectives

At this point we can ask what appropriate responses in light of suffering ought to be and what steps might be logical in a pandemic. What would a thorough biblical account of suffering and thus of providence entail? How are African religious-cultural mores primed to extend biblical insights and shore up and sustain Christians during times of suffering, especially since such attitudes should be ingrained in us? What we know in the OT account of the Fall and the Flood are clues that great grace already precedes our suffering. Not only is it

---

[24] The Akan concept of the soul, like many traditional concepts, is multilayered and spoken of periphrastically. Perhaps the concept of the soul is not that unambiguous in Christian theology either, as indicated in the lack of clarity of this entity in our theological anthropology. See further elaboration of this thought in Esther E. Acolatse, *For Freedom or Bondage: A Critique of African Pastoral Practices* (Grand Rapids, MI: Eerdmans, 2014).

[25] Chinua Achebe, *Things Fall Apart* (New York, NY: Penguin Books, 2017), ch. 4. Here the narrator reflects on the tragic hero Okonkwo's life and suggests that he is the master of his own fate and may be responsible in some way for the calamities that befall him and for his death.

clear that we suffer, but we must not be annihilated so that humankind and all the created order continues. Paul phrases it well when he very aptly breaks out in what might be a doxology:

> 8 We have troubles all around us, but we are not defeated. We often don't know what to do, but we don't give up. 9 We are persecuted, but God does not leave us. We are hurt sometimes, but we are not destroyed. 10 So we constantly experience the death of Jesus in our own bodies, but this is so that the life of Jesus can also be seen in our bodies. 11 We are alive, but for Jesus we are always in danger of death, so that the life of Jesus can be seen in our bodies that die. (2 Cor. 4:8-11, ERV)

Interestingly, Paul begins the chapter with the first creative utterance of God, in which light is called forth out of darkness (which is never eradicated but set apart from the light). It is that same light that needs to be shone on the present and indeed all predicaments. It is how we will be offered the right perception and thus an appropriate stance and course of action. Everything may look like it is going to hell in a hand basket, but the scriptural injunction is for hope that sees the present as temporary. Both in the African religious-cultural and biblical sense, the temporariness of the present circumstances, coupled with the sense of time as circular rather than linear, frames attitudes to disasters.

The reason for the different attitudes in the current COVID-19 pandemic, both in the US and parts of Africa, is the politicisation of the pandemic. First, politicians have something to gain by dismissing the seriousness of the virus. They work in cahoots with the self-styled pastors of some of the independent churches who unapologetically express the urgency of the congregants to bring in their tithes, adducing scripture (Heb. 12:25) and demonstrating their obedience to the Spirit by congregating. The political aesthetics of the "spirit," to which I have alluded previously, is at play here. This is a "spirit" of God that is not recognisable in scriptures or even the immediate history of the church. For, in this political era, the gentle Spirit (even conceived as water and fire in the scriptures) is portrayed as an aggressive warlord focused on ensuring the good life for only a particular kind of people identified as God's people on this earth, especially those who will go to church during this pandemic. This spirit (who is called the giver of life in the scriptures) seems intent on displaying power regardless of loss of life to the "men of God."[26]

What is worrisome is the fact that Africa, who in geo-spiritual perspectives is elder, is following the footsteps of the West in its approach to the pandemic. Africa in some ways is dancing to the discordant strains of a foreign tune, to its detriment. From her philosophic-linguistic arsenal to her collectivistic understanding of humanity that embraces nonhuman entities, Africa has a wealth

---

[26] The report of the death of a pastor who claimed power to heal those ailing with the virus calls to question how some of these pastors and many of the people they lead understand providence. See the full story available at:
https://www.huffingtonpost.ca/entry/frankline-ndifor-pastor-cameroon_n_5ec60a00c5b6dfc078e0f7ee?ri18n=true [Last accessed: 1st March 2022]

of ideas for navigating suffering and this pandemic, even if she may not have the requisite scientific resources. From these cultural resources – a way of being human that continues in pockets of the population removed from city states – she can dole wisdom that will sustain people in bearing under the weight of the ravages of the virus.

Some African Traditional Resources for Enduring the Pandemic

Africa's *ubuntu* – I am because we are ethos[27] – continues getting touted even though we do not consistently demonstrate it in practice. At the times and places where its collectivistic ethos is most needed for good, it sometimes veers into individualistic mode. The collectivistic stance acts as a herd mentality under manipulative leadership (even from the church) and thus works against the common good. The pandemic situation was one such moment where the collectivistic ethos could be mined for good, but somehow the notes of that call seem muted because the din from the camp that invites people to demonstrate their faith by being bold and ignoring public safety measures was louder.

Two other uniquely African traditional elements are important to navigating this pandemic. One is the concept of time and its relation to history, and the other is relationship to authority. I have already mentioned the sense of the fluidity of time akin to the biblical concept of *kairos*. This concept, which is also a lived experience, is a boon for Africa in the pandemic when time as we know it shifted and distorted people's temporal perception.[28] It is likely that the negative effect of time intervals on those whose inner clocks are not rigidly tuned to the mechanical one willbe minimised even in a heightened situation of the pandemic, thus offering psychological benefits, especially in the more rural areas untouched by the effects of the pace of life in the cities.

Additionally, despite the acknowledged patriarchy and respect for authority that underlies familial and even social relationships, traditional culture eschews autocracy and has in-built structures to ensure that the power of those in authority enhances the life of all. Many of the benefits of this system have been lost due to the endless reach of colonialism and the formation of nation states according

---

[27] I have had occasion to problematise this concept in lived experience in postcolonial times and call for a rethinking of the collectivistic ethos, which is getting lost where people are being primed to live at the junction of Western and African culture. "Unravelling the Relational Myth in the Turn Toward Autonomy: Pastoral Care and Counselling with African Women," in J. Stevenson-Moessner and Teresa Snorton (eds), *Women Out of Order: Risking Change and Creating Care in a Multicultural World* (Minneapolis, MN: Fortress, 2009), pp. 218–229.

[28] See recent research reported by Duke neuroscientist Kevin LaBar about perception of time in stressful situations. Leslie Nemo, "How the Coronavirus Pandemic Is Warping Our Sense of Time," *Discover Magazine*, 1st May 2020 [Available at: https://www.discovermagazine.com/mind/how-the-coronavirus-pandemic-is-warping-our-sense-of-time], [Last accessed: 28th June 2023].

to Western democratic structures which have not been well assimilated into the culture. We witness the failed democratic process in both civil government and the church, where leadership is almost autocratic, especially in the Independent Evangelical Charismatic (IEC) churches. With the colonial legacy of the supremacy of the West, we are witnesses to the overarching oppressive shadow of whiteness that continues because of current media allowing free flow of information, even to within the church.[29] Globalisation is both a promise and a challenge in this information highway and Africa needs to learn how to navigate that free flow of information and be wise about borrowing, not only in the pandemic, but for the many unforeseeable occurrences that might happen as long as humans exist.

Concluding Thoughts and a Tentative Proposal

Although the pandemic has receded, the questions the religious ask may never find full answers. The attempt I have made here to uncover some of the false understandings of God's overarching governance of all things (and its coincidence with human responsibility) and to offer a corrective, especially in the African context, and to bring African resources in tandem with the biblical and theological teachings of the Christian faith, is still exploratory. But lessons also transcend the bounds of the African geopolitical and ecclesial space. These are lessons first about our common humanity, and how we read human progress and humanity's future theologically in a technological and modern world. The postmodern move of collapsing the rigid line between past and present[30] and encouraging the church, and thus the public it serves, to look to the future from which the Spirit of Christ, the founding spirit of the church, calls her forward (Rev. 22:17) is to be appreciated. The pandemic has demonstrated that the past, despite the technological advances of the present, is not as different as assumed. Humankind may have made progress, but perhaps in humility it ought to own that the leaps may have been more lateral than vertical or forward, as we have reached into the past and the survival kit of previous epochs to navigate this pandemic. At the least, yet more visible, is the interconnectedness of all created reality – a fact that traditional cultures like Africa have known since the beginning of time.

---

[29] I refer here to the numbers of conspiracy theories carried to and fro via social media about the causes and course of the virus and any vaccine therapy. This is especially closely tied to how some people perceived who would win the US 2020 presidential elections and how all that is tied to the purposes of God for the world, which are still on-going, with ever deepening twists on the theme of apocalyptic signs.

[30] Gabrielle Spiegel, "The Future of the Past: History, Memory, and the Ethical Imperatives of Writing History," *Journal of the Philosophy of History* 8(2), (2014): especially page 169.

Future Directedness and Caring Practices for Church and World

What does a future directedness look like, and how does it create the pastoral theological logistics to navigate not just the pandemic but other natural disasters? A question such as the above places us in the realm of public theology, and while the limitations of this paper do not allow for extensive engagement with the subject of theology in the public square, the prophetic word as well as the politicisation of the prophetic in this moment calls for attention to the impact of theology in the public square. In this regard, many questions come to mind on how to understand and navigate the assumed movement and logic of the Spirit in the world. For one, we must ask what the judicious word should be and what form it should take in this moment? How may it be spoken without the address falling prey to easy answers, some of which might land us opposite scripture (I Thes. 5:19-22). The world witnessed prophetism gone awry in the political world when a moment and a word borrowed from the North American scene was re-clothed in African psychospiritual garb and transmigrated back and forth.[31]

In our pastoral responses for this moment, we follow what the OT approach to pandemics demonstrates: not an excavation of "whys" and "whos" but "people giving concrete expression to loving their neighbour" (Lev. 19:13-18) and here the neighbour, rightly so, includes our enemy. Moreover, the song book of Israel, the Psalms, offers a public worship model for crying out in lament. The psychosomatic benefits alone might shore us up for the long haul of this pandemic.

[31] The most visible prophetic utterance is the one by Paula White that has made the rounds on social media. But the origin of the prophesy that made reference to aid from African angels started most likely from a word of knowledge by a Ghanaian prophet who passed on the message to a well-known archbishop with access to Paula White. The most damning aspect of the prophetic prayer by Paula White is how not only Black bodies are used in high places but how it is Black Angels who might yet again come to the aid of the white masters so they might continue to denigrate and run roughshod over Blacks. Beyond this are the numerous prayer meetings and marches in some African cities in support of Trump's re-election. See also: Adelakun, "'Thank God for Amazon.Com'."

Theorising Pandemics, Africa, and Christianity: Apocalyptic/Eschatological Re-Mapping in African Pentecostalism

Nimi Wariboko

Introduction

Many scholars and ordinary folks think that the terror of pandemics is primarily about death – the fear of death, how to cope with death, stopping death – or not being freighted by the bacteria or viruses causing diseases. However, the association of pandemics with the fear of death is only valid if the most fundamental discomfort with pandemics is seen as inciting fear instead of inflaming our ontological anxieties. The association is too quick, superficial, and ignores a basic lesson we have learned from some of the best thinkers the world has ever produced. Søren Kierkegaard, Martin Heidegger, and Paul Tillich all taught us that there is a huge difference between fear and anxiety. Fear has an object. You are afraid of dogs or heights. Anxiety has no object; it is a self-awareness of our finitude. We know that we are bracketed by non-being; there was a time when we were not and there will be a time when we will not exist. In between these two "nots," we are wracked by non-being, which manifests as anxiety that reminds us that we came out of nothing, created *ex nihilo*. Anxiety has no object simply because it is a concern about the whole world that surrounds the person in total. The world is not "here" or "over there" in the way an object is. It fills the whole of the person's "space and time." It occupies the whole space; it is omnipresent.

Pandemics force us to confront ourselves as *nothing*; they compel us to come to the awareness that our being incorporates non-beingness into itself. Pandemics bring us to the *shock* of non-being, as Tillich is wont to put it. Pandemics deliver us to this shock, but not through an ontological route or any means of making us aware that our being is slipping away – although we certainly know that death upon us is the demise of our corporeal being. This shock happens through being *thrown* into a deepening and increasing knowledge of *contingency*, a form of vertigo of existence. Contingency is a realisation of "the artificiality of all arrangements, our increasing preconscious recognition that the world does not have to be organised or constituted the way it is. This recognition of increasing contingency – this recognition of our condition's radical non-naturalness –

becomes [...] the growing knowledge that things do not have to be this way, and the effects of that knowledge on ourselves and our society."[1]

Let us now take a moment to describe some of the effects, the terrors, of the deepening knowledge of contingency that pandemics inflict upon society and how its major institutions are likely to respond to the spectres of such terrors. In a situation of uncertainty and numerous possibilities, the self feels like every moment and every day is unrepeatable. The past appears to have failed to cast its shadow on the present and the future; and future (coming) events cannot be said to cast their shadows before them,[2] and the present hardly lasts long enough. There is a sense of fragility in the face of all this and, consequently, an anxiety (in the narrower sense of the word) that one may not arrive in the future. Under these conditions, it may feel like the past is literally lost and one feels continuously late because one cannot live up to the possibilities and uncertainty. One's response always appears slow and out of date.

Given this combination of "transitoriness" and temporal instability, the "managers" of society may have a pervasive feeling of time running out. The society itself and its major institutions appear not to be able to oversee human history, or to stand the test of time, and are thus bereft of their sacred trappings. They can no longer defer the passage of time and do not have a surplus of time. Even the best of institutions begins to appear provisional. No one can claim to be the same today, yesterday, and forever. No one can anticipate a collective destination for all. As sociologist of religion Richard Fenn forcibly remarks:

> In societies where institutions themselves are clearly provisional and therefore likely to change or disappear in time, it is difficult for a people to imagine a collective future that encompasses everyone. There is no single vision of the future, no common fate, and, hence no shared sense of mission or destiny [...]. As the state's claims to transcendence [and to call for public sacrifices[3]] come to be regarded as questionable, its charisma appears to be false: an artificial halo gilded

[1] Charles Mathewes, *A Theology of Public Life* (Cambridge: Cambridge University Press, 2007), p. 225.

[2] I have borrowed this phrasing from Paul Samuelson. He wrote: "We would expect people in the marketplace, in pursuit of avid and intelligent self-interest, to take account of those elements of future events that in a probability sense may be discerned to be casting their shadows before them. (Because past events cast their shadows after them, future [coming] events can be said to cast their shadows before them)." See Paul Samuelson, "Proof that Properly Anticipated Prices Fluctuate Randomly," *Industrial Management Review*, 6 (Spring 1965), p. 44.

[3] "Any attempt to require a sacrifice of the self needs to suggest that there is a larger temporal framework in which no sacrifice is ever lost or unrewarded. To demand that others link their personal fates with the destiny of the larger society and to disregard their personal needs or desires, it is necessary to evoke more than a time that 'wears away' and takes all its sons and daughters to their graves; it is necessary to evoke a common belief in a shared time that enshrines collective memory" (Richard Fenn, *Time Exposure: The Personal Experience of Time in Secular Societies* (Oxford: Oxford University Press, 2001), p. 109.

by time, burnished by scholars who reinterpret the founding documents according to special interests and pragmatic considerations.[4]

Now that we have laid out how the self and the institutions of society respond to pandemics, to the increasing knowledge of devastating contingency, let us turn to how religions, specifically Christianity, respond to crises of contingency forced on society by pandemics like COVID-19.

Christianity and Pandemics: A Tentative Map of Theological Response Patterns

Confrontation with maddening contingency provokes three major responses in Christian theological thought: eschatological attitude, apocalyptic attitude, and "closed predicament" (unyielding texture of thought in the face of contrary evidence).[5] Eschatological attitude towards pandemics demands, as Charles Mathewes puts it, an endurance of the present time and standing "fast into the indeterminate future. The fact that the world will one day end, that it is not our ultimate frame of reference, does not entail the apocalypse's imminent arrival."[6] The world will end one day, but Christians must continue to live and not call for its immediate end, or arrogate to themselves the interpretative powers to name an event as the beginning of the end. The Bible says only God the Father knows when the last day will come. In the meantime, Christians must continue to live and live well at the *edge* of the end time, *eschaton*. "Eschatology without imminent apocalypse: that is the tensive structure of commitment and longing

---

[4] Fenn, *Time Exposure*, p. 61.

[5] Using closed predicament in reference to Robin Horton, *Patterns of Thought in Africa and the West: Essays on Magic, Religion and Science* (Cambridge: Cambridge University Press, 1993), pp. 221–237. Closed predicament is used here to mean when a religious specialist either rejects or displays a lack of awareness of their established theoretical tenets. According to Horton, "absence of any awareness of alternatives [or deliberate rejection of alternative tenets, lack [of] incentive to agnosticism, or epistemic humility/defeasibility] makes for an absolute acceptance of the established theoretical tenets, and removes any possibility of questioning them. In these circumstances the established tenets invest the believer with a compelling force" (pp. 222–223). E.E. Evan-Pritchard describes closed predicament among the Azande people with regard to their witchcraft beliefs in this way: "I have attempted to show how rhythm, mode of utterance, content of prophecies, and so forth, assist in creating faith in witch-doctors, but these are only some of the ways in which faith is supported, and do not entirely explain belief. Weight of tradition alone can do that […] There is no incentive to agnosticism. All their beliefs hang together, and were a Zande to give up faith in witch-doctorhood, he would have to surrender equally his faith in witchcraft and oracles […] In this web of belief every strand depends upon every other strand, and a Zande cannot get out of its meshes because it is the only world he knows. The web is not an external structure in which he is enclosed. It is the texture of this thought and he cannot think that his thought is wrong." (E.E. Evans-Pritchard, *Witchcraft, Oracles, and Magic among the Azande* [Oxford: Oxford University Press, 1937], p. 195).

[6] Mathewes, *A Theology of Public Life*, p. 18.

that should shape human life here, during the world."[7] This contrasts with the apocalyptic attitude, which seeks finality and is not open to further becoming of the world and not waiting for the completion of the world in the *eschaton* by God. It is a fundamental temptation towards thinking of the ending of the world and a form of escapism. Charles Mathewes argues this point and I want to quote him at length here:

> Apocalypticism is not only a fundamental human temptation; it is one proper description of the root of human fault itself, the attempt to usurp God's power as the Lord of time, and as such should always be resisted [...] Apocalypticism is a fundamentally an epistemological attitude, a claim already to know. The Greek word *apokalypto* means "to unveil" or "disclose"; it suggests a mindset that basically looks at the future as an already determined and knowable reality. On this definition, "apocalypticism" is a form of eschatological meteorology, of forecasting; in a weird way, to be apocalyptic is to be *post*-apocalyptic – to know already what is going to happen, and so to treat it in the past. This is a deep human temptation, and illuminates how we seek to understand history. Our desire to understand history is actually a desire to be able to say what it meant "in the end," a desire to have it finished, over – to say that this desire entails a desire is actually to escape history.[8]

One of the major differences between the eschatological attitude towards pandemics and the apocalyptic one is that of waiting. Eschatology relies on waiting. The acute awareness of the openness of the pandemics-drenched world and the existential anxieties it generates often elicit the response of *waiting*. Waiting is problematic in a world of pandemics. Waiting as a strategy may point to a belief that all things will work out right in the end, indicating a certain belief in providence (religious or not). This belief does not go well with the conceptual underpinnings of a contingent, pandemic world that does not dispense existential guarantees. Time may not heal all things, and one may be a fool for missing opportunities. "The modern hero is the one who seizes the moment and exposes himself or herself like Faust to the 'torrents of time'."[9] All this notwithstanding, the eschatological attitude imposes waiting on all and forces all to experience their existential anxiety without the usual anaesthetics provided by some "sacred canopy," transcendent power, or apocalyptic presumptuousness that can administer grace or bring order to chaos. In a world of uncertainty and immense possibilities, even belief in providence does not relieve one of the pressures of exposure to time. There is always a dilemma of the length of the waiting period, knowing where it ends and when the time has come to act.

The third response – *closed predicament* – is particularly relevant to explore because the organising theme of the Centre for the Study of Christianity in Africa (CESCA) conference in 2021 was "Africa, Christianity, and Pandemics." The response pattern I have named closed predicament, following the eminent

[7] Mathewes, *A Theology of Public Life*, p. 18.
[8] Mathewes, *A Theology of Public Life*, pp. 38–40.
[9] Fenn, *Time Exposure*, p. 65.

English-Nigerian anthropologist Robin Horton, will enable us to draw insights from African traditional religion (ATR) that can help us to properly interpret the words and actions of African Pentecostals. Closed predicament has been well studied in ATR. In the 1960s, Horton brilliantly analysed how the problem of closed predicament affected practitioners of ATR. It limited their awareness of or search for alternatives to the theoretical tenets they held dear. This insight is important for understanding how Pentecostals are responding to the COVID pandemic that challenges the theoretical tenets about the world that they hold dear.

I make this connection between ATR and African Pentecostalism (AP) not because I want to argue that AP is ATR in new clothes or that AP is a bearer of the ethos and worldview of ATR, but rather to show that closed predicament is a core religious response, especially when such religions are in their phase of evolution, and where they therefore reject the scientific (questioning) outlook of the world. Closed predicament as a response pattern to perceived crises is rooted in the very belief structure of faith or religion. Often believers – whether in Christianity or ATR – do not want to question the validity of their faith even in the face of repeated failures of their belief system to explain the pandemics or any other crisis. They consider their beliefs as having absolute validity. For instance, we see this with African Pentecostal pastors who have come up with various explanations and predictions about when the current COVID crisis will end or how it will end. Their explanations and "prophecies" have all or mostly turned out to be wrong and irrational, yet their followers are notably reluctant "to register the repeated failures of prediction and to act by attacking the belief involved. Instead, other current beliefs are utilised in such a way as to 'excuse' each failure as they occur, and hence to protect the major theoretical assumptions on which the prediction is based."[10]

Are African Pentecostals dumb in their response to pandemics? Not at all. Their blindness, according to Horton, speaks to something that is supremely at stake which blocks their path (and, in general, religious believers in similar circumstances) to properly consider sound alternative models of explanation. The path of questioning the very spirituality (the Christian faith or mystical belief) upon which their predictions and theoretical tenets are based is not open to African Pentecostals, like many other groups of believers. As Horton expounds:

> [The] weighing up of successes [of predictions] against failures are just not among the paths that thought can take. They are blocked paths because the thinkers involved are victims of the "closed" predicament. For them established beliefs have an absolute validity, and any threat to such beliefs is a horrific threat to chaos. Who is going to jump from the cosmic palm-tree when there is no hope of another perch to swing to?[11]

---

[10] Horton, *Patterns of Thought*, p. 235.

[11] Horton, *Patterns of Thought*, p. 236.

Seriously questioning the absolute validity of their predictions and theoretical constructs risks the abandonment of their God (gods) and spirits in their spiritualist model of explanation. This is a frightening thought or proposition, a slippery slope towards chaos and abyss of unbelief. This kind of emotion is not peculiar to Pentecostals.

Many decades ago, a missionary asked a man from my ethnic group in Nigeria – Ijo/Ijaw of the Niger Delta – to convert to Christianity and throw away his gods. His response is a classic example of the fear of jumping into chaos that characterises believers of all religions when they are under the influence of the closed predicament, when they have absolutely accepted the established theoretical tenets of their belief systems and are either opposed to or unaware of alternatives. The Ijo man said to the Christian missionary: "Does your God really want us to climb up to the top of a tall palm tree, then take off our hands and let ourselves fall?"[12]

African Pentecostals and the COVID-19 Pandemic

Pandemics are particularly threatening to African Pentecostals because they attack the root of their spirituality. (This attack might produce a paradoxical effect: the very feeling of being attacked at the roots of one's belief system might catalyse that spirituality as a way of hunkering down or engaging in counter attacks.) Pentecostals are noted for their quest for power, as in mastery of their environment, physical and spiritual. The pandemic has demonstrated that they are powerless, or their pastors' claim to access God's power at will to explain, predict, and control events is hollow. Their often-discussed "spell of the invisible," their capability to pierce the phenomenal barrier and dredge up knowledge from the noumenal realm hit a brick wall with respect to predicting the advent and trajectory of the coronavirus. They pitifully resorted to comic causal explanations of 5G, a secret Illuminati group manipulating the world, moved over to believing unproven medical methods for healing those infected with the virus, and declared the whole pandemic as "noisome pestilence." Below, I provide an example of a Pentecostal pastor's response to the coronavirus. Hear what the highly respected Bishop David Oyedepo of Winners' Chapel said as he responded to the unverified claim of a Cameroun-American medical practitioner and a Pentecostal pastor, Dr Stella Immanuel, who said on 28th July 2020 that she was able to heal COVID-19 patients in the United States with hydroxychloroquine.

> If somebody comes out and say we have treated 350 people with this drug and none died, they say, No, that's not necessary. So, what's necessary? To kill them is necessary or to force your demonic vaccines on human race? Who knows what you have inside it? To turn human beings to properties for wealth's sake, for political reasons? The same way Pharaoh perished because he won't let people go, these evil

[12] Horton, *Patterns of Thought*, p. 223; see also p. 156.

> men will disappear into shame and ignominy wherever they may be and whatever forces are behind them. It [COVID-19] is mere noise. The Bible calls it noisome pestilence.[13]

I must quickly add that the likes of Bishop Oyedepo and Dr Immanuel do not exhaust the range of Pentecostal pastors' responses to the pandemic. While the likes of Oyedepo and Immanuel do not maintain epistemic humility, there are others like Pastor Ituah Ighodalo, the senior pastor of Trinity Church, Lagos, Nigeria, who defer to science.[14] But by and large, Pentecostal pastors like Ighodalo are few. Even the *Sahara Reporters*, who carried the report of Ighodalo's accommodation of medical science and his taking the vaccine, expressed some kind of surprise at his science-driven stance on the pandemic with these words: "The position taken by Ighodalo clearly contradicts the general view of some of his colleagues."[15]

It is easy to interpret the efforts of Pentecostal pastors to explain away COVID-19 or their failures to account for their own failures of explaining, predicting, and controlling the virus as anti-science or religious obscurantism. While I am not rejecting this explanation or theorisation, my interest is to locate the battlefield of their engagement with COVID-19 on a different terrain. They are caught in the web of their apocalyptic attitude to the pandemic. They believe or think they can force a closure upon COVID-19, bring some "redemption" (closure) to it, but the pandemic refuses to come to a closure. COVID has proved that it is not amenable to the Pentecostal pastors' concept of "redemption," especially the type that bypasses the halls of science or the creative and rational faculties God has bestowed on human beings. COVID-19 does not take orders from the claimed/acclaimed anointing of Pentecostal pastors; an enduement of enablement that they say is an unadulterated transcription of God's power, volition, and mind. It is not in the nature of the virus to truck, barter, and exchange with their anointing, which is the *general equivalent* of their trade (profession), a medium of exchange that is exchangeable for all commodity forms (including private jets and fat bank accounts), noumenal information, secrets, healing, and access to political power.[16]

---

[13] Africa News, "Oyedepo Backs Stella Immanuel, Says Coronavirus Has a Cure," 1st August 2020, *Ghana Web* [Available at: https://www.ghanaweb.com/GhanaHomePage/africa/Oyedepo-backs-Stella-Immanuel-says-coronavirus-has-a-cure-1023037], [Last accessed: 30th June 2023].

[14] Sahara Reporters, "It's Foolish to Reject COVID-19 Vaccine, Clerics Should Seek Knowledge – Pastor Ighodalo," 7th April 2021 [Available at: http://saharareporters.com/2021/04/07/it%E2%80%99s-foolish-reject-covid-19-vaccine-clerics-should-seek-knowledge-%E2%80%93-pastor-ighodalo], [Last accessed: 30th June 2023]. Adelakun has a comprehensive study of the pandemic and religious responses in *Powerful Devices*.

[15] Sahara Reporters, "It's Foolish to Reject COVID-19 Vaccine."

[16] All this is not to say that they did not sense an opportunity for a different kind of trade or transaction. Beyond their being confounded was also the chance to affirm themselves as a bearer of power and affirm their mastery of certain epistemologies.

The apocalyptic mindset is not a viable way of thinking about or interacting with the coronavirus. Pastors' anointing could not coerce the virus to reveal its secrets to them and, therefore, allow them to claim mastery over it and portray themselves as distinguished bearers of Godly powers. The power of their *general equivalent* has disappeared or been pulverised in the "network culture" of the variants of the virus or in the relational play of variants of the virus "backed by nothing other than themselves."[17] While the virus will eventually be fully contained, its world of self-referentiality speaks to or is a metaphor for the kind of knowledge system that not only rejects the apocalyptic mindset, but also increases the stress of our increasing awareness of contingency. Only God can pronounce the onset of the *eschaton*. There is no possibility of (forced) closure in this system as interconnections that are self-organising, self-regulating, and coevolving increasingly create ever-expanding webs of countless relations. Hence, we are in a brave new world of no redemption where order is not imposed from outside by either a prophetic man (or woman) of God or an institution. Mark C. Taylor sums up this argument in these terms:

> Since redemption presupposes closure as well as satisfaction, however it is figured, the ceaseless flux of life in network culture renders redemption impossible. Rather than the sign of certain death, the impossibility of redemption is the mark of endless life. To affirm this life is to embrace the infinitely complex networks that make us what we are and are not […] In the final analysis, the problem is not to find redemption from a world that often seems dark but to learn to live without redemption in a world where the interplay of light and darkness creates infinite shades of difference, which are inescapably disruptive, overwhelmingly beautiful, and infinitely complex.[18]

In a world that rejects Pentecostals' forced closure of issues and disapproves of their need to short-circuit scientific research and rational reasoning, as well as their incessant, vociferous attacks and, sometimes, ridiculous vituperations, we demonstrate four crucial weaknesses of African Pentecostal spirituality or epistemology. First, as stated above, there is always an escape hatch for their explanation except that, this time, the invisible coronavirus has made a public spectacle of that escape hatch. While the frequent deployment of the escape hatch since the onset of COVID-19 seems outrageous from a scientific or rational (modernist) point of view, it is not very surprising to anthropologists of religion. It is in the very nature of religious explanations or models of supposed supernatural intervention in the affairs of concrete human lives to have in them built-in escape routes and to plead the presence of complicating factors such that the models or explanations are always right within the "domain" of their operations and are "self-protective to a high degree." Horton, in the 1960s,

---

[17] Mark C. Taylor, *Confidence Games: Money and Markets in a World Without Redemption* (Chicago: University of Chicago Press, 2004), p. 326.
[18] Taylor, *Confidence Games*, pp. 330–331.

named this as "converging causal sequences" based on his study of African (Kalabari) traditional religion:

> By and large, if a diviner attributes a disease to a certain spirit aroused by certain antecedent circumstances and if the remedy based on this attribution fails, another diviner can always say the first attribution was a mistake, and that it was really another spirit, aroused by another set of circumstances, who caused the trouble. […] Faced with a theory postulating several possible causes for a given event, and no means of inferring the actual cause from observable evidence, divination [or Pentecostal explanatory model] goes, as it were, "over the head" of such evidence.[19]

Second, over the years, Pentecostal pastors and their enablers have succeeded in raising their utterances (including coughs, sighs, and throat-clearing exercises) to the infallible oracles of God, giving all their vocal undulations absolute validity. But right now, they sense that the *evental* appearance of the virus, their colossal failure at predicting its coming, their feeble attempts at praying it away, and their abject resort to the *converging causal sequences* of unending attributions of causation constitute a formidable attack on their worldview. A chink in their armour is taking in enemy fire. So, they are fighting back with all kinds of outlandish explanations; some saying the vaccine for COVID-19 will turn heterosexual Christians into homosexuals or vampires. Simply put, Pentecostal pastors are not accepting the reality of the pandemic. Many of them still believe it is a hoax or even something worse. Accepting the reality of COVID-19 is akin to asking them to climb to the top of a tall palm tree and let go. COVID is anxiety-generating for them in special ways because they are trapped in apocalyptic thinking. No wonder some of them are predicting that the pandemic portends the end of the world. And they are using the fear of imminent end-time judgement to corral, control, and fleece their congregations. Some even coupled the ongoing pandemic with the ascendance of the first (black) woman, Kamala Harris, to the office of the vice president of the United States to categorically state that it is past time for God to end all things on earth. Once again, let me return to Mathewes for some clarity.

> [T]he eschatological imagination opposes all apocalypticisms, all temptations to anticipate the end of time. The eschatological imagination is most fundamentally ontological, for the Greek word *eschaton* means "a limit," "an edge," or "an end." It is in a way to refuse a false knowingness about the future and hence to enable real knowledge by keeping us open to the future and hence to the "new thing" that God is always almost about to accomplish. This imagination identifies the apocalyptic temptation as a temptation toward endings, and in response to this temptation most fundamentally enacts a resistance to our own sinful desire to end all things. Theologically speaking, this desire for endings is an attempt to avoid God – a way of escaping our actual responsibility to understand and act in response to God's action upon us. The world will end, for the eschatological imagination: but we will not be the ones to end it. God's will is not captive to our expectations.[20]

---

[19] Horton, *Patterns of Thought*, p. 239.

[20] Mathewes, *A Theology of Public Life*, p. 40.

Third, it is hard for Pentecostal pastors who identify with supernatural powers and privileged access to God's wisdom to acknowledge the limits to their knowledge. What should any scholar of religion expect them to do? Cooperate with science and lose the chance to assert their prophetic and all-knowing identity? They must hold on to their obscurantism because it is the source of their power. History is replete with information about religious leaders not stepping down for science. Ask Galileo for his theory of the earth rotating around the sun and you would get an earful. African Pentecostalism needs its moment of reformation and enlightenment.

Pentecostal pastors in Africa now largely occupy the position intellectuals should occupy in our society. The pandemic is only one event in a series of events and crises on the continent that gives Pentecostal pastors the chance to play their cherished role of "public intellectuals," "public theologians," and servants. The way their attitude of apocalyptic finality has played out cannot be totally divorced from the pre-existing condition of epistemological crisis, precarious existence, and an acute awareness of the *contingency* of our lives. All of these exacerbated our terror of the pandemic. We as Africans occupy the top of the metaphorical palm tree, and we are afraid to let go because there is no reliable (consensus) epistemological cushion that might catch us. Christians or Pentecostals in the United States or Europe can resort to apocalypticism all they want, but they still have a solid enterprise of science and medical facilities to fall back on. For Africans, we were already long trapped in ontological anxiety before the pandemic. And most of our people were already used to receiving the answers to existential questions from Pentecostal pastors.[21]

Finally, the turn towards apocalypticism, apocalyptic finality (not being open to the further becoming of the world), is also a turn away from human creativity at some fundamental level. Apocalypticism rejects human creativity, which is always standing at the edge, *eschatos*, of previous human accomplishments and straining to move forward.[22] Humans are the true *eschatos* (in the original meaning of a spatial or a temporal end/edge). Human lives do take place at this edgy and porous boundary; and in the words of eminent theologian Catherine Keller, they exist at the "horizon that always recedes again into a 'not-yet' that 'already is' or nothing at all."[23] To reject eschatology is to be apocalyptically impatient with human creativity – and ultimately divine creativity as it undergirds all human creativity. Or, at least, I can state that all human creativity participates in divine creativity obliquely. The sense of apocalyptic finality does

---

[21] I acknowledge the assistance and insight of Dr Abimbola Adunni Adelakun (University of Texas at Austin, USA) in nudging me to make this third point.

[22] Nimi Wariboko, *The Charismatic City and the Public Resurgence of Religion: A Pentecostal Social Ethics of Cosmopolitan Urban Life* (New York: Palgrave Macmillan, 2014), pp. 16–17; Nimi Wariboko, *The Principle of Excellence: A Framework for Social Ethics* (Lanham, MD: Lexington Books, 2009), pp. 103–106, 109.

[23] Catherine Keller, *Apocalypse Now and Then: A Feminist Guide to the End of the World* (Boston, MA: Beacon, 1996), p. xiii; see also p. 134.

not recognise or wants to terminate this interplay of human and divine creativity. The absence of recognition reflects Pentecostal pastors' failure to recognise the sovereignty of God to make the call on the onset of the *eschaton*. Now we see that African Pentecostalism is a subversive movement under the cover of loyalty. It is a challenge to orthodox Christianity. The challenge regarding the ongoing pandemic is especially rooted in fatalism. This is the fatalism of not being open to the dynamism of the present, of not accepting the "new" that human ingenuity can bring forth in its open and ongoing interplay with divine creativity, and of not receiving the new gift that "time constantly delivers to us (or delivers us to)."[24] Many African Pentecostals are enthralled by the inevitability or fatalism of their fantastic projection of apocalyptic finality.

Conclusion

The absolute commitment to apocalyptic finality, coupled with the Pentecostals' belief in their ability to completely decode the "texts" of the world and the Bible, gives Pentecostalism its tragic fatalism. Pentecostals bind their fate to these two wheels of certainty (finality and decoding), and they are willing to roll with them. They think that, in this matter, they are helpless or have no choice. One needs to be outside this mindset to appreciate this tragedy. The tragedy is the tragedy of fanaticism, binding oneself to a self-proclaimed omniscient interpretative paradigm.[25]

African Pentecostal fanaticism is wrapped in a mystical belief inside an apocalyptically realised epistemology, but perhaps there is a key to unlock the epistemological suit of armour that is not only set against the so-called liberal cultural despisers of religion, but also ultimately against God. That key is the Christian faith. "Christian faith resists apocalyptic conclusion, and cultivates an eschatological attitude toward it, by continuing to question and by remaining open to those who would question it," according to Mathewes.[26]

---

[24] Mathewes, *A Theology of Public Life*, p. 243.

[25] "Fanaticism is a tragedy, but it cannot be seen as such by fanatics." See Mathewes, *A Theology of Public Life*, p. 179.

[26] Mathewes, *A Theology of Public Life*, p. 196.

Prophets, Pandemics, and Parousia: Neo-Prophetic Movements in Kenya and the Apocalyptic Interpretation of COVID-19

E. Okelloh Ogera

Introduction

The onset of COVID-19 created a lot of anxiety within many circles, including religious ones. Many people attempted to find meaning in a situation that seemed senseless and religion, being one of the key drivers of worldviews by providing answers to many of life's questions, became a recourse for many. In sub-Saharan Africa, Christianity is highly influential. Many contemporary Africans who identify as Christians are especially oriented towards the Pentecostal/Charismatic wing. This paper explores how a newer branch of the Pentecostal/Charismatic Churches (PCCs) in Africa, the Neo-Prophetic Movements[1] (NPM) sought to interpret and make sense of the COVID-19 pandemic within Kenya. The paper draws attention to recent events preceding the pandemic that set the stage for a Neo-Prophetic apocalyptic interpretation of the coronavirus. Using the Ministry of Repentance and Holiness (MRH) of Prophet Edward David Owuor[2] as a case study, the paper presents how Prophet Owuor utilises an apocalyptic narrative to explain the reasons for the continued presence of COVID-19. The paper also analyses the characteristics of this apocalyptic rhetoric, concluding that the aim is to authenticate Owuor's prophethood, maintain the authority of the prophet, and at the same time encourage the adherents to participate in spiritual exercises. In doing so, the paper will point out that, for the NPMs, the understanding of the apocalypse is a world-ending cataclysm or the end of the world.

---

[1] Cephas Omenyo and Atiemo Abamfo, "Claiming Religious Space: The Case of Neo-Prophetism in Ghana," *Ghana Bulletin of Theology* 1(1), (2006), pp. 55–68; Cephas N. Omenyo, "The Bible Says! Neo-Prophetic Hermeneutics in Africa," *Studies in World Christianity* 19(1), (April 2013), pp. 50–70.

[2] Prophet David Owuor runs the Repentance and Holiness Ministry (RHM), which he founded in 2004. The ministry is headquartered in Nakuru town in Kenya and has a large following all over the country. Owuor was a scientist holding a PhD in Molecular Medicine before turning to preaching.

Apocalypticism and Neo-Prophetic Movements

It is worth noting here that, even though there is a considerable presence of apocalyptic doctrines in the Christian scriptures,[3] there seems to be a tendency to minimise their importance by mainstream Christianity. Today, many churches rarely include passages from Revelation in their services, evident from the book's scant presence in the lectionaries.[4] However, the NPMs seem to be changing this script by attempting to mainstream apocalypticism. This is evident in how the apocalyptic ideology is understood and propagated among the NPMs. Apocalypticism is intricately intertwined with prophetism. Perhaps the reason for NPM's affinity with the Book of Revelation is because of how it frames an apocalyptic rhetoric that divides its narrative world into good and evil. On the one hand, the reader finds God and his agents and on the other, the devil and agents that do his work.[5]

The ideological understanding of apocalypticism as propagated by the NPMs in Kenya emanated from biblical apocalyptic literature, texts written or revised during times of perceived or real social, religious, or political crisis.[6] Mirrored in the contemporary context of Africa, they give rise to the apocalyptic narratives prevalent within NPMs. Africa is a continent that is continuously experiencing social, religious, and political crises. African people, on a communal as well as individual level, are subjected to these crises. These crisis scenarios feed into the way NPMs appropriate apocalyptic ideology in the sense that current contexts of the crises are interpreted as the struggle that "believers" must face before the end of the world. In other words, these crises are meant to test the faith of the true believer, and only those who will "obey till the end will be saved" (Matt. 24:13).

Such interpretations of the apocalyptic ideology help to serve two major purposes. The first is to authenticate the prophethood by helping them exhibit their spiritual acumen and prowess. In doing so, the prophet seeks to prove they have the spiritual wherewithal to help their adherents manoeuvre through difficult times and emerge triumphant. The second purpose is to maintain the adherents in the practice of spiritual exercises such as fasting and prayers among others as a sign of unwavering faith. This also serves the postulated purpose of maintaining the prophet's authority over the adherents as it is the prophet who determines the manner of spiritual exercises to be undertaken. For example, Prophet Owuor directed his followers not to fast during the COVID-19

---

[3] See for example Mark 13:1-2 where Jesus talks of the destruction of the temple or Thessalonians 4:15 where Paul talks of what will happen when Jesus returns.

[4] C. Koester, *Revelation and the End of All Things* (Grand Rapids, MI: Eerdmans, 2001), p. 32.

[5] Michael Labahn, "The Book of Revelation – an Early Christian 'Search for Meaning' in Critical Conversation with Its Jewish Heritage and Hellenistic-Roman Society," *In Die Skriflig* 48(1), (20th March 2014).

[6] D.E. Aune, T.J. Geddert, and Craig A. Evans, "Apocalypticism," in Craig A. Evans and Stanley E. Porter (eds), *Dictionary of New Testament Background: A Compendium of Contemporary Biblical Scholarship* (Downers Grove, IL: InterVarsity Press, 2000).

pandemic, arguing that fasting would reduce their immunity when they need it most.

One of the major ways in which the NPMs in Kenya appropriate apocalypticism is through the element of revelation. Several researchers such as Gerhard von Rad,[7] W.S. Vorster,[8] André LaCocque,[9] P.A. Verhoef,[10] and David P. Murphy[11] argue that the most prominent characteristic of an apocalyptic worldview is the fact that it contains the aspects of revelation as given by supernatural or divine mediators to a human recipient in relation to salvation and redemption from the pains and problems of the present world. The prophetic figures among the NPMs in Kenya portray themselves as the human recipients of divine revelation that they then pass on to their adherents. "These revelations are verbalised and themed towards the expectation of life after death expressed in terms of a lasting kingdom."[12] Thus, the essence of apocalypticism as appropriated by the NPMs is the hope that the new order will ultimately be brought about by divine intervention. This intervention is already in motion, evidenced by the fact that God has sent His messengers, the prophets of the NPMs, to inform the people about the impending salvation. These ideologies are propagated through apocalyptic rhetoric depicting the NPMs as a response to the crisis, enabling suffering people to see that God is in control of their circumstances and that ultimate deliverance is assured. The way the NPMs therefore propagate their apocalyptic ideology seems to suggest that apocalypticism is the product of a prophetic movement, which claims to reveal the way things really are both in heaven and on earth.

Apostasy, Pandemics, Apocalypse

One of the key features of Prophet Owuor's ministry is calling for repentance. His message has always been that the world is living in apostasy and must therefore repent or experience the wrath of God. Any observer of Owuor's ministry will know that, for Owuor, his is the voice of the one "crying in the wilderness for everyone to repent and prepare the way" for the second coming of Jesus. However, his call for repentance is often marked with threats of calamities, plagues, and disasters if people do not heed his word. Owuor was

---

[7] Gerhard von Rad, *Old Testament Theology, Vol. 2: The Theology of Israel's Prophetic Traditions*, trans. D.M.G. Stalker (Edinburgh: Harper & Row, 1965), pp. 301–302.

[8] W. Vorster, "'Genre' and the Revelation of John: A Study in Text, Context and Intertext," *Neotestamentica* 22(1), (1988), pp. 158–159.

[9] André LaCocque, *Daniel in His Time* (Columbia, SC: University of South Carolina Press, 1988), p. 88.

[10] P.A. Verhorf, *Profete En Profesie* (Cape Town : Lux Verbi, 1993), p. 83.

[11] David P. Murphy, *The Doomsday Survival Handbook: Bucket Lists for Every Conceivable Apocalypse* (Naperville, IL: Sourcebooks, 2012), p. 14.

[12] J.J. Collins, *Encounters with Biblical Theology* (Minneapolis, MN: Fortress, 2005), p. 163.

therefore very quick to take credit for "foretelling" the calamities that befell Kenya in 2019. These calamities bore an uncanny resemblance to some biblical narratives, such as the famine in which many people died of hunger, followed by a locust invasion described to be of biblical proportions. The *East African* newspaper reported in August 2019 that, according to the National Drought Management Authority (NDMA), more than 2.5 million Kenyans were facing starvation as the drought and food security situation in the country continued to deteriorate.[13] Even before the famine dissipated, a swarm of locusts invaded Kenya from her eastern and northern neighbours, Somalia and Ethiopia respectively. The locusts started swarming into Kenya in December 2019, triggering the worst locust outbreak the country had experienced in 70 years. Writing for the *National Geographic* magazine, Madeline Stone intimates that "East Africa is in the midst of a crisis that sounds like something out of the book of Exodus: A plague of locusts is spreading across the region, threatening the food supply of tens of millions."[14]

From the very beginning of the locust invasion, news outlets would compare it with the locust plague recorded in the Bible. Headlines such as "Apocalyptic Moment Locust Invasion Turns Sky Dark as Worst Infestation in Decades Hits" or "Pictures of Locust Swarms in East Africa are Truly Apocalyptic" were plastered across several newspaper outlets. Such reporting helped to drive the narrative of an apocalyptic understanding of the locust invasion among the people. The onset of the COVID-19 pandemic ensured a more frenzied linkage between the "plagues," the pandemic, apostasy, and an impending apocalypse among NPMs. Prophet Owuor, for instance, claimed that the locust invasion and the COVID-19 pandemic were ways in which God was punishing people for refusing to heed his call for repentance. It was reported in March 2019 that Prophet Owuor had claimed to have warned the government on the impending plague, saying, "I am seeing God's judgement upon Kenya, I have talked to high profile leaders about the coming judgement for them to prepare."[15] Whether Prophet Owuor was merely claiming credit for a naturally occurring event, or whether it was indeed an act of God in response to Kenyan's apostasy, is not the issue here. What is known for a fact is that, with the onset of the COVID-19

---

[13] Collins Omulo, "Worsening Drought Puts 2.5m Kenyans at Risk of Starvation," *The East African*, 28th August 2019 [Available at: https://www.theeastafrican.co.ke/tea/news/east-africa/worsening-drought-puts-2-5m-kenyans-at-risk-of-starvation-1425908], [Last accessed: 4th July 2023].

[14] Madeline Stone, "East Africa's Plague of Locusts and the Bizarre Climate Science behind It," *National Geographic*, 14th February 2020 [Available at: https://www.nationalgeographic.com/science/article/locust-plague-climate-science-east-africa], [Last accessed: 4th July 2023].

[15] Bosco Ondieki, "Prophet Owuor Predicts Disaster If Kenyans Don't Repent," *The Standard*, 25th March 2019 [Available at: https://www.standardmedia.co.ke/ureport/article/2001318076/], [Last accessed: 4th July 2023].

pandemic, Prophet Owuor once again claimed that he was the one who struck the world with coronavirus and the locusts. He reportedly said that because he is a true prophet of God, he can punish the world according to Revelation 11:5-6 due to the blackmails and disrespect he has received in the past few years.[16]

Such opportunistic interpretations of disasters magnify the stature of prophets. To highlight this point, Prophet Owuor later claimed that there would be a more devastating and scarier calamity in the coming days that would replace the dreaded coronavirus. In a privately recorded video shared widely online, the prophet states that the world should be prepared for the pandemic that will completely wipe out humans. In the video recording, Prophet Owuor says that "There is a tremendous plague worse than the coronavirus that you see in Asia. The Lord has commanded me to strike the earth and I have struck the earth, so there would be a lot of painful boils which are round and would become ripe full of fluid […]"[17] What is important to note is that Prophet Owuor's claim of prior knowledge of these "plagues" and pandemics are proof that he is indeed a "true" prophet of God sent to warn people against the evil ways prevalent in the world. And therefore, people should turn away from sins such as homosexuality, fornication, and adultery, among others, or they will face God's punishment just like the people of Sodom and Gomorrah.

Apostasy is not a surprise for Prophet Owuor because, according to him, the current crop of church leaders in Africa have contributed to the status quo by preaching about money rather than holiness. Owuor's public spats with other church leaders are well documented, where he accuses them of being "false teachers and preachers of prosperity."[18] Again, the narrative is aimed at bolstering the image of Owuor as a prophet of God by shaming, scandalising, and criticising others, while painting himself in a positive light. The narrative of false teachers causing apostasy in the last days is not new and certainly did not begin with Prophet Owuor. Indeed, the Didache alludes to the same when it states that:

> For in the last days false prophets and corrupters shall be multiplied, and the sheep shall be turned into wolves, and love shall be turned into hate; for when lawlessness increases, they shall hate and persecute and betray one another, and then shall appear the world-deceiver as the Son of God, and shall do signs and wonders, and the earth shall be delivered into his hands, and he shall do iniquitous things which have never yet come to pass since the beginning.[19]

---

[16] Ministry of Repentance and Holiness website [Available at: www.repentandpreparetheway.org], [Last accessed: 17th May 2021].
[17] Getty Soila, "Prophet Owour Predicts Worse Pandemic After Coronavirus (Video)" *GOTTA.News*, 21st March 2020, https://gotta.news/prophet-owour [Last accessed: 17th May 2021].
[18] Charles Ronald, "Inside Prophet Owuor and Bishop Margaret Wanjiru's War," *HiviSasa*, 29th April 2018 [Available at: https://hivisasa.com/posts/inside-prophet-owuor-bishop-margaret-wanjirus-war], [Last accessed: 4th July 2023].
[19] George Cantrell Allen, *The Didache* (London: Astolat Press, 1903).

Conventional understanding of apostasy in Christianity parallels Prophet Owuor's understanding as the total rejection of Christianity by someone who, having at one time professed the Christian faith, publicly rejects it. For Owuor, the fact that the country has most people who claim to be Christian, yet the hallmarks of sin and evil are prevalent in their society is a clear sign of apostasy. In other words, there cannot be a "Christian community" with high levels of sin and evil.

In Prophet Owuor's understanding, the locust invasion and the COVID-19 pandemic are signs of human apostasy. The only way to mitigate these calamities is to heed his message of repentance. Interestingly, Owuor's understanding of apostasy in the last days seems to stem from a literal interpretation of several New Testament passages warning about apostasy, such as 1 Timothy 4:1-3; 2 Timothy 3:1-5; 4:3-4; James 5:1-8; and 2 Peter 2:1-22; 3:3-6. Such an understanding of apostasy has a strong tinge of pre-millennialism in understanding eschatology. This is evidenced in narratives about the end times or last days which are used interchangeably,[20] indicating that this present age will end with the rapture. Accordingly, the rapture is to be followed by the tribulation which will end with the second coming of Jesus Christ, also known as the Parousia. The Parousia then ushers in the millennium, Christ's thousand-year-long reign on earth (Rev. 20). This is an indication of NPMs understanding that the "pandemics," especially COVID-19, are signs of apostasy and are therefore part of a process setting in motion a series of events culminating in the Parousia.

Apocalyptic Interpretation of COVID-19

That the current COVID-19 pandemic has led to an existential crisis is not in doubt. As Simon Dein notes, pandemics indicate the fragility of life and the world; they cause chaos, engender paralysing anxiety that the world is dissolving, lead to a sense of detachment, and raise significant issues of meaning, resulting in such existential crises.[21] It must be noted that this is not the first time apocalypticism is being equated with a pandemic. In the past, apocalyptic rhetoric was used during previous incidences such as the swine flu and bird flu, as well as the millennium bug at the dawn of year 2000 and the September 11th terrorist attack in New York. Thus, to find meaning within the context of the current crisis, NPMs, among others, have turned to apocalyptic narratives and rhetoric. In interpreting the COVID-19 pandemic, clear apocalyptic aspects emerge: symbolism, eschatological perspectives, and pre-millennialism.

---

[20] A quick glance at the messages posted on the RHM YouTube channel will indicate this.

[21] Simon Dein, "Covid-19 and the Apocalypse: Religious and Secular Perspectives," *Journal of Religion and Health* 60(1), (1st February 2021), pp. 5–15.

Symbolism

The close affinity between symbolism and apocalypticism cannot be overstated. In apocalyptic literature, the use of symbolism and symbolic language is predominant. Therefore, it is no surprise that the NPMs in Kenya utilise the symbolism found in the Bible, especially the Book of Revelation. The symbols in Revelation, although enigmatic, are intended to reveal meaning rather than conceal it. Symbols represent a metaphor in which a visual, numerical, or linguistic sign of a known object or concept is used to express an unknown object or concept. A symbol may be defined as "a relatively stable and repeatable element of perceptual experience, standing for some larger meaning or set of meanings which cannot be given, or not fully given, in perceptual experience itself."[22] Bearing this in mind, it is essential to note that the presence of symbolic imagery in the apocalyptic rhetoric of the NPMs in Kenya serves two major purposes: revelation and explanation.

The revelatory aspect of symbolism is one of the key factors of Neo-Prophetism. Over the years, people have tried to explain the cryptic messages found in the Bible, especially the Book of Revelation. Contemporary prophets such as Owuor claim that God has revealed to them the meaning of the symbols in the Bible. This is an aspect of direct revelation, distinct from general and special revelations. Direct revelation is understood to mean incidents where God supposedly reveals things to particular people by divine decree, special understanding of the scriptures, inspiration, and special guidance from the Holy Spirit. Other aspects of direct revelation include instances where someone sees visions, dreams, or hears the voice of God directly. Such revelations are predominant among the AICs as well as the NPMs. No wonder contemporary prophets prefer to make their "prophetic pronouncements" using symbols and imagery. Owuor is often at pains to prove that he hears directly from God, and the "prophecies" that he gives come directly from God. This is the reason why Prophet Owuor claims that he "prophesied" about the COVID-19 pandemic in 2015.[23] The significance of such claims demonstrates that Owuor is seeking to show or prove to his followers that God can reveal things to him before they happen. This emanates from a literal understanding of Amos 3:7, which feeds many aspects of prophetic foretelling.

These prophetic foretelling aspects have been used to explain the origin of COVID-19. On this, Prophet Owuor claims that God forewarned him about the impending pandemic and that, unless the people repent, God will authorise him to "release" the pandemic as a sign of God's displeasure. In a video message circulated online, Owuor claims that, since he is a true prophet of God, he is capable of punishing the world according to Revelation 11:5-6, which states that

---

[22] P. Wheelwright, *Metaphor and Reality* (Bloomington, IN: Indiana University Press, 1962), p. 92.

[23] Ministry of Repentance and Holiness, available at www.repentandpreparetheway.org [Last accessed: 17th May 2021].

"If anyone seeks to do them harm, fire pours from their mouths and consumes their enemies; and thus shall the man die who seeks them harm. These two have the power to shut up the sky, so that no rain may fall during the time of their prophesying; and they have the power to turn water into blood and to strike the earth at will with every kind of plague." Perhaps to put this into context, it is significant to point out that Prophet Owuor claims that he is a witness mentioned in Revelation 11. In a series of messages, photos, and videos[24] posted on the MRH website and YouTube channel, Owuor interprets the two witnesses of Revelation 11 to be Moses and Elijah. He claims that he is, or at the very least has the powers of, both Moses and Elijah. The resultant feature of these claims is that he can order plagues on earth.

The interpretation of the symbolism and imagery found in the biblical Book of Revelation is used to show the "potency" of the prophet, such that those who refuse to believe his word or mock him can suffer his (or God's) wrath. This interpretation implies that since people have not heeded Prophet Owuor's call for repentance, God instructed him to "strike" the world with the deadly pandemic. In his Online Global Service broadcast live via *Jesus is Lord* radio and the internet, Prophet Owuor claims to be a "spiritual" treasure to the world and having him in the country is a blessing.[25] He said that the blackmail and insults being thrown at him will just bring more harm to the people, adding that his prophecy about coronavirus was given on 1st December in 2015.[26] Ultimately, such interpretations lead to the development of an apocalyptic worldview. The apocalyptic worldview leads to the belief that history is moving towards a cataclysmic crisis, and that the *eschaton* will come about within the lifetime of the current generation. Such a worldview emphasises the capability of certain individuals to possess certain revelations which gives them special knowledge about the present age. This special knowledge is divinely revealed through symbolism to the prophet, who then shares it with the rest of the community, having first decoded the symbols.

Eschatological Perspectives

One cannot discuss apocalypticism without eschatology, which is basically a doctrine of the last things or end times. The "end" with which eschatology is concerned can be the purpose or goal as well as the endpoint towards which human life or history more generally is heading.[27] As has been stated, Africa is a continent that has undergone numerous socio-economic and political

---

[24] It is important to note that these images seem to have been edited in order to show that there are two people instead of one. In the images, the prophet appears as if he is two people, yet the image is the same.

[25] Soila, "Prophet Owour Predicts Worse Pandemic."

[26] Soila, "Prophet Owour Predicts Worse Pandemic."

[27] Mikel Burley, "Dislocating the Eschaton? Appraising Realized Eschatology," *Sophia* 56(3), (1st September 2017), pp. 435–452.

challenges. All these have contributed to an eschatological interpretation of the current age and events. This understanding largely stems from a literal interpretation of Matthew 24:7-8 which states that "there will be famine and earthquakes in various places. All these are the beginning of birth pains." In other words, the happenings and events in the world all point to the end of age as described in Matthew 24. The COVID-19 pandemic has helped propel eschatological perspectives into the apocalyptic rhetoric of NPMs and other evangelical Christians. COVID-19 is seen as a definite continuation of the events that precede the Parousia. This leads to the understanding of eschatology as realised – that is "the *eschaton* has moved from the future to the present, from the sphere of expectation into that of realized experience."[28] It is significant to note that in apocalyptic rhetoric or writings, crisis plays a central role in interpreting events. It simply means that a crisis takes on a redemptive quality due to its ability to bring about ideal conditions never experienced and believed to be beyond reach. Although crisis prompts fear, it also opens new opportunities. Rather than seeing crisis as something to avoid, the apocalyptic mindset welcomes it as a disruptive event necessary to wipe away corruption and create a perfect society. In other words, the contemporary crisis and corruption being witnessed in the world are parts of a larger plan by God to overcome evil once and for all. Perhaps this larger plan idea is best exemplified by the fact that the pandemic has drawn people towards God as they seek answers and solutions.

It is therefore no wonder that most of the prophetic pronouncements made by prophets within the NPMs in Kenya focus on death, destruction, and pain. Prophet Owuor, for example, is famous for "prophesying" tsunamis, earthquakes, floods, accidents, drought, bloodshed, and currently the COVID-19 pandemic, among other calamities.[29] All these calamities ostensibly point towards an imminent apocalypse. It does appear that, for Prophet Owuor, COVID-19 is proof that the plagues of the Book of Revelation are occurring now, and Jesus' return is imminent. For him, strangely, Revelation 6:1–8:1 predicts the COVID-19 pandemic, as the virus is associated with the fourth horseman.

Pre-Millennialism

The third aspect of the prophetic interpretation of COVID-19 and other pandemics is pre-millennialism. Listening to Prophet Owuor's messages, pre-millennial undertones emerge. Owuor may not use the term millennial or pre-millennialism; however, aspects of the same are evident in his messages. Pre-millennialism asserts that the Parousia is imminent and that biblical prophecies provide clues as to when it will take place.[30] Most importantly, the Parousia will usher in the rapture, where "believers" will be taken to heaven while at the same

---

[28] C.H. Dodd, *The Parables of the Kingdom* (London: Nisbet, 1936), p. 193.
[29] This has accorded Prophet Owuor the nickname "prophet of doom."
[30] Dein, "Covid-19 and the Apocalypse."

time the great tribulation for everyone else will begin. It is therefore not a wonder that movements such as MRH maintain that the apocalypse is imminent and continuously seek to understand contemporary events through the lens of biblical prophecy.

In this light, the Repentance and Holiness Ministry (RHM) and Prophet Owuor argue that the world is too pervaded with evil and sin, such that only a direct intervention from God can save humanity by preserving the "elect" and ushering in Christ's millennial Kingdom on earth. Like many other pre-millennial movements, the RHM calls for a return to the fundamentals of true religion, belief in the inerrancy of the scriptures, and the necessity of believers to maintain their faith and morals. Pre-millennialists have been awaiting the catastrophic hand of God while seeking to win as many people, sometimes referred to as the elect, to their side. The emergence of COVID-19 soon after other calamities indicates that God is indeed about to intervene by ending the evil and perversion in society and ushering in the millennial Kingdom. COVID-19 and other pandemics such as the locust invasion, Ebola virus, and civil wars in Africa are just the birth pangs of the imminent Parousia. This narrative is partly enhanced by the close affinity of millennialism and conspiracy theories. COVID-19 has seen the rise of numerous conspiracy theories that aid the imagination of an apocalyptic end of the world. Such conspiracy theories include linking COVID-19 and 5G cellular networks, COVID-19 as a genocidal tool against Africans, the COVID-19 vaccines as meant to make certain races, especially Africans, sexually impotent, among others. Although there is no indication that these conspiracy theories are believed or propagated by Prophet Owuor, the religious connotation of the same cannot be ignored.

Summations on Prophets, Pandemics, and Parousia

Any pandemic with the magnitude of COVID-19 must affect and disorganise life in society, including religious life, which is one of the manifestations of social activity. Religion produces faith that can be beneficial as well as detrimental in a pandemic such as the one occasioned by COVID-19. Faith provides vital coping mechanisms as well as answers to some of the ultimate questions in life, such as why the pandemic came in the first place. But faith can also be detrimental in that some people may feel that the pandemic is a sign that they are being "punished" by God; or, as has been discussed in this paper, that the end of the world is at hand. Thus, the connection between contemporary prophets in Africa, experienced pandemics including COVID-19, and the heightened levels of an expected Parousia raise pertinent questions that need to be answered. These include the question of sin and evil in African Christian thought, the place of eschatology in African Christianity and theology, and the relationship between prophecy and apocalypse.

Sin and Evil in African Christian Thought

Sin is understood in two significant ways within African Christianity. The first is the definition of sin as alienation or estrangement from God. Sin, then, is when one is selfish, self-centred, proud, or disobedient towards God. Secondly, sin is a deliberate act that is morally wrong not necessarily before God, and violates acceptable communal values too. In this context, therefore, when someone speaks about sin, they may be referring to what society considers as being wrong.[31] That would include such actions as smoking, drinking, fighting, and dressing inappropriately, among others. Significantly, the debates surrounding the origin of sin and evil and their repercussions, as well as ways of dealing with sin, are issues that have plagued religions since time immemorial.

What needs to be interrogated further is the connection between sin and evil and, more importantly, aspects of the divine justice of the same. Regarding the current COVID-19 pandemic, the questions that emerge are: is the pandemic because of sin and/or evil? Is God "punishing" the world due to apostasy? Can genuine repentance avert the pandemic? Such questions seem legitimate in the current socio-religious dispensation, yet it must be noted that they are lopsided in theological orientation. Christianity is a faith based on hope. As such, during a pandemic such as COVID-19, it is prudent to preach hope rather than despair. Christianity and Christian theology should provide hope by promoting acts and messages of compassion, solidarity, and care to a hurting world. Christianity should not castigate humanity as being averse to sin or evil but seek to reconcile humanity to God. However true this might be, some believe that the Christian teaching of "other-worldly" punishment for sin has also contributed to the moral decay of society. Joseph Donders, for example, argues that the Christian message of "heaven" or "eternal salvation" deludes people into indifference towards their earthly responsibilities and that the message of the "last judgement" confuses people as far as their moral duties on earth are concerned.[32] This might, however, not be true for the NPMs. The understanding of the pandemic because of apostasy and God's intervention seems to drive adherents of NPMs to practise the spiritual exercises as prescribed by the prophet. It is believed that engaging in these spiritual practices faithfully will achieve two major things: the first is that they (the elect) will be preserved beyond the current pandemic; and secondly, the authority of the prophet over the adherents is maintained, if not magnified.

Eschatology and Crises in Africa

Van Wyk argues that, although the notion of the "final" or "last" judgement is an important aspect of the biblical message, in the growing African Christianity,

[31] C. Wethmar, "Conceptualization of Sin in African Christian Theology," *Acta Theologica* 1 (2006), pp. 249–268.

[32] Joseph G. Donders, *Non-Bourgeois Theology: An African Experience of Jesus* (New York: Orbis Books, 1985), 51-6.

it is not a high priority.[33] This understanding could not be further from the truth. The current dispensation of African Christianity propagated by Pentecostal and Charismatic churches strongly fronts the ideology of eschatology. In fact, eschatology and associated themes such as death, the return of Christ, judgement, rewards, heaven, and hell, fascinate and frustrate people because they have only a limited imagination of the "other world."[34] It is important to interrogate how some branches of Christianity in Africa can link the crises facing the continent with the *eschaton*. In addition, there is need for a further interrogation of the nature of the apocalyptic rhetoric in connection with eschatology, bearing in mind that the apocalyptic rhetoric of NPMs in Kenya consists of an eschatological dualism. This dualism has a clear differentiation between two spheres: the present versus the eternal; the reign of evil versus the triumphant salvation; the earthly and death versus the heavenly and life; the unrighteous and evil people versus the elect and righteous; and this-worldly space versus an other-worldly space. Prophetism and apocalypticism clearly fuel an eschatological understanding of contemporary events such as the current COVID-19 pandemic.

The Relationship Between Apocalypse and Prophecy

Apocalypticism and prophecy are intricately intertwined. Prophecy, just like apocalypticism, relies heavily on imagery, symbolism, and mythology. In ancient Israel, apocalyptic literature arose as a crisis-management endeavour to reassure and strengthen the Jews by instilling a strong faith that God would intervene to vindicate them and punish their oppressors. The traumatic experience of the exile, which had the most profound effect on the thought patterns and lifestyle of the people, had to be countered with an equally strong and effective message of consolation and rehabilitation. The prophets had to speak with a different diction and tenor. Their style of speaking and writing, naturally, underwent a dramatic change: the prophetic preaching was transformed into apocalyptic writing. Whether this is the case in contemporary Africa is yet to be seen. What is clear is that contemporary prophets in Africa such as Owuor utilise apocalyptic literature in the Bible as a source of, and the basis of, their prophetic pronouncements. However, the strength of the apocalyptic ideology lies in its ability to communicate its prophetic message.

Conclusion

The human quest for meaning via transcendence, in the face of a monstrous and inexplicable natural disaster, catastrophe, or plague, is an instinct. It is the way

[33] I.W.C. van Wyk, "The Final Judgment in African Perspectives," *HTS Teologiese Studies/Theological Studies* 62(2), (2006), pp. 703–729.

[34] Elias Bongba Kiffon, "Eschatology in Africa: The Imperative of a Transformative Social Praxis," *Svensk Teologisk Kvartalskrift* 4 (2018), pp. 245–266.

to cope or deal with the panic, fear, and uncertainty created by the catastrophe; faith in the supernatural is an essential part of the human arsenal of either fight or flight. People's quest for transcendence explains their faith in the ultimate spiritual authority in the face of the pandemic. As this paper has shown, one of the Christian theological explanations for the COVID-19 pandemic is rooted in the apocalyptic end-times devotion and rhetoric, supported with end-time prophetic writings, and invoking modern-day doomsday prophets. This perception feeds the narrative that some Christians think that the COVID-19 pandemic is caused by human sin, igniting God's anger upon humanity. It needs to be noted that this current dispensation is not new. Indeed, Christian history is replete with groups maintaining that the end of the world is imminent, such as Jehovah's Witnesses, Mormons, Seventh Day Adventists, and Christadelphians, among others. It is telling that a pandemic of the magnitude of COVID-19 caught many "prophets" unawares. In many African countries south of the Sahara, there are numerous "prophets" and religious leaders who at the beginning of every year predict events that will occur that year. That even Prophet Owuor "belatedly" claimed credit for correctly foretelling the pandemic some five years prior is telling. But more significant still is the association of the pandemic with apostasy and the Parousia as a means of explaining the pandemic.

Understanding Science and Eschatology Relations and its Role in Overcoming Neo-Apocalyptic Falsehood and Negative Impact on COVID-19 Management

Charles Amarkwei

Introduction

This paper establishes that an understanding of empirical science and eschatology, no matter how paradoxically correlated, serves to prevent the use of neo-apocalypticism so that the management of the COVID-19 pandemic cannot be undermined. Such a view demands that the paper first outlines the essential meaning of eschatology in the light of the concrete revelation of God in history in Jesus Christ and in the Holy Spirit. This revelation of God is not a whimsical and capricious selection of meaning that has no basis in the life, suffering, death, and resurrection of Jesus Christ. This approach also requires a look at the nature of African Christian eschatology that takes on board not only apocalyptic content but also issues such as death, Parousia, resurrection, judgement, hell, and eternal life.

That knowledge of Christian eschatology specifically is then critically employed to engage with the neo-apocalyptic interpretation of Pastor Chris Oyakhilome during the emergence of the COVID-19 pandemic. The nature of neo-apocalyptic interpretations and the danger they pose to Christian eschatological life shall be discussed. The paper will assert that the lack of a proper understanding of Christian eschatology needs to be addressed for African Christianity to partner science in order to move Africa out of unnecessary superstition into a reasonable and meaningful existence that is founded on the experience of the ground of being who is in Christ, is in the power of the Holy Spirit, and is moving history to God's end at the end of the world.

What is Christian Eschatology? An African Perspective

I define Christian eschatology as the doctrine about the end and the goal of creaturely existence as it is based on the knowledge of Jesus Christ in his historical death and resurrection objectively, and the subjective experience of him as the Saviour. The word eschatology is derived from two Greek words, *eschata* and *logos*, meaning the "last things" – the end/goal/purpose/reason/meaning of history/the cosmos and science/study, respectively. The former has a double meaning that relates to things that will happen at the end of the cosmos on the one hand, and the purpose of life, or the meaning of life, or the reason for life, or the fulfilment of life on the other.[1] Creaturely life is in ambiguity, which simply means all creatures live in imperfection. This is what is known as the predicament of creation and for which reason there is the longing to overcome it.[2] Christian eschatology teaches that the end and/or the goal of the cosmos is God, who is revealed to Christians in Jesus Christ as the Creator, Redeemer, and the One who makes all things new. The end of the cosmos also means the coming of God in Jesus Christ our Lord and his Kingdom in the power of the Holy Spirit.[3] It is the purpose of God from the beginning of creation that makes creation's existence meaningful, and that will be fulfilled in the future at the end of the cosmos when Jesus appears in his Kingdom.[4]

The above expectation of the end is not utopian but based upon the revelation of God to the cosmos as the absolutely concrete in history, objectively and subjectively, through grace and by faith in Jesus Christ as One who died and rose again. The experience of conversion following the revelation, known both in Protestant and African Christian circles as pneumatic experience, leads to the acknowledgement, confession, and proclamation of the Lord Jesus Christ as the goal, meaning, and the end of history or cosmos. Conversion is also from the power of the resurrection and makes the ambiguities underlying the human predicament overwhelmed and conquered. Moreover, a new life emerges by participating in or living in the work of God through the Son in the power of the Holy Spirit. Thus, conversion is referred to as renewal or the born-again experience in traditional theology and pietistic theology, as well as Pentecostal and Charismatic theology.

Moreover, conversion is an affirmation of the eschatological God who is, who was, and is to come (Rev. 1:8).[5] It is an experience that awakens the faculties of

---

[1] Paul Tillich, *Systematic Theology, III: Life and the Spirit: History and Kingdom of God* (Chicago, IL: University of Chicago Press, 1976), 394-398.

[2] Tillich, ST, III: 339–406.

[3] Karl Barth, *Credo: A Presentation of the Chief Problems of Dogmatics with Reference to the Apostles' Creed*, trans. James Strathern McNab (London: Hodder & Stoughton, 1936), p. 120; Karl Rahner, "The Hermeneutics of Eschatological Assertions," *Theological Investigations* Vol. 4, trans. Kevin Smyth (Baltimore, MD: Helicon, 1966), p. 342; in John C. McDowell, "Karl Barth Having No-thing to Hope For," *Journal for Christian Theological Research* 11 (2006), p. 15 [Available at: http://digitalcommons.luthersem.edu/jctr/vol11/iss2006/2], [Last accessed: 11th July 2023]. See also Jürgen Moltmann, *The Coming of God: Christian Eschatology*, trans. Margaret Kohl (London: SCM Press, 1996), p. xi.

[4] Tillich, *ST*, III: 394-406; Wolfhart Pannenberg, *Theology and the Kingdom of God* (Louisville, KY: Westminster Press, 1969), p. 52; in Carl Braaten, "The Kingdom of God and Life Everlasting," in Peter C. Hodgson and Robert H. King (eds), *Christian Theology: An Introduction to Its Traditions and Tasks* (Philadelphia, PA: Fortress Press, 1982), pp. 291–292.

[5] Tillich, *ST*, III: 395–96.

the creature to appreciate its past fallenness or spiritual death by virtue of the renewal and the new life that has been experienced. It awakens the convert to understand that God is the creator of all things and God is the only reason why life is worth living, because God has a plan for all creatures. In particular, the meaning derived from this efficacious pneumatic experience rests chiefly in the death and resurrection of God, which is executed in Jesus Christ in the Holy Spirit.[6] It brings about a conviction of faith that there is hope and that the ambiguities associated with all creatures shall come to an end on the day of the Lord. Thus, in effect, the end, purpose, or meaning for creation dwells in God alone, who is Father, Son, and Holy Spirit from the beginning. God as the source of meaning drives history and every creature paradoxically to that very end. Seriously, the goal of life is not in things[7] nor, for that matter, any part of the whole of creation. It is not the unreasonable or irrational acquisition of material things that should be deemed the goal or the purpose of life. It is in the meaningful acquisition of material things and the purposeful and responsible utilisation of materials of the created order. Therefore, it is the life associated with God that resides in the Triune God and moves with meaningfulness and responsibility for the whole cosmos.

The life subsisting in God positively acknowledges the good in the whole of creation and gives a person a reason to live responsibly. It encourages the enjoyment of what is in the created order and its management towards the goal of the whole of creation. It is motivated by an *agape* love that is found in God through Jesus the Son, who is revealed and experienced in His death and resurrection in the power of the Holy Spirit (I Cor. 15:1-11). Therefore, its power is revealed in a dominating power that is vulnerable and self-sacrificing in the creation, redemption, and renewal of the whole of creation. Moreover, life subsisting in God is contrary to the dominating power that does not honour the good of creation; that is, the beloved community of God.

Hence, for Karl Barth, Jürgen Moltmann,[8] or perhaps African Christians, eschatology must be axiomatic to the Christian faith interpretation. And rightly so, because eschatology is fundamental to dealing with the human predicament and is the basis upon which the Christian gospel is preached. Eschatology is not abstract; it is an embodiment of the Trinitarian economy of the cosmos, which is

---

[6] Particularly, in Ghana Pentecostalism, Elder Mireku's Song "*Se mewo Yesu a, mewo ade nyinara; se Yesu bo me a ade nyinaa abo me* ..." meaning "If I have Jesus, I have everything; if I lose Jesus, I have lost everything ..." and other similar songs and medleys capture this genuine experience in the Ghanaian Christian experience. This great Christian experience also accentuates the Akan eschatological concept of *Nyame* and *Gye Nyame*. *Nyame* as God is the One who, when encountered, brings about ultimate satisfaction. And *Gye Nyame* means the One without which nothing holds together.

[7] Daniel Migliore, *Faith Seeking Understanding: An Introduction to Christian Theology* (Grand Rapids, MI: Eerdmans, 2004), pp. 342–343.

[8] Braaten, "The Kingdom of God," p. 273.

experienced in life. It is a life that comes based on God's love for us; our faith response to the work of the Son and the meaningfulness we experience in hope in the Holy Spirit (I Thes. 1:3; 5:8). It is the hope of the resurrection after death, the vindication after judgement in eternal life at the coming of Jesus Christ (Parousia), marking the end of history and ushering in of the new heaven and earth (I Cor. 15:12-28, Rev. 21:1, 5). And so, it is a hope that works with the principle that Jesus Christ is present and is working through, with and under, but also above and ahead, of the whole cosmos. Moreover, from the beginning, meaningfulness in the whole of all existence, which is driving every creature as an ultimate concern, does not exclude empirical science.[9] This is because science itself is part and parcel of the good creation of God. How, then, does the Creator fight against the creature, except when it is distorted? And even then, God works for its redemption and renewal. So, this non-escapist attitude to life and existence in general is the basis upon which Christians live courageously in confronting evil and injustice, and that is because it is worthwhile to live here and now.

Eschatology is a this-worldly disposition based on what God has done (Acts 10:38). Thus, Christian life is about the *eschaton* which is here "already" as the Kingdom manifesting in the hearts of all believers and in the faith community of Jesus Christ and ensures that the Kingdom of God is tangibly and holistically experienced. But then, it is also other-worldly, in the sense that, having experienced the subjective truth of redemption and renewal and having knowledge of the objective truth about Jesus' resurrection from the dead, there is an absolutised faith or hope for the new earth and new heaven. It makes room for the Christian to understand the present fragmented fulfilment and to anticipate the "not yet" as the final fulfilment in the Parousia (I Cor. 13:12).

The understanding of eschatology stands on the Lord Jesus, who reveals to people the will of the Father in the power of the Holy Spirit in His death and resurrection and is linked to empirical science as concomitant to the Trinitarian economy. The assumption is that science is initially rejected by some African Christians for its inherent ambiguities but can be accepted and transformed and used to advance God's purpose of life in fullness as an eschatological pointer of eternal life at the end of history.

Eschatology is an acknowledgement of the limitedness in all existence, including the existence of the Christian. The coming of Jesus Christ is the persuasion that Christians have about the fact that they do not possess all knowledge in view of their limited capacity in the presence of the Son of God. This limitation, revealed through faith and life in Jesus Christ in the Spirit, does not restrain itself in the realm of what is commonly called "spirituality." The lack of knowledge reveals itself in the empirical sciences, gestalt sciences, and all other sciences. A good Christian eschatological understanding of the Christian limitation in accepting all knowledge leads to an unperturbed posture. It also

---

[9] Tillich, *ST* I:9-10; Paul Tillich, *Dynamics of Faith* (New York: HarperOne, 2009), 4-22.

points to the human frailty constantly, which needs redemption, and at the same time, points to God in Jesus Christ in the Spirit as the Creator, Redeemer, and Sanctifier. So, the Christian constantly lives in humility, ascribing all knowledge to God and endeavouring to live in God. This is also the disposition expected of the church. So, the church does not make room for the Grand Inquisitor[10] who takes the place of Jesus Christ, retiring and making a ridicule of Jesus. Indeed, the church is not Jesus Christ who is the Lord. And the church cannot worship itself but only God in Jesus in the power of the Holy Spirit. The church cannot arrogate to itself absolute powers with which it cross-examines everyone and pretends to possess all knowledge, including in the realm of empirical science. Yet, the church in Christ and in the Spirit will interrogate and seek to learn to know more until the coming of Jesus Christ. Similarly, it sees apocalyptic ideas as symbolically rich and that which the human capacity cannot grasp fully until the return of the Lord.

Moreover, unlike the general African worldview that there is life after death, Christian hope goes beyond death to hope in the resurrection of the body and the renewal of the whole of existence itself.[11] Christianity goes further to assert the Parousia, which is not the cyclical renewal or fragmented fulfilment in existence but a once-andfor-all coming of God that will end all creaturely struggles. Nevertheless, Christian eschatology corroborates the worldview that there is eternal life and eternal death after some form of judgement based upon the life that is lived before death or the life that was lived before the *eschaton*.

Upon the above rests the Christian life and the life of the church, indicating that, from the beginning of the Christian's life, there is an animation with an eschatological purpose. Thus, life in the present in Jesus has a lot to do with life with Jesus in the future. Living in Jesus in the Spirit thus secures life even in the face of suffering, pain, and death. It is a life that has no room for fear of suffering, pain, and death; rather it has the courage of confidence (Rom. 8:35-39), and the peace that surpasses all understanding (Eph. 4:7). Thus, having Jesus or living in Jesus, or participating in the life of Jesus Christ in the Spirit ends all fears and anxiety. And this understanding endures, irrespective of the symbolic apocalyptic ideas available.

The Paradoxical Relations of African Christian Eschatology and Science

Traditionally, Africans have a holistic approach to reality in general. Indeed, it is normal for Africans to combine spiritual healing with both traditional and

---

[10] Fyodor Dostoevsky, *The Brothers Karamazov* (New York: Barnes and Noble, 1995), pp. 225-243.

[11] Riemer Roukema, *Gnosis and Faith in Early Christianity: An Introduction to Gnosticism*, trans. John Bowden (Harrisburg, PA: Trinity Press International, 1999), p. 151.

orthodox medicine. There have been no qualms at all about doing this in recent times. And this holistic approach is true regarding the reality of the African traditionalist, whose mind I term "kpelelogical." This terminology is a hybrid of a word from the Ga ethnic group of southern Ghana, *kpele*, and that of the Greeks, *logos*. The Ga word *kpele* means "all-encompassing."[12] Hence, kpelelogy connotes an ontological mode of holistic thought. Interestingly, there is also what I term "Kpelelogical," which echoes the mind of the African Christian after the pneumatic experience of conversion. While the former (kpelelogical), is not capitalised, the latter is, indicating the transformation of the African primal mind. African Christians therefore engage the combinations of supernatural healing alongside orthodox medicine without any misgivings.[13] However, African Christians find it extremely strange to have orthodox medical care without spiritual healing. Every healing is ascribed to God even if it is wholly acknowledged to be orthodox. It is this relationship between both kpelelogical and the Kpelelogical in which traditional and orthodox healing seems to be relegated or rejected but embraced and utilised in the face of divine healing, and that indicates the paradoxical correlation.[14]

Thus, in a sense, the separation of science from faith is only artificial because almost all world civilisations knew that, fundamentally, science itself existed not without a purpose beyond it.[15] Nonetheless, science and faith or theology should not interfere with each other's domain. The theologian, as an interpreter of Christian faith, should positively grant scientific research its free expression (independence). The result is that there is a mutually independent relationship. But since they are both grasped by ultimate concern, which is the end or goal of history, they are all limited in themselves. In view of this situation, although they

---

[12] Marion Kilson, *Kpele Lala: Ga Religious Songs and Symbols* (Cambridge, MA: Harvard University Press, 1971), pp. 7, 18.

[13] J.S. Mbiti, *African Religions and Philosophy* (London: Heinemann, 1969), pp. 2, 15–16, 169; Kwabena Asamoah-Gyadu, "Therapeutic Strategies in African Religions: Health, Herbal Medicines and Indigenous Christian Spirituality," *Studies in World Christianity* 20(1), (2014), pp. 70–90; Kwame Gyekye, *African Cultural Values: An Introduction* (Accra: Sankofa, 1996), p. 3; cf. Paul Tillich, *The Philosophy of the Sciences According to Objects and Methods* (Lewisburg, PA: Bucknell University Press, 1981); Ken Wilber, *A Theory of Everything: An Integral Vision for Business, Politics, Science and Spirituality* (Boston, MA: Shambhala, 2000), pp. 33–80.

[14] Charles Amarkwei, *Paul Tillich and His System of Paradoxical Correlation: Forging a New Way for Science and Theology Relations* (Eugene, OR: Wipf and Stock, 2020).

[15] Thomas Wendell, *On the Resolution of Science and Faith* (New York: Island, 1946), p. 3; Paul Tillich in Robert C. Kimball (ed.), *Theology of Culture* (New York: Oxford University Press, 1959), pp. 11–12; Frank Thilly and Ledgar Wood, *A History of Philosophy* (New York: Holt, Rinehart & Winston, 1957); George G.M. James, *Stolen Legacy: Greek Philosophy is Stolen Egyptian Philosophy* (Bensenville, IL: Lushena, 2014), p. 7; Charles Thaxton and Nancy Pearcey, *The Soul of Science: Christian Faith and Natural Philosophy* (Wheaton, IL: Crossway, 1994), p. 43; Gordon H. Clark, *The Philosophy of Science and Belief in God* (Nutley, NJ: The Craig, 1977).

seem in conflict, both science and theology could enlighten each other. And this enlightenment could be seen as guesses or hypotheses in science, on the one hand, and enlightenment of theology in the promotion and utilisation of science and technology for a responsible attainment of life in fullness on the other.

Yet, on the Christian front, the responsible utilisation rests on the revelation of God in Jesus Christ in his death and resurrection in the Spirit. When we look at Jesus Christ in his death and resurrection, there is the revelation of how God, fully divine and fully human, relates. First, the created order, including science, represented by humanity in suffering and death, is rejected or separated from God. Yet, God in Jesus Christ accepts and renews the whole of creation represented by humanity in his resurrection. Similarly, science is seemingly rejected yet accepted, transformed, and utilised in the light of the resurrection. Therefore, the ethical values of the ground or goal of existence seen in Jesus is the sure means or standard of accepting responsible scientific knowledge and rejecting irresponsible scientific knowledge. It is a relationship that has resonance with the Chalcedonian Creed, as it affirms the paradox of grace on the one hand and the paradox of faith on the other. It is the testimony that God revealed in Jesus Christ in the Spirit is the One who is with the transformed science today and was with it from the beginning and will appear with a fully transformed science. Moreover, this action of God will take place without change or confusion, without separation or division, regarding the essential nature of science and God. This is because it is only through the accommodation made to science that science itself will be healed from its ambiguities in consonance with the conviction that, "that which he has not assumed, he has not healed."[16]

The crux of the matter at stake is whether a particular science and technology should be accepted or not because of a neo-apocalyptic interpretation of reality. Our position is that neo-apocalyptic interpretation fundamentally distorts the knowledge of God in Jesus Christ and stifles the attainment of divine economy for the cosmos. So, in the discussion following, I wish to take a view of neo-apocalypticism and then follow up with how its application today has effectively undermined COVID-19 management.

Neo-Apocalypticism and Pastor Chris Oyakhilome's View

Neo-apocalyptic understanding is really an offshoot of the Jewish eschatology that developed from this-worldly to other-worldly convictions. Although a this-worldly strain of eschatology dominates Jewish thought, the other-worldly strain that is captured by the apocalyptic imagery of the end of the world or the cosmos equally persists in Christianity.[17] Traditionally, in Christianity, it is seen as the

---

[16] Gregory of Nazianzus, "Epistle 101," in Edward R. Hardy (ed.), *Christology of the Latter Fathers* Vol. 3, Library of Christian Classics (Philadelphia, PA: Westminster, 1954), p. 218.

[17] Braaten, "The Kingdom of God," pp. 276–278.

revelation of God through Jesus, the Son of God, and the Holy Spirit on the one hand, and the hope that Jesus Christ will come again, which is engendered by the former experience, on the other hand. In contrast, neo-apocalypticism focuses on interpretation of the imageries of the apocalyptic in the Bible (cf. Rev. 7:1–20:15).

Particularly, neo-apocalyptic interpretations dwell chiefly on the rapture and the thousand-year reign of Jesus Christ.[18] Neo-apocalypticism chastises traditional eschatology for not dealing with the issues of the rapture and the thousand years of Jesus' reign. And it may be right so long as eschatological millennialism is part of traditional theology.[19] Two views of neo-apocalypticism are: firstly, those who believe that the Lord will come before the thousand-year reign (pre-millennialism); and secondly, those who think that Jesus will come after his thousand-year reign (post-millennialism).[20] Both Pre-millennialists and Post-millennialists have an idea of conflict in the end times based upon apocalyptic ideas in the Bible in common.

Pre-millennialists believe that the rapture will mark the coming reign of Jesus Christ. And they believe in two major conflicts at the time of the end. The first conflict is associated with the coming of the Anti-Christ and the tribulation. Thereafter, the thousand-year reign of Jesus Christ will follow. After the thousand-year reign of Jesus Christ, there will be the final conflict where evil will be defeated forever.[21] Pre-millennialists also have three different variants, depending on when the rapture will take place. The first variant believes that before the tribulation, rapture will take place. The second variant believes that the coming of Christ, which is represented by the rapture, will take place during the tribulation. And finally, the third variant sees the rapture taking place after the tribulation.[22] On the other hand, Post-millennialists are of the view that the thousand-year reign of Jesus Christ is identical to the age of the church, after which there will be the conflict between good and evil and the coming of Jesus Christ.[23]

Characteristically, Millennialists are extremely vigilant, perhaps inspired by an eschatological reading of the Bible. Nonetheless, this vigilance leads them to identify every symbol used in the Bible with some extreme idea in history. It has led them to the point of identifying the exact times at which the rapture will take place or the time the second coming of Christ will take place. This deterministic attitude of neo-apocalypticism undermines the truth of the Christian message as,

---

[18] Moltmann, *The Coming of God*, pp. 147, 159.

[19] Moltmann, *The Coming of God*, pp. 192–194.

[20] Moltmann, *The Coming of God*, p. 147.

[21] James H. Evans Jr., "Eschatology, White Supremacy, and the Beloved Community," in Rebecca S. Chopp and Mark Lewis Taylor (eds), *Reconstructing Christian Theology* (Minneapolis, MN: Fortress, 1994), pp. 352–353.

[22] Moltmann, *The Coming of God*, p. 159.

[23] Evans Jr., "Eschatology, White Supremacy, and the Beloved Community," p. 353.

on major occasions, it has proved to be false.[24] Millennialist interpretation of the end times leads into labelling occurrences, organisations, people, certain structures, and systems as evil. This labelling denies the gospel of its centrality in the life, ministry, death, and resurrection of Jesus Christ, because it fails to understand that the Christian message stands for hope for all who are in despair and sin. Thus, the Millennialist division of the world into true believers and infidels represents a determination ahead of God at the very end. And instead of preaching and representing love and hope through faith in Jesus Christ, they become messengers of hatred, despair, and godlessness through their extremely destructive actions.[25] Daniel Migliore's description of Millennialists cannot be overemphasised when he wrote, "Most conspicuous in this neo-apocalyptic depiction of the end time is the absence of a theology of the ministry, cross and resurrection of Jesus Christ. Eschatology is torn away from the person and work of Christ, Armageddon replaces Golgotha."[26]

Because of their propensity to labelling and tagging, Millennialists are highly prone to isolationist tendencies. And they tend to arrogate to themselves the very powers that belong to God. These powers include the ability to know, understand, and explain every reality in human history, including the present. Thus, this neo-apocalyptic understanding and disposition betray the very essence of eschatology, which is pre-eminently an acknowledgement of our limitation in every sphere of life and knowledge, and our faith and hope in the one and only person, Jesus Christ.

Indeed, Christians are called to bear witness to what the Lord is doing, what he has done, and what he will do in responsible living. Responsible living cannot be related to the escapist "responsibility" of preaching fear, anxiety, and destructive tendencies in the name of the rapture.[27] Rather, responsible living is a life that is held accountable by God through the death and resurrection of Jesus Christ and hopes for the new earth and new heaven. It is the hope that confronts the evil of death by deploying the gift of human knowledge and wisdom as God's tool for the experience of life in fullness. And it is deploying scientific knowledge as God's gift and tool which is to be used to bring healing to the world during a pandemic.

The neo-apocalyptic depiction of the end of the world and the manifest actions of Millennialists show a denial of the failures in Christian history. Christian history has shown that an apocalyptic interpretation of reality, whereby the church predicted that the reign of Jesus had come and thus exercised Jesus' authority as if it were Christ Himself, was a betrayal. Hence, anytime the church assumed the position of Christ, it became an inquisitor looking out for its enemies and pretending to know all. Yet, the inherent ambiguities in the

---

[24] Migliore, *Faith Seeking Understanding*, p. 336.
[25] Migliore, *Faith Seeking Understanding*, pp. 335–337.
[26] Migliore, *Faith Seeking Understanding*, p. 37.
[27] Moltmann, *The Coming of God*, pp. 158–159.

medieval church, which arrogated to itself the powers of Jesus Christ and pretended to know everything, were made evident through the knowledge of science.[28] The falsehood and inconsistency associated with the created order, which the church is part of, became clear down the line.

The results of the Renaissance and the Enlightenment teach the church today to live in humility, acknowledging what it knows and what it does not know as it looks to the Lord's coming when everything shall be plain.[29] Moreover, knowing where the Protestant Reformation has come from, it is important for neo-apocalyptic interpreters to remember their pasts for them to reposition themselves. The view today, whereby science and technology are labelled as the Beast, or the Anti-Christ, shows the embarrassing inconsistencies associated with their initial position in history. The point is that a major action for which Roman Catholicism was criticised is acting upon the same body who opposed Roman Catholicism for similar actions.

One typical example of how African Christianity nearly succumbed to the onslaught of neo-apocalyptic interpretation of the times during the wake of COVID-19 is accentuated by Pastor Chris Oyakhilome. He is the leader of the church denomination commonly known as the Christ Embassy, but officially named LoveWorld Incorporated. Pastor Chris is more likely a Post-millennialist who believes that we are in the age of the church. This means that, in his view, the church is enjoying its thousand-year reign with Jesus Christ. He states as follows:

> We are still in the age of the Church and the Anti-Christ cannot advance his plans yet. The Bible is clear that after the Rapture of the Church, the son of perdition will be revealed. Brothers and sisters, this isn't a time to play with Christianity. Give your life to Christ now while you still can because these things will happen, but after the Church is raptured.[30]

For him, right after the thousand-year reign, the rapture must take place, followed by the coming of the Anti-Christ. Although he seems not to be explicit in his statements, we must understand that, for Millennialists, the coming of the Anti-Christ means ushering in the period of tribulation. Surely, this will also be followed by conflict and the second coming of Christ. Therefore, being a "vigilant" Christian, Pastor Chris sees in the light of a neo-apocalyptic interpretation the whole idea of coronavirus and its management as a ploy. The ploy is that COVID-19 is just a smokescreen that is used to introduce a fifth-

---

[28] William R. Shea, "Galileo and the Church," in David C. Lindberg and Roland L. Numbers (eds), *God and Nature: Historical Essays on the Encounter Between Christianity and* Science (Berkeley, CA: University of California Press, 1986), pp. 114–133.

[29] Moltmann, *The Coming of God*, pp. 159–165.

[30] Kareem Ugbodada, "Oyakhilome Reveals Frightening Story About Coronavirus and New World Order," 2 *PM NEWS* (5th April 2020) https://www.pmnewsnigeria.com/2020/04/05/oyakhilome-reveals-frightening-story-about-coronavirus-and-new-world-order/ [Last accessed: 17th April 2022].

generation (5G) technology into human bodies via vaccination to manipulate people in fulfilment of what the Bible says about the Anti-Christ. Thus, for him, it is most probable that COVID-19 was manufactured somehow to foster that evil agenda that will prepare the way for the Anti-Christ. He is quoted as saying the following:

> Don't think what is happening right now has to do with a virus. It's not a virus. The world has chosen to be deceived. As they have been deceived many times before.
>
> […] This is not a pandemic. Question: where did the other ones go? No one is asking. I have asked the question, "Where do viruses come from?" They are not found in nature, it means they're created. I'm trying to let you know the reason you're in your house. I call it a global siege.
>
> […] What they don't tell you is that your body can be connected. Did you know that once that happens you can also be controlled as your devices are controlled, meaning that signals can be sent to your brain, your brain can be controlled. Once that happens, you are no longer yourself. The idea is controlling the new race.
>
> […] So, since they can't vaccinate everyone, they started vaccinating children and raising them that way. You wanna know what's going on in the world? There's a movie called *Divergent* from 2014. That's what the groups that are interested in the new world order are up to, to put a vaccine in your body containing a digital ID, by which you as a human being can be controlled, you cease to be yourself.
>
> […] they use two things: 1. They created a pandemic (COVID-19) in order to create fear and panic. 2. They use the internet of things (IOT) and created 5G (people can easily embrace it), which causes health issues, but you wouldn't know because they made you love the high internet speed.[31]

Pastor Chris reportedly made similar comments on a live programme on 29th December 2020.[32] He said that "the vaccine introduces into your body a nano-chip which the 5G connects to, and somebody from somewhere can alter your DNA. They can get into your system, into your life and you are no longer what God created."[33]

So far, in Pastor Chris's statements, I identify two main areas that effectively seek to undermine COVID-19 management in Africa and beyond. Firstly, I identify in his statements the suggestion that the quarantine was a channel for 5G technology to be rolled out. Plainly, this suggestion has the power to embolden numerous Christians to flout quarantine rules in their respective nations and especially in Africa. Apart from the consequences pertaining to the undercutting and destruction of 5G investments, the health management plan of many nations is severely undermined. Now, there is the need to remember the Shincheonji Church, which was the cause of about over 72.4 per cent of infections in South

---

[31] Ugbodada, "Oyakhilome Reveals Frightening Story About Coronavirus."

[32] For a broad study, see Adelakun, *Powerful Devices*.

[33] News Ghana, "COVID-19 Vaccine Will Work With Nano-Chips, 5G to Control You," *News Ghana*, 1st January 2021 [Available at: https://newsghana.com.gh/covid-19-vaccine-will-work-with-nano-chips-5g-to-control-you-pastor-chris/], [Last accessed: 20th July 2023].

Korea's city of Daegu and about 93 per cent of the root cause of the national infection in March 2020.[34]

The second mode of undercutting the COVID-19 management by Pastor Chris was the neo-apocalyptic interpretation that the 5G technology to be introduced through inoculation is a precursor to the Anti-Christ. For Christians who chose to believe in Pastor Chris's statement above, vaccination is surely not an option. And even when he attempted to douse the flames of anti-vaccination Christians by saying the time was not yet up, he was only preparing and arming them against future management schemes as well as those presented at that time.

Standing by the two areas above sends the clear message that science itself is the sure means through which the Anti-Christ will manifest. And, looking at the way it is presented, there seems some suggestion that any scientific and technological advancement ought to be part of the grand scheme of the Anti-Christ. This also implies that the Christian message has nothing to do with science, or that science conflicts with the Christian faith. However, the latter's statement is a half-truth, because the church of the future is the church that can utilise science and technology most effectively and efficiently to propagate the Christian message.[35]

Pastor Chris, nonetheless, tried to clarify his statement by asserting he was on the side of science by stating that, "the lockdown was not science." He cited the United States of America (USA) as evidence of failed lockdown measures. Moreover, he says that wearing a face mask was not scientific because it was only a political measure. Pastor Chris stated that, "in fact, scientifically, [wearing a mask] is dangerous to health […] and that's the truth."[36] It could be surmised that Pastor Chris's goal was to put the blame not only on science, but also on geopolitics and its local political allies. Of course, firmly behind that idea is the assumption that the Anti-Christ is working with and is within the powerful political systems in the world. However, learning from the Shincheonji Church's experience in Korea, it is very plain that the lockdown was to effectively enforce social distancing as a scientific control of the spread of disease. Face masks prevent the spread of the virus from one person to another. Vaccination is also a scientific measure to provide protection against infection. These measures taken to ensure good health are logical, and the neo-apocalyptic interpretations only seek to undermine them.

---

[34] Yun-Jung Kang, "Lessons Learnt from Cases of COVID-19 Infection in South Korea," *Cambridge University Press Public Health Emergency Collection* (7th May 2020), pp. 1–8. DOI: 10.1017/dmp.2020.141.

[35] See, for instance, Adelakun, *The Healing of Maseko.*

[36] Akelicious Media, "Wearing Facemask 72bout is an Embarrassment to Science," 6th May 2020 [https://www.youtube.com/watch?v=VEiatmfWxvw&feature=emb_imp_woyt], [Video taken down] [Last accessed: 16th April 2022].

African Christianity and the Management of Pandemics

Having noted that traditional theological relations with science for the well-being of every creature are founded on the paradox of the grace of the Trinitarian God revealed in the life, ministry, death, and resurrection of Jesus Christ in the Spirit, and having also identified that there is more assurance in believing and hoping in the love of God revealed in Jesus Christ, it is only reasonable to look to Him in times of crisis.

The good creation of God is entrusted with a rationality that involves the use of both wisdom and knowledge acquired through meaningful existence. Moreover, this beautiful knowledge bequeathed to all creation and epitomised in human knowledge, which includes science and technology, are to be utilised responsibly as a demonstration of goodness in the creation of God. Therefore, scientific knowledge obtained to be utilised for the renewal of the creation of God is also the work of God to end the human predicament. Thus, even though we expect this goal of existence to take place at the end of the cosmos, we also believe that the goal existed at the beginning, even as it exists in our present world. Nonetheless, we reckon with the fact that human knowledge, including science and technology, is so limited and could not be advanced without the revelation of God's love in Jesus Christ.

Again, it is the same reason why it is important to avoid hasty conclusions about what science will do to help the whole creation of God through arguments not anchored in Jesus Christ. Churches in Africa must understand their human incapacity to know even all the mysteries of God on the one hand, and the mysteries of science on the other hand. Since, as Christians, our knowledge of God is not in full (although it is enough for our salvation to be guaranteed), it will finally be brought to fullness at the coming of the Lord Jesus and the end of the cosmos. So, the inherent ambiguity in science and technology should always be exposed as we preach the gospel of the crucified but risen Lord. Nonetheless, the church, based on its limited knowledge, should understand the beauty of the knowledge of God within the cosmos that is hidden, but which, when found, could be the very platform God in Jesus Christ will ride on as He appears in His Kingdom at the end of the cosmos. And in doing this, the scrutiny ought to be whether it is performing an act of love, although, on its own, it has no room for value as a subject of epistemology.

The COVID-19 pandemic has exposed how "handicapped" our world is. Everything that exists has been challenged. Both science and religion have been challenged and their limitations glaringly exposed. Many people continue to die and, as people of God, this ought not to be a time for escapist ambitions where helpless Christians only pray without doing practically anything to salvage the situation. Christians who believe in Jesus Christ and who do not wait for the end of history to appear to end the human predicament must get involved to the point of death by doing good deeds. The church today can do no less. Hence, the church in Africa is called upon to join the fray by using their gifts of knowledge and abilities and resources to save lives and thereby glorify God with faith in Jesus Christ. Practically, medical science and technology ought to be vigorously championed by churches as a hope to the people of the continent and as a challenge to governments to invest more in those areas.

People lose hope when medical services get reduced to demonic activity that will potentially destroy Africans. It is important not to forget where Africa has come from. Africa and its renewal for life in fullness should not be steeped in and aggravated by Christian superstition that is contrary to the gospel of the saving Jesus Christ. The churches in Africa must promote the future of their people through science and technology (because Africa cannot live in its past) but constantly renew itself in the light of the work of Christ in the Spirit. If African Christianity could see the great opportunities in COVID-19 to develop the diverse talents of the African youth and channel them into great scientific advancements, there will be hope. The gloom will be apparent when African scientists cannot see a reason to utilise their gifts as nurses, doctors, biomolecular scientists, virologists, and laboratory workers. Africa cannot be saved by science only, but God has a plan for science for the salvation and renewal of Africa in holistic terms.

Consequently, proclaiming a message that undermines the manufacture, distribution, and administration of vaccines to end the COVID-19 pandemic based on the fear of the control of the Anti-Christ undermines and contradicts God's purpose. The call of Jesus Christ is not a call that creates anxiety, panic, and fear. Rather, it is a call to believe in Him who alone saves, and in whom alone there is the courage, that even in death there is life in Him. The call is for everyone to believe and live in Jesus Christ in the Spirit. Anyone who does this always has life, and that life in Christ Jesus conquers all ambiguities, including the evil of the Anti-Christ.

Moreover, the Christian call is not a life of courage that lacks wisdom. Courage is the power of God operating in wisdom, knowledge, and common sense. For faith in God is not an irrationality but is full of purpose and meaningfulness. Therefore, African churches ought to be wary of diving into the depths of contradictions in the name of prophecy and new revelations. The reason is that whatever God does is right in the light of its reasonability (that is, it makes sense). Sometimes the sense it makes goes beyond human comprehension. God's way seems contradictory, but is not contradictory in essence, because God cannot contradict God's self whatsoever.

Conclusion

The interpretation of apocalyptic imagery in the Bible can be very emotional and the risks of making false claims are extremely high. Its very nature is not new; it has existed in the life of the church through almost all denominations. However, time and time again, the church's interpretation and behaviour regarding historical millennialism are a stark embarrassment. Scientists were killed while others had all their works destroyed because the church falsely assumed they judged them rightly.

The church ought to learn from the lessons of church history and admit its need for redemption. Thus, views about eschatology should constantly remind all to understand that, as Christians and churches, we have extremely limited knowledge and that it is only in Jesus Christ that life becomes meaningful. This does not mean that Jesus Christ is not working in the processes and systems of the world. And if Jesus is working in the cosmos and through the cosmos, all may have to admit in humility the need for the church to work with other systems, such as science. This should not lead to the worship of science. Rather than admitting that science itself always needs to be improved and updated, African Christians should proclaim Jesus as the fulfilling agent at the end of the cosmos.

More importantly for Africans, there is a long way ahead in terms of science and technology. African churches must promote responsible scientific studies to improve health and socio-economic well-being. Africa without science will go into pitch darkness and the grace of God could be extremely difficult to perceive. And knowing that science is not an enemy, although it has the potential of an irresponsible utility, the church is called upon to promote its responsible use, especially after experiencing the COVID-19 pandemic. Hence, a good appreciation of the dangers associated with neo-apocalyptic interpretations of biblical metaphors and sound eschatological understanding may help manage the aftermath of COVID-19 pandemic.

A Theological Response to Understanding Human Suffering in an African Context from the Viewpoint of God's Omnipotence

Elizabeth Olufunmilayo Akinbobola

Introduction

Suffering is prevalent in the world and has been from time immemorial. Humans have been plagued and terrorised by all kinds of suffering, always threatening their lives and existence. Most of the time, this unexplainable and inescapable reality comes in the form of disappointments, mental disorders, accidents, possession of evil spirits, sicknesses, diseases, pestilences, and sometimes death, such as from the experience of COVID-19 and Ebola.

Despite its varying causes, suffering usually results in pains and agonies of heart; these various experiences of pain caused by suffering transcend our human minds and imaginations. They stand as formidable and insurmountable forces that cannot be overcome by mundane powers. Therefore, humans have always turned to both terrestrial and celestial powers such as gods, spirits, ancestors, magic, diviners, and witch doctors for help and deliverance. The unpalatable and unannounced suddenness of this phenomenon has also made some individuals question the existence, the power, and love of God.

Various religions have different interpretations of human suffering, its sources, and the solutions. For example, African religions are aware of the presence of evil in the world and, in various ways, Africans always endeavour to fight it.[1] From theological and religious points of view, God is omnipotent and He is good. This can be seen especially in the salvation history that cumulated in the event of Jesus Christ becoming the incarnate Son of God for the redemption of the whole world (Jn. 3:16).

African religions also believe that God is omnipotent; this is revealed in the various names ascribed to him by the various societies in Africa. The Akan of Ghana call God *Odomankoma*. God is also referred to as *Oboadee*, *Obo-nkwa*, *kwasi-Asi a daa awisi*. God has several names in Ghana that indicate that He is all-powerful, everlasting, and a grandfather.[2] He is called *Lubanga* among the Acholi, *Umlungu* among the Nyika, *Kazah* among the Bajju, *Chukwu* among the

---

[1] John S. Mbiti, *African Religions and Philosophy* (London: Heinemann Educational Books Ltd, 1969), p. 204.

[2] E. Kofi Agorsah, *Religion, Ritual, and African Tradition: African Foundations* (Bloomington, IN: Author House, 2010), p. 3.

Igbos, *Leve* among the Mende, *Mawu* among the Ewe, *Dagun* among the Birom, and *Ngai* among the Kikuyi. Whatever name this Supreme Being is known by, God has the attributes of being the creator, king, and judge who is omnipresent, omnipotent, all-wise, all-knowing, all-seeing, and immortal.[3]

The traditional Africans believe that God is also involved in the world. God is the one who provides food, sunshine, rain, children, health, and protection.[4] This paper aims to examine an African perspective of suffering rooted in the African context and provide a theological response to the understanding of suffering in that context from the viewpoint of God's omnipotence as it discusses suffering from biblical, theological perspectives and an African worldview.

Suffering is an Inevitable Reality in Human Experience

From Christian religious faith, the scriptures identify several reasons for suffering. God uses suffering as punishment; God also uses suffering to demonstrate His power (Ex. 3:20). Suffering also builds perseverance and strength of character (Job 13:15).[5] Suffering can be God-inflicted, Satan-inflicted, or even self-inflicted. Such was the experience of King Saul, who was being tormented by evil spirits from God for his disobedience (I Sam. 16:14). Job also faced all kinds of afflictions from Satan because God permitted them to demonstrate his Almightiness in the life of Job (Job 1:12).

Self-inflicted injury or pain is intentionally harming one's own body without expecting the injury to be fatal. People who engage in self-inflicted injuries hardly consider that, when they purposely do so in an attempt to cope with anger, stress, and other emotional problems, it can cause harm on a long-term basis, resulting in physical and emotional harm, and may lead to unintended consequences such as severe injury or accidental death.[6] Some of the same humans believe that Satan is the major cause of evil, even though God is aware of the presence of evil in the world; yet God is not the author of evil in an individual's life (Jas. 1:13).[7]

---

[3] Samuel Waje Kunhiyop, *African Christian Ethics* (Nairobi: WordAlive, 2008), 16.

[4] Richard Gehman, *African Traditional Religion in the Light of the Bible* (Bukuru: African Christian Textbooks, 2013), p. 179.

[5] Stephen F. Saint, "Sovereignty, Suffering and the Work of Missions," in John Piper and Justin Taylor (eds), *Suffering and the Sovereignty of God* (Wheaton, IL: Crossway, 2006), p. 112.

[6] Nicole Washington, "What is Self-Inflicted Injury?" *Medical News Today* [Available at: https://www.medicalnewstoday.com/articles/self-inflicted-injury], [Last accessed: 19th July 2023].

[7] C. Ogunkunle, "Evil Man's Apprehension of Contrary Situation," *Ado Journal of Religions* 2(2), (Dec 2003), pp. 1–11.

In the traditional African context, suffering is also thought to be inflicted by the gods on people to punish offenders.[8] In the face of this reality, some people believe in the existence of an omnipotent and loving God who is immutable, while others have doubted His omnipotence and His loving nature. One of the pertinent questions individuals usually ask is, why should humans experience pains and agonies, caused through suffering, when there is God? This profound question in human experience has been answered in various ways by philosophers and theologians across the ages. The question re-occurs from generation to generation.

Those who believe in the omnipotence of God also ask questions such as: Why is God silent? Where is God in this matter? Why me, Lord? D.W. Amundsen asserts that the reality of suffering, especially when it affects the helpless or innocent, is a problem for anyone that affirms the existence of an omnipotent and benevolent deity.[9] Carol Troupe affirms that the personal experience or witnessing of suffering can cause some to draw closer to God as a source of strength and comfort. However, for others, it can be the reason that they lose their faith in God altogether.[10] While Simeon Kolawole corroborates Troupe while discussing those who deny God's goodness and power in the face of evil, this is a major reason for naturalism as a viable explanation of the world, which has also contributed to the growing secularism of the modern world and the tendency to reject God and religious viewpoints as a means of attributing the world's existence to an omnipotent God.[11] The assertion of God's omnipotence from the Christian faith and African religion is a contradiction of His powerful and loving nature for a secular mind; the understanding of God's omnipotence has been revealed in the Incarnation, which can help the unbeliever turn to God for comfort and deliverance in the face of suffering.

A Philosophical Origin of Evil

The origin of evil has been viewed from many perspectives, such as biblical, philosophical, theological, and social to mention but a few. Evil is defined as any case of undeserved pain or suffering by one or more beings.[12] Notably, not all evil is undeserved, because it is possible for someone to experience one kind of suffering or another due to their irrational behaviour.

---

[8] Celestine Chukwuemeka Umeh, *The Human Suffering: Concept Nature and Cause: Any Way Out?* (Onitsha: Rex Charles and Patrick, 2006), p. 152.

[9] D.W. Amundsen, "Suffering," in Sinclair B. Ferguson, David F. Wright, and J.I. Packer (eds), *New Dictionary of Theology* (Leicester: The Bath Press, 1988), p. 667.

[10] Carol Troupe, *Human Suffering in Black Theology* (Sheffield: Equinox, 2011).

[11] Simon Adebayo Kolawole, "An African Philosophy of Evil and its Implications for the Mission of the Church," (PhD thesis, Nigerian Baptist Theological Seminary, Ogbomoso, 2002), p. 18.

[12] Jeff Jordan, "Divine Love and Human Suffering," *International Journal for Philosophy of Religion*, 56(2), (Oct–Dec 2004),pp. 169–178.

In the Greek world, the question of the meaning and the origin of evil was answered in many ways over the course of the centuries. There are, however, two basic concepts of constant thought on the meaning and origin of evil. First, evil was seen as a metaphysical principle, e.g. among the Pythagoreans and in Plato's later writings. Second, it was believed that human ignorance is the source of all evil: Democritus, Socrates, and Plato subscribed to this. They maintained that an unenlightened and ignorant human does evil involuntarily, and this is the basis of all ruin and corruption. Getting enlightened leads to knowledge and frees humans from evil, causing them to do good, thus creating the moral being.[13] The weakness of this concept is that the suffering that emanates from evil cannot be eliminated, nor can it be solved by only philosophical principles. Suffering is real, concrete, physical, and spiritual; it is not an abstract principle. Therefore, it must be solved physically, mentally, and spiritually. The second concept, that human ignorance is the source of all evil, also presumes that knowledge can caution humans away from doing evil. However, knowledge cannot totally free them from doing evil; neither can it make them morally good or upright. This is because many have gained enlightenment and knowledge through education and yet do evil, and even in greater proportions.

Neil Ormerod also expresses his opinion that evil arises when humans fail to live according to the purpose of their existence – that's when humans fail to act according to the dictates of intelligence and reason. The outcome of such evil usually results in the suffering that causes pain.[14] One may also experience evil or suffering when one behaves ineptly and unreasonably. John M. Frame observes that some have argued that the possibility of evil is necessary for an orderly universe ruled predictably by natural law. The law of gravity, for example, takes no account of persons. If someone jumps from a high cliff, s/he will be hurt, whether righteous or wicked. If God miraculously protected everybody (or those who are righteous) who took foolish chances, it would be difficult to prevent events of nature scientifically.[15] God has endowed humans with wisdom to be able to make moral choices that will be useful for their existence; that is why He created humans as moral and rational beings.

John David Weaver explains that, according to one dimension of evil, the self-centred freewill of people could be seen as leading to immoral acts and the suffering of innocent and guilty alike.[16] This is true in the sense that when one misuses the free will given to humans by God and becomes self-centred, the

---

[13] Ernest Chilles, "Evil, Bad, Wickedness," in Colin Brown (ed.), *The New International Dictionary of New Testament Theology* (Grand Rapids, MI: The Paternoster Press, 1986), p. 561.

[14] Neil Ormerod, *God and the Problems of Pain, Suffering and Evil* (Augsburg, MN: Fortress Press, 2015), p. 25.

[15] John M. Frame, *Systematic Theology: An Introduction to Christian Belief* (Phillipsburg, NJ: P&R, 2013), p. 284.

[16] John David Weaver, *In the Beginning God: Modern Science and the Christian Doctrine of Creation* (Oxford: Regent's Park College, 1994), p. 168.

outcome is usually a disaster for the person and his neighbours. From the scriptural point of view, the sin of Adam and Eve led to their doom and the doom of their posterity.

P.G. Nelson states that, among the incidents in human life that God allows, there are what we should describe as tragedies or disasters. When Jesus was asked about the tragedies experienced by the Galileans whose blood Pilate had mixed with their sacrifices and the case of the man who was born blind (Lk. 13:1-5, Jn. 9:1-3a), Jesus' response showed that these were not as a result of an individual's sin but that they belonged to an order in which all have sinned, and that God can also sometimes choose not to intervene for more specific purposes. Most especially, God can allow what can be interpreted as bad things by human beings to happen and use them in a chain of events that ultimately leads to what He wants. For example, the deliverance of Israel from famine through the sale of Joseph by his brothers to the land of Egypt.[17] Joseph himself declared later to them that it was meant to do him harm, but God intended it for good to accomplish what is now being done – the saving of many lives (Gen. 50:20).

A Biblical View of Suffering

Suffering as punishment for sin is one of the dominant themes in the Old Testament. The fall of man in the Garden of Eden through disobedience led to sin, guilt, suffering, and death (Gen. 3). God chose Abraham and raised the Israelites as a nation through him and promised to bless the nations of the world through him (Gen. 12:2-3), which has been fulfilled in Christ Jesus. God has always warned His chosen people against sin through His various prophets at varying periods and the punishments He will mete out to them for violating His law. Since the Fall, humanity has continued to sin against God.

In the beginning of the Decalogue, as an introduction to the law corpus of the Pentateuch, it is said; "I Yahweh your God, am a jealous God, punishing the children for the sin of the fathers to the third generation" (Ex. 20:5). The curse list brings to a close the entire collection of laws in Deuteronomy with the warning, "However, if you do not obey Yahweh your God and do not carefully follow all His commands and decrees, I am giving you all today, all these curses will come upon you and overtake you" (Deut. 28:15).[18] The Israelites did not find it a palatable experience each time God allowed them to be taken captive by their enemies because of their sin. They usually faced oppression, famine, and death.

---

[17] P.G. Nelson, *God's Control Over the Universe: Providence and Judgement in Relation to Modern Science* (Scotland: Whittles, 2000), p. 45.

[18] Jos Luyten, "Perspective on Human Suffering in the Old Testament," in Jan Lambrecht and Raymond F. Collins (eds), *God and Human Suffering* (Louvain: Peter's Press 1990), p. 32.

In these contemporary times, some children have reaped the evil sown by their fathers and their forefathers in line with Exodus 20:5. They are not able to excel in their endeavours until deliverance is conducted for them after they have given their lives to the Lord Jesus Christ. Likewise, a curse can bring untold suffering into a human's life. When one is cursed by God, it can come in any form as He has purposed it. It can come in the form of sicknesses, poverty, frustration, disappointment, even death. Curses in any form are not something that anyone would reasonably desire. In ancient Israel, the idea of suffering as punishment for individual guilt developed especially in post-exilic times, the time in which the law became the charter of the faithful community and in which, next to the prophets and Levites, the sages and the scribes became the spiritual educators of the nation.[19]

Robert Duncan Culver states that evil is allowed in the world for reasons God has never seen fit fully to disclose and which human wisdom has not been able to discover or explain fully. The unexplainable presence of evil in the world can be adduced from the scripture that says God raised wicked tyrants, "that my name may be proclaimed in all the earth" (Ex. 9:6; cf. Rom. 9:7), and in prophetic declarations wherein God called an oppressive and destructive emperor "my servant" (Jer. 25:9).[20] When humans are unable to interpret the suffering but God understands, man should solely depend on God.

Suffering as an undesirable experience for humans fulfils various purposes. The first explanation is given in terms of the covenant itself. God's wrath and its consequent harm and suffering of men are due to righteous retribution. Evil is just a return for evil. Any harm or threat of harm is righteously brought upon evil i.e. unfaithfulness and immorality.[21] "The people of Israel did what was evil in the sight of the Lord and served Baal […] so the anger of the Lord was kindled against Israel and the hand of the Lord was against them for evil" (Judg. 2:11-15).

Suffering also plays a vicarious and redemptive purpose. Many great prophets suffered in a representative way for their people. Moses shared his people's sufferings and felt all their burdens were laid on him (Num. 11:1-15). Hosea suffered in his marital relationship, which was an enacted parable of God's loving and forgiving relationship to errant Israel (Hos. 1–3). Isaiah, Ezekiel and, above all, Jeremiah felt the anguish of their prophetic vocation (Jer. 15:18; 20:7-12).[22]

---

[19] Luyten, "Perspective on Human Suffering in the Old Testament," p. 8.

[20] Robert Duncan Culver, *Systematic Theology: Biblical and Historical* (Ross-Shire: Christian Focus, 2013), p. 21.

[21] A.D. Verby, "Evil," in Geoffrey W. Bromiley (ed.), *The International Standard Bible Encyclopaedia* Vol. 2 (Grand Rapids, MI: Eerdmans, 1982), p. 208.

[22] R.B. Edwards, "Suffering," in Geoffrey W. Bromiley (ed.), *The International Standard Bible Encyclopaedia* Vol. 4 (Grand Rapids, MI: Eerdmans, 1988), p. 651.

Although the Israelites believed that God can allow evil to come to them, they still believed in God's loving kindness. Multiple scriptural passages confirm this: "You do not stay angry forever but delight to show mercy" (Mic. 7:18). Again, "He will not always accuse, nor will he harbour his anger forever. He does not treat us as our sins deserve or repay us according to our iniquities" (Ps. 103:9). Also, "the Lord within her is righteous; he does no wrong. Morning by morning, he dispenses his justice" (Zep. 3:5). Dorothee Soeue asserts that, in the vagaries and vicissitudes of biblical Israel's national life, the leaders of God's people retained a profound faith in the goodness of their God which nothing could shake.[23]

Kim Garchar observes that to eradicate suffering would mean that humans have become something other than human (either by somehow being able to prevent tragedy or otherwise lacking the power to choose). In her opinion, the question now is not how to eradicate tragedy and suffering, but rather how humans ought to proceed in the face of suffering, as it is part of the human condition.[24]

From the Old Testament's assertions, suffering can come to humans for different reasons, such as for retribution, as vicarious or redemptive, or to test obedience. Whichever form it takes, African Christians should live a life of obedience to God, run away from the kind of life that can cause retribution for them, and see God as a powerful being that they can depend upon for comfort and deliverance in the days of their afflictions.

The New Testament's view of suffering is focused on the suffering of Christ, especially His suffering on the cross and the kind of experience His followers will have as they pattern their lives after Him. The Greek verb *paschein* and its related forms (including *pathein* and compounds such as *synkakopathein*, to sympathise) denote the various aspects of suffering. The theology of suffering is called *paschology*. In the synoptic gospels, *Paschein* is used only for the sufferings of Christ.[25] The universal symbol of Christianity is the cross. To reflect on the life of Jesus is to remember His suffering. As the servant songs of Isaiah anticipated, Jesus was despised and rejected, a man of suffering who was acquainted with infirmity. Likewise, this has been the experience of those who follow Jesus and are no strangers to suffering.[26]

Paul emphasised the gracious, saving work of God on behalf of His human creation through the fully human mediator between God and human beings: Jesus. Thus, Paul gave to God the title "God our Saviour" and said that God

---

[23] Dorothee Soeue, *Suffering* (Philadelphia, PA: Fortress, 1975), p. 177.
[24] Kim Garchar, "Sin, Sorrow and Suffering: A Roycean Response to These Deeper Tragedies of Life," *American Journal of Theology and Philosophy* 33 (2012), p. 59.
[25] F.P. Cotterell, "Suffering," in T.S. Desmond Alexander and Brian S. Rosner (eds), *New Dictionary of Biblical Theology* (Leicester: InterVarsity Press, 2000), p. 804.
[26] Alan Neely, "Suffering," in A. Scott Moreau (ed.), *Evangelical Dictionary of World Missions* (Grand Rapids, MI: Baker, 2000), p. 915.

wants everyone to be saved.[27] Jesus' suffering and death are a pointer to what His followers will experience in the world, which has been authenticated by Jesus Himself. Jesus said that there would be many trials and sorrows for His followers (Jn. 16:33). Paul and Barnabas taught that entrance to the Kingdom of God comes with many tribulations (Acts 14:22) which must not shake a Christian's faith (I Thes. 3:3).[28] Paul's call was unavoidably linked to the fact that he must suffer greatly for the sake of the Lord's name (Acts 9:15). The reality of this calling to suffer is attested to in his epistles. Hence, rather than questioning the legitimacy of his apostleship because of his suffering, Paul considered suffering to be a characteristic mark of his apostolic ministry (Gal. 6:17; I Cor. 2:1-5; II Cor. 11:23-29; Phil. 1:30). In addition, Paul's willingness to suffer on behalf of his churches also provided a model of Christian love, so that Paul could call his churches to follow his examples of giving up their right for others, even when this meant undue suffering and hardship (I Cor. 4:8-13; 6:7; 9:1-27).[29] John Enyinnaya asserts that, in Paul's thought, suffering is a legitimate part of Christian experience (II Cor. 1:5, 3:10), and is in fact a proof of our sonship and a guarantee that we share in Christ's glory. Enyinnaya, quoting from John Stott's comment, said that the suffering is not only the opposition of the world but also all our human frailty, both physical and moral, and which is due to our provisional, half-saved condition.[30]

In the New Testament as well, suffering fulfils various purposes. Suffering may come to believers to test their love for Christ. God sometimes brings us into testing times. This tests the character, the maturity, and the reality of one's Christian claim. The tests of God in life may take believers through experiences of persecution (I Pt. 4:12) and sickness (II Cor. 12:7).[31] Joel R. Beeke observes that our sufferings are "for our education and instruction in his family." Beeke, quoting Owen and Willard, states that "all our afflictions are helps towards heaven." They contribute to the "increase of their eternal glory; every reproach and injury doth but add weight to their crown. God's chastening is a badge of our sonship and of the father's love (Heb. 12:3-11)."[32]

---

[27] Frank Theilman, *Theology of the New Testament* (New York: Zondervan, 2005), p. 188.

[28] Comfort Phillip and Walter A. Elwell (eds), "Suffering," in *Tyndale Bible Dictionary* (Leicester, IL: Tyndale, 2001), p. 1227.

[29] S.J. Hafeman, "Suffering," in Gerald F. Hawthorne, Ralph P. Martin, and Daniel G. Reid (eds), *Dictionary of Paul and His Letters* (Leicester: InterVarsity Press, 1993), p. 919.

[30] John Enyinnaya, "The Bible Meets Human Need: Reading Romans in the Light of the HIV/AIDS Pandemic," *West Africa Journal of Education* (2012), p. 28.

[31] P.H. Lewis, "Temptation," in David J. Atkinson and David H. Field (eds), *New Dictionary of Christian Ethics and Pastoral Theology* (Leicester, IL: Intervarsity Press, 1995), p. 837.

[32] Joel R. Beeke and Mark Jones, *A Puritan Theology: Doctrine for Life* (Grand Rapids, MI: Reformation Heritage, 2012), p. 549.

Suffering can also come to believers so that they can learn obedience. Jesus learned obedience as he endured temptation, trials, persecution, suffering, and death (Heb. 5:8).[33] The Christian who takes up a life of suffering (*Pathon*) with Christ is thereby dedicated to a moral life which rejects sin (cf. I Jn. 3:6, Rom. 6:1-11).[34] Jesus says, "If any man will come after me, let him deny himself and take up his cross daily and follow me" (Lk. 9:23, c.f. Matt. 16:24). The believer is to deny his flesh and old selfish nature and is to walk the path which Christ directs him to take with the particular suffering which forms that particular cross.[35]

Alister McGrath argues that if God can be said to suffer through his incarnate Son Jesus Christ, it means that a point of contact is immediately established between God and the pain of the human world.[36] This means that God is not far away while humans suffer, especially the believers in Christ. The scripture says that we have a high priest who suffered with us (Heb. 4:15). The involvement of God with human anguish is one way to affirm the meaningfulness of suffering and to sustain hope amid affliction.[37]

From the New Testament perspective, Jesus died an ignominious death to reconcile humanity who had been lost in sin to God. Jürgen Moltmann remarks that, since Jesus was condemned and executed on the cross, He did not die a natural or accidental death.[38] He was despised and rejected and experienced sorrow. The death of Jesus Christ on the cross has brought humanity into a close relationship with God. Jesus Christ suffered, leaving us an example; this means that every believer should see suffering as part of their Christian experience. Today, Christians are experiencing various forms of sufferingin many nations of the world, such as kidnappings, banditry, poverty, persecutions of all sorts, and even killings. As God did not spare Jesus from suffering and death but He was with Him, Christians should know that God is with them in all their trials and tribulations. As Christ had victory over death, they too will triumph.

---

[33] Tesfaye Kassa, "Jesus Christ, Supreme Over All," in Tokunboh Adeyemo (ed.), *Africa Bible Commentary* (Nairobi: WordAlive, 2006), p. 1496.

[34] Raymond E. Brown and Joseph A. Baumgarten, "The Christians Through Suffering Renounce Sin," in *The New Jerome Biblical Commentary* (Newark, NJ: Prentice Hall, 2011), p. 907.

[35] R. Allan Killen, "Suffering," in Charles F. Pfeiffer, Howard F. Vos, and John Rea (eds), *Wycliffe Bible Dictionary* (Peabody, MA: Hendrickson, 2008), p. 1630.

[36] Alister E. McGrath, *Christian Theology: An Introduction*, 2nd ed (Oxford: Blackwell, 1998), p. 248.

[37] L. Bregman, "Suffering," in Rodney J. Hunter (ed.), *Dictionary of Pastoral Care and Counselling* (Nashville, TN: Abingdon Press, 1990), p. 1231.

[38] Jürgen Moltmann, *The Crucified God* (Minneapolis, MN: Fortress Press, 2015), p. 180.

Human Suffering in an African Worldview

Suffering is not alien to African people's experiences. Africans are aware of suffering and look for solutions whenever they experience it. From an African perspective, religious, social, and natural causes of suffering are inseparable and interconnected.[39] This is because Africans do not just believe that suffering or affliction comes to them by chance. Something must be responsible for it, and they tend to look for the root cause of their problems, which is often more spiritual than physical. Newell Booth observes that Africans are quite aware of the physical causes of problems as well, and they take practical steps to deal with them anytime the diviner diagnoses them.[40]

An illness, for instance, is hardly considered to be merely natural and so is not treated in isolation, as in modern medical practice. An illness is treated as part of the person suffering within the context of the community, which includes both the people alive and the spirits of the ancestors.[41] African people understand suffering as wrapped up in what is called "evil." There are different kinds of myths, proverbs, riddles, and ethical teachings that support this assertion. Despite this understanding, Africans still emphatically say that God did not create what is evil, nor does He do them any evil whatsoever. For example, the Ila hold that God is always in the right, and "cannot be charged with an offence, cannot be accused, cannot be questioned. He does good to all at all times."[42]

Some societies see evil as originating from, or associated with, spiritual beings other than God. Part of this concept is a personification of evil itself. For example, the Vugusu say that there is an evil divinity which God created good, but who later turned against him and began to do evil. This evil divinity is assisted by evil spirits and all evil now comes from them. Thus, a kind of duel exists between good and evil forces in the world.[43] Celestine Chukwuemeka Umeh, expressing a similar view, said that, in a typical African setting, the Supreme Being should be exonerated of any responsibility for evil in creation. For instance, the Igbo traditional attitude excludes *Chukwu* (God) from all blame for any fault or imperfection in the world: *Chukwu* is holy and always good.[44]

Different causes are responsible for suffering in the African worldview, such as sin, ethical violation, the concept of choice, and the like. Worldview, as defined by Donovan, means a person's way of understanding life and the world

---

[39] Daniel Kasomo, "An Investigation of Sin and Evil in African Cosmology," *International Journal of Sociology and Anthropology* 1(8), (December 2009), pp. 145–155.

[40] Newell Booth, "African Religion," in R. Pierce Beaver, Jan Bergma, and S. Langley (eds), *A Lion Handbook of World Religions* (Herts: Lion, 1982), p. 161.

[41] Joe M. Kapolyo, *The Human Condition: Christian Perspectives Through African Eyes* (Leicester: InterVarsity Press, 2005), p. 127.

[42] John S. Mbiti, *African Religions and Philosophy* (London: Heinemann, 1969), p. 204.

[43] Mbiti, *African Religions and Philosophy*, p, 204.

[44] Umeh, *The Human Suffering*, p. 152.

in which they live.[45] According to many stories of creation, humanity was originally in a state of happiness, childlike ignorance, immortality, or the ability to rise again after dying. God also provided humans with the necessities of life; they lived in a state of paradise. God made other things for their use and protection. There are a number of people, including the Bambuti, Banyarwanda, Barotse Bushmen, Chayga, Pare, Eleyo, and others who tell of God giving humans a particular rule to observe. When they broke it, the separation took place.[46]

Apart from the sin which caused a separation between God and humanity in their blissful state, L.O. Lawal observes that sin in traditional religions is described by various terms, one of which is *eewo* or "forbidden thing." It connotes the act of breaking laws or taboos. Sin constitutes various vices, such as adultery, cheating, false oaths, incest, robbery, wickedness, and all offences which humans commit against themselves and which usually endanger the well-being of their society.[47] Taboo is defined as a prohibition that makes people or things untouchable.[48] Therefore, African people frowned at all of these misdeeds and it was not until recent times that all kinds of laxity that virtually eroded the ethical values upheld by the Africans came in.

In most African cosmologies, all strange diseases, abnormal occurrences, physical disorders, ailments, accidents, untimely deaths, inability to gain promotion in office, failures in examination, disappointments in romantic relationships, barrenness in women (both long-term and short-term), impotence in men and life, failure of crops, and all unexplainable problems of life are attributed to witches and other spiritual agents of malevolence. Diseases are viewed as a direct intervention by the deities or the malevolent spiritual beings.[49]

Most religions in Africa attribute the creation of the universe to the all-powerful, loving God but the presence of evil is an incursion upon His absolute sovereignty. The problem of evil has often been seen as a dilemma and the idea of a loving Creator or an omnipotent God seems implausible.[50] It is believed that the traditional Africans recognise the existence of only one God, the Supreme Creator and absolute sustainer and controller of all beings and things.[51] God's

---

[45] Wilbur O'Donovan, *Biblical Christianity in Modern Africa* (Waynesboro, GA: Paternoster Press, 2000), p. 4.

[46] Mbiti, *African Religions and Philosophy*, pp. 95, 97.

[47] L.O. Lawal, "Sin and Punishment in Yoruba Traditional Religion," *Ibadan Journal of Religious Studies* 62(9), (June & December 2014), p. 213.

[48] Lawrence B. Ekundayo, "Taboo in the Biblical Context," *Ado Journal of Religions*, 2(1), (July 2003), p. 42.

[49] Afe Adogame, "Healing" in Moleffi Kete Asante and Ama Mazama (eds), *Encyclopaedia of African Religion* Vol. 1 (Washington DC: Sage, 2009), p. 309.

[50] P. Ade Dopamu, *Esu, The Invisible Foe of Man: A Comparative Study of Satan in Christianity, Islam and Yoruba Religion* (Ijebu-Ode: Shebiotimo, 1992), p. 10.

[51] P. Yakubu Otijele, "Understanding the African World View: A Religious Perspective," *Ogbomoso Journal of Theology* 6 (1991), p. 8.

omnipotence is spoken of among some people, like the Yoruba, Ngombe, Akan and Ashanti. One of the names for God describes Him as “the All-powerful or the Almighty.” God’s omnipotence is seen in His exercise of power over nature.[52] The Yoruba believe that *Olodumare* is the most powerful in heaven and on earth, that He can do all things.[53]

Since Africans know through creation that God is all-powerful, they should come to God through redemption, through the God who has revealed Himself as Father, Son, and the Holy Spirit. Africans are to receive the grace freely given to them by God through Jesus Christ. This will deliver them from the power of suffering, hell, and death. It is only those who accept the grace of God who will have continuous victory over their pains and sorrow. The acceptance of Africans that suffering results from sin and consequently breeds chaos for humanity is a touchstone for their need to turn from appeasing the gods to accepting the Christ event.

Conclusion

This paper has discussed suffering within the context of the African worldview and has shown how God’s loving response to suffering in creation and redemption is made known through His omnipotence. African religions teach that suffering came to the world through sin. It has also been discovered through this paper that Africans understand God’s omnipotence in creation but not in redemption. A theological understanding of who God is through redemption will help Africans fully turn to God for comfort and deliverance in the days of their adversities, having the understanding that they have an advocate with the Father and that they are not alone in their suffering, and that suffering has its blessings when yielded to God in Christ Jesus.

[52] Mbiti, *African Religions and Philosophy*, p. 31.

[53] Samson A. Fatokun, “African Traditional Belief Systems,” in Ademola Ajayi (ed.), *African Culture and Civilization* (Ibadan: Atlantis, 2005), p. 132.

“Where Is God in Times of Crisis?”: Trends, Trajectories, and Possibilities for Theological Rethinking Among Christians During the COVID-19 Pandemic

Kwaku Boamah

Introduction

The desire of humankind to know and understand the environment is a natural search for answers to mind-boggling existential questions. Although difficult to accept, crisis is a part of life. However, in times of crisis, such as pandemics, a lot of questions are asked, including the place of God in these moments.[1] The early Christians asked such questions, including the reason Christians should die with non-Christians during the outbreak of smallpox in 165 AD and measles in 251 AD. These devastating questions pushed the exiled Bishop Cyprian to respond in his text *On The Mortality*.[2] At the outbreak of COVID-19, many Christians asked similar questions, with so much dismay and hopelessness. Rodney Stark observes quite aptly that “frequently in human history, crisis produced by natural or social disasters has been translated into crisis of faith.”[3]

This paper therefore explores the outbreak of pandemics in the early Roman Empire and Christian reactions to these pandemics. It evaluates the nature and extent of the pandemics compared to COVID-19 and the attendant Christian responses in coping with the diseases. The central focus of the study is to assess how Cyprian’s *On The Mortality* addresses the many questions of Christians. It also uses Dionysius’ response to the pandemics to evaluate and compare the nature, impact, and response of the Christians during the pandemics to the COVID-19 pandemic, particularly in 2020.

---

[1] J. Kwabena Asamoah-Gyadu, “Dealing With a Spiritual Virus: Whither the Prophetic?” *Religious Matters in an Entangled World,* 13th April 2020 [Available at: https://religiousmatters.nl/dealing-with-a-spiritual-virus-whither-the-prophetic/], [Last accessed: 16th July 2023].

[2] Iris M. Smith, “The Contributions of St Cyprian: Perspectives on Epidemiology and Early Christianity,” *Young Historian Conference* (2014), p. 2

[3] Rodney Start, *The Rise of Christianity* (New York: HarperCollins, 1996), p. 77.

COVID-19 in Perspective

Coronavirus is one of the most devastating pandemics in world history, after the influenza pandemic in the early twentieth century. It is generally known as COVID-19, which was first acknowledged to have appeared in 2019 in Wuhan, China. It causes acute respiratory diseases.[4] The World Health Organization declared the outbreak as a public health emergency of international concern in January 2020 and a pandemic in March the same year.[5] By 4th March 2021, more than 127 million cases were confirmed the world over, with over 4.7 million deaths recognised to have been caused by COVID-19, making it one of the most dreadful plagues ever known in history.[6] Symptoms of the COVID-19 virus are varied, and can be barely perceptible or fully life-threatening. Local and international news on both traditional and social media has been about deaths, disease, fear, panic, cities blockaded and locked down, flights cancelled, widespread disruption, conferences suspended, economic impact, religious centres closed, etc., portraying the picture of the devastation created by COVID-19.

It was really scary to think about the closing of churches, which pushed them to hold online services, including the hosting of Communion/ Eucharistic services online, even by the historic mainline churches, while members stayed at home for fear of infection and spreading the virus.[7] It was unthinkable that Easter festivities were celebrated behind screens; there were no Palm Sunday, Maundy Thursday, Good Friday, and Resurrection Sunday services.[8] Even when the restrictions were eased, many of the members were still afraid to attend church services. Some were relaxed about going to work, attending funerals, going to the marketplace, or sitting on the bus, but were suspicious of attending church services. The irony is that many were comfortable attending funeral services but refused to attend Sunday services in the same church. During this period of ease, the church services were regulated in terms of duration, frequency, activity, and structure. They were altered from the usual ways of doing things in the church, adopting the "New Normal" services, which could not extend beyond a certain time frame to reduce the time members spent sitting,

---

[4] Isaac Boaheng, "Christianity and the COVID-19 Pandemic: A Pastoral and Theological Reflection from the Ghanaian Context," *Journal for Pastoral Theology* (2021), p. 1.

[5] World Health Organization, n.d, "Timeline: WHO's COVID-19 response" WHO website [Available at: https://www.who.int/emergencies/diseases/novel-coronavirus-2019/interactive-timeline?gclid=CjwKCAiAp4KCBhB6EiwAxRxbpIIA2sok1TrgaFGDxUPNqnAVnOtrIg7ggUBSQgc-Ubz0ba_miMMFjxoCfpYQAvD_BwE#event-115], [Last accessed: 19th July 2023].

[6] Boaheng, "Christianity and the COVID-19 Pandemic," p. 1.

[7] J. Kwabena Asamoah-Gyadu, *Christianity and Faith in the COVID-19 Era* (Accra: Step Books, 2020), p. 29.

[8] Asamoah-Gyadu, *Christianity and Faith*, p. ix.

and therefore their human interaction, and limit their time spent wearing face masks. Participation in church services had to be reduced to give room for social distancing measures, thereby pushing church managers to hold multiple services, including screening the services online so that those who could not attend could still participate anywhere they were.[9]

Pandemics in Rome and the Christian Response

Pandemics have been an eventful part of world history and, whenever they occurred, the church was not spared. There are examples of pandemics in the early Roman period that affected the church greatly. In the days of the emperor Marcus Aurelius, what has been noted as the smallpox pandemic appeared around 165 AD[10] in Mesopotamia and, within a year, it was already present in Rome.[11] It is usually referred to as the "Plague of Galen," which started among the armies and spread to the cities.[12] It is sometimes also referred to as the "Antonine Plague."[13] The disease caused a lot of deaths in the empire, estimated at a quarter to a third of the empire's population, including the emperor himself, within 15 years. Others even argue that half of the Roman population were killed by the disease.[14] In some cases, it is estimated to have killed over five thousand people a day.[15] It is, however, certain that although these projections may be too high, the numbers were indeed overwhelming and human beings became vulnerable.

Cyprian wrote that many Christians died because of the disease,[16] and Dionysius, Bishop of Alexandria at the time, also posited: "But after the shortest breathing space, disease struck us, which was more terrifying to them than any terror."[17] This statement shows that the pandemic was unexpected, dreadful, and novel – which are all characteristic of the coronavirus pandemic in 2019. The impact was indeed felt in all households. Therefore, Dionysius described the situation in these words: "there is no house without one dead, and would that it

---

[9] See, for instance, Adelakun, *The Healing of Maseko*.

[10] Jennifer Manley, "Measles and Ancient Plagues: A Note on New Scientific Evidence," *The Classical World* 107 (2019), p. 395; Stark, *The Rise of Christianity*, p. 73.

[11] R.J. Littman and M.L. Littman, "Galen and the Antonine Plague," *The American Journal of Philosophy* 94 (1973), p. 243.

[12] Stark, *The Rise of Christianity*, p. 76.

[13] Rebecca Flemming, "Galen and the Plague," in Caroline Petit (ed.), *Galen's Treatise (De indolentia) in Context: A Tale of Resilience* (Leiden: Brill, 2019), pp. 219, 226; Manley, "Measles and Ancient Plagues," p. 395.

[14] Littman and Littman, "Galen and the Antonine Plague," p. 244; Stark, *The Rise of Christianity*, p. 73.

[15] Smith, "The Contributions of St Cyprian," p. 2; Stark, *The Rise of Christianity*, p. 77.

[16] Cyprian, *On Mortality*, p. 15.

[17] Eusebius, *The Church History*, 22:2.

were only one!"[18] He pictured the pandemic as a type of persecution and martyrdom which affected both the Christians and non-Christians.[19]

Furthermore, in 251 AD, beginning in the rural towns, another pandemic emerged, which scholars maintain was the outbreak of measles.[20] At the peak of that pandemic, the church could not celebrate Easter. It is revealing that Asamoah-Gyadu argues that some major incidents in scriptures which the church celebrates today, such as the Triumphant Entry, the Last Supper, Feet Washing, Transfiguration, Night of the Betrayal (Good Friday), Passover, the Resurrection, Ascension, and Pentecost among others all happened in some lockdown mode.[21] Dionysius, according to Eusebius, "gave a rule based on an eight-year cycle, proving that Easter should not be celebrated at any other time than after the vernal equinox."[22] On the other hand, according to Cyprian, the disease attacked the eyes, limbs, and gave fever.[23] It was quite interesting that, at the height of that pandemic, many took flight to other places for cover, including priests and notable physicians at that time in Galen in 165 AD,[24] all because, like with COVID-19, many notable people, including political and religious leaders, were killed.[25]

The Christian response to these pandemics during the period of the Early Church was quite positive, which helped them to grow. For instance, Stark identifies a few Christian reactions to the pandemics that aided the spreading of the faith more widely.[26] In the first place, the Christians had a better explanation of the reason for the pandemics than the philosophers at the time. It is without a doubt that, in times of crisis, people ask questions about why such calamities have befallen them. During these pandemics, when the question of why was raised, while the Roman pagan Hellenistic culture could not explain it, the Christians saw it as a sign of the end of time and therefore a need to remain faithful. Cicero is said to have responded to the question of why with: "it depends on fortune or (as we should say) 'conditions' whether we are to experience prosperity or adversity. Certain events are indeed, due to natural causes beyond human control."[27] This explanation does not address the question but leaves the situation hanging. However, the Christian explanation helped them to develop some positive attitudes towards the pandemics and made them calm, unlike the non-Christians.[28] The Christian explanation of the apocalypse gave them hope

---

[18] Eusebius, *The Church History*, 22:1.
[19] Eusebius, *The Church History*, 22:1.
[20] Stark, *The Rise of Christianity*, p. 73.
[21] Asamoah-Gyadu, *Christianity and Faith*, pp. 1–107.
[22] Eusebius, *The Church History*, p. 20.
[23] Cyprian, *On Mortality*, pp. 8, 14.
[24] Flemming, "Galen and the Plague," pp. 222, 225.
[25] Stark, *The Rise of Christianity*, p. 85.
[26] Stark, *The Rise of Christianity*, pp. 74–75.
[27] Stark, *The Rise of Christianity*, p. 80.
[28] Smith, "The Contributions of St Cyprian," p. 2.

for the future. The understanding that the pandemics were a sign of the end of the age made the Christians hopeful of the return of Christ. Additionally, due to the understanding of the early Christians of the pandemics as eschatological, they extended a value of love and care even to those infected by the diseases. Dionysius observed that:

> Most of our brethren showed love and loyalty in not sparing themselves while helping one another, tending to the sick with no thought of danger and gladly departing this life with them after becoming infected with their disease. Many who nursed others to death, died themselves hence transferring their death to themselves.[29]

He wrote, therefore, to eulogise the many fallen Christians who fell victim to the sickness and had to lose their lives from nursing infected victims.[30] It is quite likely that the Christians who ministered to the victims were women because both Adeloye and Kupolatin assert that women play essential roles towards recoveries during pandemics.[31] On the other hand, the non-Christians exhibited a lot of fear and individuality during the period, but the Christians showed love and care. Dionysius notes:

> The heathen were the exact opposite. They pushed away those with the first signs of the disease and fled from their dearest. They even threw them half dead into the road and treated unburied corpses like refuse in hopes of avoiding the plague of death, which for all their efforts, was difficult to escape.[32]

Therefore, while the early Christians in the face of the pandemics ministered to the victims, the non-Christians maltreated them. Stark argues that solidarity, especially by showing care, was a characteristic feature of the early Christians; in the fourth century, the Emperor Julian sought to establish pagan charities to match the Christian standards.[33] It must be pointed out, however, that during the coronavirus pandemic in 2020, a strategy of isolation from victims of the virus was adopted all over the world, but care was duly given. Both the Christian and non-Christian organisations, including individuals, made donations of supplies in terms of food, personal protective equipment (PPE), and monies to help the plight of those affected directly or indirectly by the disease. Yet from the example of the Early Church based on the Emperor Julian's concern and the action of the Christians in times of crisis, it is evident that caring for the existential needs of people cannot be excluded from the missionary efforts of the church if growth is ever anticipated. As was the example of the Early Church even from the time of the apostles in Acts 2:47, caring for the needs of members

---

[29] Eusebius, *The Church History* 22:3, Stark, *The Rise of Christianity*, p. 82.

[30] Eusebius, *The Church History* 20:3.

[31] J.O. Adeloye, "From the Pulpit: COVID-19 in a Time like This," *Trinity Journal of Church and Theology* 20 (2020), p. 109; Lawrence O. Kupolati, "From the Pulpit: COVID-19 Pain," *Trinity Journal of Church and Theology* 20 (2020), p. 115.

[32] Eusebius, *The Church History* 22:4, Stark, *The Rise of Christianity*, p. 83.

[33] Stark, *The Rise of Christianity*, pp. 83–84.

and non-members should not only be during crisis eras, but in good and bad times alike. The responses of the Christians to the situation led to an increase in the membership of the Christian fraternity.[34] According to Stark, humans are predisposed to join the winning team. Since the Christians had a better explanation of the situation and did not desert her members, including those who contracted the disease, the faith became attractive to the non-Christians.[35]

The picture where the non-Christians are said to have abandoned their loved ones for fear of being infected by isolating and quarantining them was similar to the coronavirus in 2020. However, the early Christians showed love and care which invariably attracted many non-Christians to the faith due to the Christian reception and communal activities. They provided social services and solidarity to their members, extending this even towards non-Christians.

Reflections from Cyprian's *On Mortality*

Cyprian, whose full name was Thascious Caecilius Cyprianus, is believed to have been born in the Roman North African region in Carthage in the third century.[36] He fled into exile due to persecution targeted at the leadership of the church by Emperor Decius around 249–252 AD.[37] He fled with Dionysius of Alexandria when the bishops of Rome, Antioch, and Jerusalem, including the revered Church Father Origen, were martyred.[38] Murphy describes the reign of Cyprian as "marked by persecutions, schism and plague."[39] While in exile, Cyprian administered his diocese with several letters to address specific issues.[40]

One of the major epistles of Cyprian to the church in Carthage during the plague is *On Mortality*. During the persecutions, the Christians asked an age-long question of why? The most crucial question that disturbed many of the Christians was why they had to die along with the non-Christians. The Christians thought that because they were loved by God, they were not expected to die in the company of the unrighteous. They anticipated that, since God was the Creator and Master of the universe and they were disadvantaged in the empire, God would protect them from natural disasters. Cyprian captures the worries of the believers and his response generally in a sarcastic way that "it disturbs some that

---

[34] Smith, "The Contributions of St Cyprian," pp. 6–7.
[35] Stark, *The Rise of Christianity*, p. 75.
[36] Smith, "The Contributions of St Cyprian," p. 2; Daryl Aaron, *The 40 Most Influential Christians ... Who Shaped What We Believe Today* (Ada, MI: Baker, 2013), p. 65; G.A. Oshitelu, *The African Fathers of the Early Church: The Contributions of the African Church Fathers to the Development of Christian Thought in the Early Church* (Ibadan: Sefer, 2002), p. 49.
[37] Henry Chadwick, *The Early Church* (Middlesex: Penguin Books, 1993), p. 118.
[38] Oshitelu, *The African Fathers*, p. 50.
[39] Edwina Murphy, "Death, Decay and Delight in Cyprian of Carthage," *Scrinium* 15 (2019), p. 79.
[40] Aaron, *The 40 Most Influential Christians*, p. 66.

the power of this disease attacks our people equally with the heathen, as if the Christian believed for this purpose, that he might have the enjoyment of the world and this life free from the contact of ills."[41]

The situation of hopelessness in the life of some Christians in times of such widespread crises was equally expressed by many Christians in the year 2020 when the coronavirus was at its peak.[42] In the context of Ghana, when similar questions were raised during the COVID-19 era, four main interpretations were provided, according to Boaheng. The interpretations ranged from spiritualisation of the virus to apocalyptic interpretation and to the pandemic ushering in the Anti-Christ, and many Christians were confused about their faith and asked the question "why?"[43] They, in many respects, asked why the sickness was ravaging every aspect of life without divine intervention, why God has allowed the pandemic, etc. It is therefore in this light that Cyprian's letter addressed to the Early Church in the time of a pandemic is still relevant today, when the world is also asking similar questions in the face of a pandemic. Cyprian's *On Mortality* is a useful text which helps to deal with the many questions of Christians in times of crisis.[44] Murphy explains that *On Mortality* "was written to address those whose faith has been shaken by the plague and returns us to the prophetic wisdom of the aged Simeon."[45] The letter began with an introduction which affirms the fact that the disease, unlike the persecution and martyrdom, did not attack only Christians, but all. He affirmed that the plague affects Jews and Gentiles alike.[46] He cited the examples of Job and Tobias to suggest that Christians must develop positive attitudes and not murmur. In all this, Cyprian emphasised the difference between Christians and non-Christians, and said life after death is the most important issue that Christians should consider, instead of how they will die. He established that, as long as Christians remain on earth, the troubles of the flesh would affect them – they are only different to the non-Christians in the spirit.

> It disturbs some that this mortality is common to us with others; and yet what is there in this world which is not common to us with others, so long as this flesh of ours still remains, according to the law of our first birth, common to us with them? So long as we are here in the world, we are associated with the human race in fleshly equality, but are separated in spirit. Therefore, until this corruptible shall put on incorruption, and this mortal receive immortality, and the Spirit leads us to God the Father, whatsoever are the disadvantages of the flesh are common to us with the human race.[47]

---

[41] Cyprian, *On Mortality*, p. 8.
[42] Adelakun, *Performing Power*; Adelakun, *Powerful Devices*.
[43] Boaheng, "Christianity and the COVID-19 Pandemic," pp. 2–4.
[44] Smith, "The Contributions of St Cyprian," p. 9.
[45] Murphy, "Death, Decay and Delight," p. 84.
[46] Cyprian, *On Mortality*, p. 15.
[47] Cyprian, *On Mortality*, p. 17.

By these words, Cyprian sought to encourage the Christians to look beyond this world and focus on the world to come. The admonishment by Cyprian here concerns the mortality of the body on earth and, although being Christian is affected by the frailties of this life, it is very important to cut down on some expectations of the community of faith. The essence of managing the expectations of people is crucial because it brings acceptance of the circumstances and does not make them anxious in crises.

Notwithstanding, it is also interesting that Cyprian deals with the theology of the form of death in this letter. This was important because many of the Christians preferred to die as martyrs than to fall to the plague, yet Cyprian argues using the Christian idea of predestination. He argues that, in the first place, martyrdom is not in one's power; neither can one claim to have lost what one does not know whether they deserve to receive.[48] His argument here is further emphasised by using the example of Cain murdering his brother after making a sacrifice. Cyprian admonishes his readers that God already knew Cain was going to kill his brother and had cautioned him against it. To this end, Cyprian posits that "It is one thing for the spirit to be wanting for martyrdom, and another for martyrdom to have been wanting for the spirit."[49] Cyprian makes a strong case: "For God does not ask for our blood, but for our faith."[50] It implies that, if the Christians have faith in God, they will leave their lives, including how they die, to God's providence. The idea of God determining the form of death of the Christian is equally important to encourage the church in a crisis to hold on with the understanding that if God does not permit it, it will not happen, and that God is the determinant of the destinies of humanity. This gives hope to a community in a crisis to hold on despite the challenges of the time.

A major Christian theology exposed by Cyprian to admonish Christians' concern in the time of crisis in this text is the understanding that there is nothing good here on earth. The Christians had an understanding that life here on earth is a transit and this world is full of miseries. In light of this, Cyprian argues that "It is for him to wish to remain long in the world whom the world delights, whom this life, flattering and deceiving, invites by the enticements of earthly pleasure."[51] He argues this way to stress the point that Christians are not expected to love the world; therefore, when they worry that they are dying, it becomes problematic. He further cites I John 2:15 in the letter to buttress the suggestion that Christians are not to love the world or anything in it. To him, therefore, since the world does not love Christians, they must be happy leaving it. Upon sounding these positions, Cyprian further admonishes the Christians to see the pains of the plague that are leading to death as an opportunity to enter into the Father's

---

[48] Cyprian, *On Mortality*, p. 17.
[49] Cyprian, *On Mortality*, p. 17.
[50] Cyprian, *On Mortality*, p. 17.
[51] Cyprian, *On Mortality*, p. 24.

glory.[52] He makes this point strongly because the Christian apocalyptic theme suggests that this world will soon be destroyed.[53] Cyprian's argument here is to be positively minded and look forward to a better world in view, which helps a people in crisis to hold on to faith knowing that the world has nothing good to offer after all.

Another major theology in Cyprian's text is the Christian understanding of suffering. He argues that the Christian calling includes suffering.[54] Suffering, he argues, is foretold in scriptures in many places. Therefore, the Christians must accept current predicaments.[55] He identifies some examples of Christian characters from both canonical and apocryphal texts, such as in Job, Tobias, Abraham, and some statements from Paul to affirm the understanding that suffering is an important part of being Christian.[56] He talks about Job losing his wealth, wife, and children and being stricken with a terrible disease, yet he remained faithful in the midst of his storm,[57] and Tobias, for all his excellency to the things of God, suffered to the extent of blindness but is praised by the angel Raphael for his steadfastness.[58] Abraham held on to God and was ready to sacrifice his son due to his love for God.[59] Cyprian then recounts the example of the Israelites murmuring on the desert, where God was not very pleased with their constant complaints. Cyprian admonishes the Christians to learn from the example of the Apostle Paul, who after many sufferings for the gospel, is assured of God's grace which is "sufficient" for him.[60] These canonical and apocryphal accounts employed by Cyprian to encourage the Christians were intended to let them know that they are not the only ones who have ever suffered. These examples further affirm the Christian theology of suffering as an integral part of the Christian calling. Therefore, it must be accepted in good faith while looking into the future.

Furthermore, a major theology that is laudable in this text is the Christian idea of the end time, the apocalypse. Cyprian encourages the Christians in times of crises to have hope and faith in God because, even when they die, they will not be lost.[61] He cites Paul in I Thessalonians 4:13 to inspire the Christians that they should not sorrow for brothers and sisters who die because of the hope of the resurrection and because those who sorrow exhibit a lack of hope which is not

[52] Cyprian, *On Mortality*, p. 25.
[53] Smith, "The Contributions of St Cyprian," p. 7.
[54] Cyprian, *On Mortality*, p. 9.
[55] Smith, "The Contributions of St Cyprian," p. 7.
[56] Cyprian, *On Mortality*, pp. 10-12.
[57] Cyprian, *On Mortality*, p. 10.
[58] Cyprian, *On Mortality*, p. 10.
[58] Cyprian, *On Mortality*, p. 10.
[59] Cyprian, *On Mortality*, p. 11.
[60] Cyprian, *On Mortality*, p. 13.
[61] Cyprian, *On Mortality*, p. 20.

Christian.[62] In doing this, Cyprian quotes Jesus' words in John 11:25 and comments: "If we believe in Christ, let us have faith in His words and promises; and since we shall not die eternally, let us come with a glad security unto Christ, with whom we are both to conquer and to reign for ever."[63] To this end, Cyprian held that death is a vehicle unto immortality and should be seen as an enjoyment rather than a vanquisher.[64] Cyprian cites a lot of biblical references and situations in scriptures to admonish the Christians that, in times of crises, their attention should rather be on the end of the age, when they will be glorified.[65] He then presents the Christian joy of the apocalypse in a dramatic series of rhetoric questions to excite the Christians into building a sure hope in the coming of the Lord and not paying full attention to their current dilemma occasioned by the plague:

> Who that has been placed in foreign lands would not hasten to return to his own country? Who that is hastening to return to his friends would not eagerly desire a prosperous gale, that he might the sooner embrace those dear to him? We regard paradise as our country – we already begin to consider the patriarchs as our parents: why do we not hasten and run, that we may behold our country, that we may greet our parents?[66]

The excitement of a child meeting their parents after a long trip sets the final picture of the Christian hope. The desire of Christian hope is established at the coming of the Lord. Therefore, he argues, "we attain the harbour of our home and eternal security, when having accomplished this death, we come to immortality. For that is our peace, that our faithful tranquillity, that our steadfast, and abiding, and perpetual security."[67]

Therefore, Cyprian contends: "Let us greet the day which assigns each of us to his own home, which snatches us hence, and sets us free from the snares of the world, and restores us to paradise and the kingdom."[68] In the light of this Christian hope espoused strongly in his text, Christians experiencing pandemics of the magnitude of the coronavirus must look to the glorification of the saints at the Lord's coming and not shiver.

A significant theology evident in Cyprian's *On Mortality* is the need not to be afraid of death.[69] The pandemic entered everywhere and the repercussions were felt everywhere, but the Christians need not despair but have faith. Cyprian, from the introduction of his work, sought to deal with the fear associated with the plague. He rather asked them to see it as an opportunity, "since you are about to be with Christ, and are secure of the Lord's promise, do you not embrace the

---

62 Cyprian, *On Mortality*, p. 21.
63 Cyprian, *On Mortality*, p. 21.
64 Cyprian, *On Mortality*, p. 22.
65 Cyprian, *On Mortality*, p. 23.
66 Cyprian, *On Mortality*, p. 23.
67 Cyprian, *On Mortality*, p. 3.
68 Cyprian, *On Mortality*, p. 26.
69 Smith, "The Contributions of St Cyprian," p. 2.

assurance that you are called to Christ, and rejoice that you are freed from the devil?"[70] He therefore cites the example of Simeon the priest, who was waiting to see Jesus before he died and who was very excited at the sight of Jesus, and hence the Christians should have the same pleasure to die, rather than fear it. The joy of the Christian death must fill the heart because they shall see Christ where there will be no affliction, pain, or torture.[71] Cyprian exhorted the Christians to be happy when death comes because it unites them to the faithful with Christ.[72] Cyprian additionally contrasted how the righteous and the unrighteous see death, saying: "The righteous are called to their place of refreshing, the unrighteous are snatched away to punishment; safety is the more speedily given to the faithful, penalty to the unbelieving."[73] This statement shows that, to the righteous, death is the gate by which they are prepared for their crown.[74] Therefore, the Christian is not expected to have any fear of death but to keep attention on immortality. "Let us be prepared for the whole will of God: laying aside the fear of death, let us think on the immortality which follows."[75]

Cyprian's *On Mortality* is therefore very useful to modern Christians who find themselves in crises such as the coronavirus pandemic. At times like these, Christians usually question their faith because, oftentimes, crises come when people are not ready or prepared. The most dominant questions in times of pandemics are borne out of the feeling of loneliness, where members feel God does not care. Therefore, pastors and preachers of the gospel must admonish members of what the faith is about. Cyprian's approach to dealing with the issues during his time was very soothing to encourage members to hold on to the faith, knowing that God has not deserted them but that sufferings are already predicted because they are part of the Christian faith. The members must appreciate that they are in transit and do not live here on earth but rather in a world that is to come. The members have to focus on the new world, the destination of their glory, and death is a necessary agent to get there. Therefore, they must not despair but stand strong because God has not deserted them.

Conclusion

Pandemics are a real aspect of life on earth and, when they come, the church is not exempted. As in the case of the Early Church, the church can gain from these predicaments if they develop the right attitudes. Learning from the Early Church implies that Christians must show solidarity, especially in times of crisis, and even towards the non-Christians to make the faith attractive to them. It is even

---

[70] Cyprian, *On Mortality*, p. 3.
[71] Cyprian, *On Mortality*, p. 5.
[72] Cyprian, *On Mortality*, pp. 6, 7.
[73] Cyprian, *On Mortality*, p. 15.
[74] Cyprian, *On Mortality*, p. 16.
[75] Cyprian, *On Mortality*, p. 24.

more crucial to maintain their hope by exhorting one another and responding to some pressing dilemmas of the faith to assure members of the presence of God. Cyprian addresses many of these questions raised by Christians, and his addresses are still relevant today because similar questions are being asked. His text addresses a lot of theological concerns of the time. Cyprian conveys to his readers the vagueness of this world to suggest that there is nothing good here. Therefore, Christians should be happy when death beckons. After all, they will be going to a better place. Furthermore, the text deals with suffering as a composite aspect of the Christian calling. Therefore, suffering, sickness, and death should not destabilise their faith. Additionally, Cyprian explains the Christian concept of the end of the age; thus, the Christian apocalypse. Finally, and even more so, Cyprian's major theme in this text seeks to encourage the Christians to have no fear of death at all, irrespective of how it comes.

Mediating the Divine During COVID-19: The Case of Perez Chapel International

Daniel Nii Aboagye Aryeh

Introduction

The effect of the COVID-19 pandemic on religious organisations has forced the Charismatic churches in Ghana to mediate the divine presence through the media on a mass basis from church auditoria. The presence of the Holy Spirit during church services, manifesting through personal contact with the man/woman of God, is a key ethos of many Charismatic churches in Ghana. In other words, COVID-19 is enhancing an already existing means of mediating the presence of the divine through the media to heal victims of the disease. Although the situation looks similar to the common practice, where Charismatic women/men preaching on radio and television ask listeners and viewers to touch the device for miracles, the COVID-19 pandemic has offered a revised and updated version of media ministry and healing through which victims of the disease were healed. This phenomenon deserves critical studies by scholars in the field of Pentecostal and Charismatic studies.

This study discusses how Bishop Charles Agyinasare of Perez Chapel International mediated the divine presence to bring healing to victims of COVID-19 and compares this with how the churches approached the influenza of 1918 in Nigeria, South Africa, and Ghana, and propounds a theory of space/distance and the divine in Charismatic Christianity in Ghana. The theory seeks to provide a solution for church services during pandemics in Africa to minister the power of God to victims of pandemic diseases, which would eventually encourage churches to adhere to lockdown restrictions.

In order to achieve my goal, my procedure is to (i) discuss how Pentecostals dealt with the influenza pandemic of 1918; (ii) discuss how Charles Agyinasare mediated the divine to heal COVID-19 victims; (iii) attempt to formulate a theory for mediating the divine for healing COVID-19 victims; and (iv) draw a conclusion. Charles Yewuraekow Agyinasare is a Ghanaian pastor and founder of the Word Miracle Church International, now the Perez Chapel International, a Pentecostal-Charismatic ministry in Ghana. The study is limited to restriction/lockdown situations where churches in Ghana were stopped from holding in-person services.

A narrative research method is used for this study. "Narrative methods can be considered 'real world measures' that are appropriate when 'real life problems' are investigated."[1] The narrative research method relies heavily on narratives concerning individuals or a particular phenomenon/issue for research.[2] The aim is to gain an understanding of a written document about issues pertaining to a particular people. The method may also include interviews to complement narratives regarding the phenomenon being studied. Although it can be used quantitatively, it is also a qualitative method that is mainly focused on library and archival research. One of the weaknesses of the narrative method from a qualitative perspective is that the text being interpreted is subjective; hence, it affects the objectiveness of the study. However, the study proceeds on the assumption that what has been written is factual and accurate and needs to be maintained by discovering the insight from the written document(s).[3]

In this paper, I engage the narrative research method in a qualitative approach. This involves archival and library research, with interviews. The rationale is to avoid over-generalisation and narrow down the discussion to a specific context. In other words, library and archival materials/documents will be consulted for an analysis of how Pentecostals handled the influenza pandemic of 1918 in Africa, and Bishop Charles Agyinasare of Perez Chapel International will be interviewed to ascertain how he deploys his healing grace to minister healing to victims of COVID-19.

Pentecostals and the 1918 Influenza Pandemic in Africa

In this section, I give a brief introduction concerning the church and the influenza pandemic in Africa and will discuss how Pentecostal Churches (AICs) in Nigeria, South Africa, and Ghana mediated with the divine to heal victims. My choice of Nigeria, South Africa, and Ghana is due to the availability of publications available to me.

The world has encountered many pandemics during which the church has devised various ways to mediate the divine to the specific location of the members of the church. The influenza pandemic/epidemic, first reported in Spain in 1918, led to the temporary closure of church services in the affected countries.[4] The influenza pandemic is also known as the Spanish flu. According to Nick Donnelly and Jim McManus, "the Spanish flu brings new challenges. Not least, it brings the challenge that the Church itself may see 25% of its ministers and faithful ill, bringing consequent issues for ministry and also possible financial strain. The numbers of very ill and dying people may overwhelm the Church's

---

[1] *ATLAS.ti, "Narrative analysis in Research," available at https://atlasti.com/guides/qualitative-research-guide-part-2/narrative-research last Accessed 9 March 2023.*

[2] *Narrative Research.*

[3] H. Jansen, "Research, Narrative, and Representation: A Post-Narrative Approach," *History and Theory* 58(1), (2019), pp. 67–88. DOI:10.1111/hith.12100.

[4] John M. Barry, *The Great Influenza: The Story of the Deadliest Pandemic in History* (London: Penguin Books, 2005), p. 17.

ability to provide pastoral care."[5] Influenza affected members of the church, including the clergy, leading to a ban on church services, the wearing of face masks, and social distancing in affected countries.[6] In this period, the Pentecostal churches in Africa and the African independent/initiated/indigenous churches (AICs) were not very popular.

During this period, Pentecostal churches emphasised the presence of the divine through the activities of the Holy Spirit to heal, following what was happening in the USA, Europe, etc.[7] As Asamoah-Gyadu argues, the Pentecostal phenomenon was reported earlier in India and Haiti before the Azuza Street experience in the USA became more popular; hence it being global in outlook.[8]

Pandemics often motivate non-religious persons towards being religious in order to seek a solution to the pandemic. According to Naomi Paget, the role of spirituality and religion during the influenza pandemic played an important role in people's response to the flu.[9] Paget's assertion suggests that during pandemic periods religion plays a key role in survival. Religious denominations that claim to have the power of God to mediate the divine presence for healing are often sought because pandemic diseases are usually novel and do not have science/drugs to effectively combat them immediately. "Any issue that defies sociological and scientific prescriptions was considered for spiritual solution."[10] Religion is crucial in every facet of life in Africa and religious solutions are equally patronised by the masses.[11] In other words, shopping for health[12] and protection from the pandemic becomes a reality.

Nigeria

During the influenza pandemic in Nigeria in 1918, some leaders of the AICs attempted to minister the power of God to victims of the pandemic to heal them.

---

[5] Nick Donnelly and Jim McManus, "Pandemic Flu: The Role of the Church," *The Furrow* 57(12), (Dec 2006), pp. 657–663.

[6] Steve Yount, "A Century Later, Have We Learned the Lessons of the 'Spanish Flu' Pandemic of 1918?" *Denison Forum*, 6th April 2020 [Available at: https://www.denisonforum.org/columns/contributor-article/a-century-later-have-we-learned-the-lessons-of-the-spanish-flu-pandemic-of-1918/], [Last accessed: 16th July 2023].

[7] J. Kwabena Asamoah-Gyadu, *African Charismatics: Current Development Within Independent Indigenous Pentecostalism in Ghana* (Leiden: Koninklijke Brill NV, 2005), pp. 11–12.

[8] Asamoah-Gyadu, *African Charismatics*, pp. 10–13.

[9] Naomi Paget, *Ministry During Pandemic: From Awareness to Implementation* (Prusia: Judson Press, 2020), p. 38. Italics in original.

[10] Daniel Nii Aboagye Aryeh, "Religion and Urban Life: Space and Patronage for Prophetic Ministry in Cities in Ghana," *Alternation* Special Edition 30 (2020), pp. 311–334. DOI: https://doi.org/10.29086/2519-5476/2020/sp30a17.

[11] David N.A. Kpobi, *Mission in Ghana: The Ecumenical Heritage* (Accra: Asempa Publishers, 2008), pp. 83–89.

[12] Asamoah-Gyadu, *African Charismatics*, p. 67.

Others were not seen to be actively involved in the attempt to heal victims of the pandemic. Omololu Ebenezer Fagunwa argues that, in Nigeria, there was a "huge pneumatic experience and spiritual awakening" that made the Aladura Church very popular.[13] The Aladura Church resisted the lockdown and held prayer meetings in the houses of members to combat the influenza.[14] The Church did not mediate the divine from a distance (virtually) but met with the members and used prayer to mediate the divine. Although it was argued that the Aladura Church was formed to heal victims of influenza,[15] I have not found any evidence that indicates that a victim of influenza was healed. Garrick Sokari Braide, a powerful faith-healing minister, was imprisoned during the period and could not mediate the divine presence to heal victims of the pandemic. Allan Anderson postulates that it is likely that Braide died of influenza,[16] while Matthew Kustenbauder is emphatic that this was indeed the case.[17]

Another means of mediating the divine to heal victims of the influenza pandemic is seen in the ministry of Sophia Odunlami, although it is not evident whether victims of the influenza were healed. Towards the end of 1918, Sophia Odunlami (later Mrs Ajayi), a 19-year-old prophetess of the Aladura Church, claimed to have had a vision in which she heard a voice that rainwater and prayer should be used for victims of the influenza.[18] Firstly, it implies that some of the victims of the influenza were not kept in isolation centres. They were allowed to look for religious solutions, probably due to the adverts by the pastors of the Aladura Church. Secondly, it seems the use of prayer as a means to mediate the divine for healing was not yielding the needed results. Hence, prayer was not abandoned, but augmented by rainwater. It is not clear how the rainwater and prayer were used concurrently. Nonetheless, based on the liturgy of the Aladura churches, the rainwater was distributed to victims of influenza after each prayer session to be used to either bathe, drink, wash the face, etc. In the words of S.A. Fatokun, Prophetess Odunlami was "a God-gifted divine healer raised in an outbreak of influenza against all charms and medicines."[19] Despite these outstanding remarks, there is no evidence of the healing of any victim of influenza through the use of rainwater and prayer directed by Prophetess

[13] Omololu Ebenezer Fagunwa, "African Pentecostalism and the 1918 Influenza Pandemic: The Supernatural Amid the Fearful and Implications for the COVID-19 Pandemic," *Christian Journal for Global Health* 7(5), (Dec 2020), pp. 52–64.

[14] Asamoah-Gyadu, "Dealing With a Spiritual Virus: Whither the Prophetic?"

[15] Fagunwa, "African Pentecostalism and the 1918 Influenza Pandemic," p. 57.

[16] Allan Anderson, *African Reformation: African Initiated Christianity in the 20th Century* (Trenton, NJ: Africa World Press, 2001), p. 82.

[17] Matthew Kustenbauder, "Prophetic Movements: Western Africa," in John Middleton and Joseph C. Miller (eds), *New Encyclopedia of Africa* 4th ed. (Detroit, MI: Thomson/Gale, 2008), pp. 273–279.

[18] Fagunwa, "African Pentecostalism and the 1918 Influenza Pandemic," p. 58.

[19] S.A. Fatokun, "Precious Stone Society 2018." https://tacnlawna.org/precious-stone-society/ [Last accessed: 24th February 2022].

Odunlami. That notwithstanding, this does not intend to discredit the ministry exploits of Prophetess Odunlami, but to find evidence of her works.

South Africa

South Africa also experienced the ravaging features of the 1918 influenza pandemic. Patterson states that "in South Africa, Durban was infected in September; the whole country was suffering within three weeks and during October the disease moved north to Bechuanaland, Southern Rhodesia, and Nyasaland."[20] The influenza spread rapidly in South Africa, probably considered as the first African country where the spread of the influenza was so fast. The influenza killed thousands in South Africa within six weeks (in October 1918) and culminated in drought and economic hardships, which were experienced mostly by peasants.[21]

Prior to the 1918 pandemic, some of the Zionist churches, such as the Christian Catholic Apostolic Holy Spirit Church in Zion and Zion Apostolic Church of South Africa, among others, had started in 1911.[22] However, there is no or scant information in the scholarly fraternity concerning how these churches that claim to have had the power of God to perform healing mediated for the healing of victims of the influenza pandemic. Nonetheless, the influenza facilitated the call of some of the leaders of the Zionist churches into ministry. For example, Prophet George Khambule, founder of the iBandla Labancwele (a Zionist church), in 1918 experienced his calling to ministry when he contracted the disease and was taken to the hospital. Jonathan A. Draper asserts that:

> Khambule was taken to hospital with influenza, died, and experienced himself looking down from on high […] burning in hell and found himself accused of adultery and murder […] Khambule's dead sister, Agnes (Agrineth), in the form of an angel, intervened on his behalf and he entered heaven and received a commission to save and heal his people.[23]

Although Khambule was infected with the influenza, he was commissioned to heal, and there were testimonies of him (Khambule) healing barrenness, eye disease, chest disease, dumbness, etc., through prayer and the use of ashes and water. However, it is not clear whether he healed a victim of influenza or not.

---

[20] Patterson, "The Influenza Epidemic," p. 500.

[21] Howard Phillips, "Why Did it Happen? Religious and Lay Explanations of the Spanish Flu Epidemic of 1918 in South Africa," *Kronos* 12 (1987), pp. 72–92; Glenda Kruss, "Religion, Class and Culture – Indigenous Churches in South Africa, With Special Reference to Zionist Apostolic," Master of Arts thesis, Department of Religious Studies, University of Cape Town, 1985, p. 142.

[22] Kruss, "Religion, Class, and Culture," p. 130.

[23] Jonathan A. Draper, "A Broken Land and a Healing Community: Zulu Zionism and Healing in the Case of George Khambule (1884–1949)," *Studia Historiae Ecclesiasticae* 36(1), (2010), pp. 1–16 [Available at: http://www.scielo.org.za/scielo.php?script=sci_arttext&pid=S1017-04992010000200004&lng=en&nrm=iso], [Last accessed: 16th July 2023].

Ghana

In Ghana, although K. David Patterson graphically illustrates that the influenza spread nationwide within three months in 1918, many scholars have not studied how the founders of the AICs/Pentecostalism in Ghana who ministered during the period mediated the divine for the healing of victims of the influenza pandemic (see below for the map).[24]

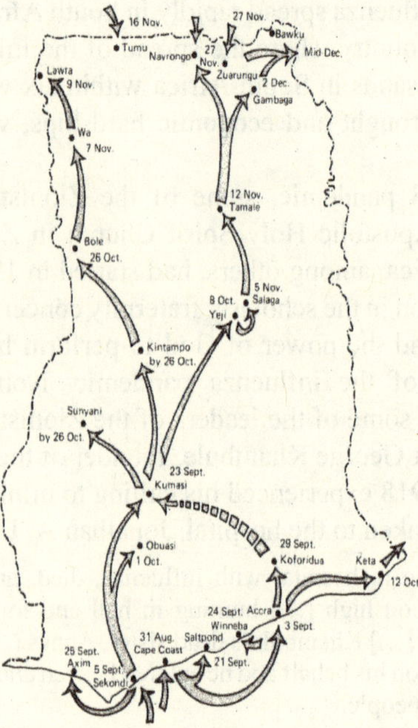

Map I

The arrows in Map I show how the influenza pandemic was brought into the country through the coast at the south of Ghana through the centre to the north of the country. It also indicates the dates at which the disease reached the major cities of Ghana.

The influenza was reported to have started in the coastal cities and towns of the Gold Coast (now Ghana) and later spread into all the then ten regions of Ghana. According to Patterson:

> On 28 August 1918, the Governor of Sierra Leone wired his counterpart in Accra that Freetown had influenza and that all ships reaching the Gold Coast from England or Sierra Leone should be considered infected. The warning was too late.

---

[24] K. David Patterson, "The Influenza Epidemic of 1918–19 in the Gold Coast," *The Journal of African History* 24(4), (1983), pp. 485–502.

> The *SS Shonga*, an American vessel outbound from Freetown, reached Cape Coast on 31 August. The town was almost certainly infected during its brief call. The *Shonga* proceeded eastward and by 3 September, when it reached Accra, virtually the entire crew was sick. Sixteen of the most serious cases were landed and hospitalised. The vessel and the crewmen were quarantined.[25]

This assertion by Patterson indicates that influenza was imported to Ghana through people who were working in vessels going from neighbouring countries to Ghana. "As the infection spread, the markets dwindled, schools closed, public meetings were cancelled and normal business came to a standstill. Waterfront districts were hard hit; cocoa loading was delayed and ships by-passed Accra."[26] Due to this, the most important decision was to impose some restrictions. Evanson Zondani Sambala stated that "the native beliefs hastened when colonial administrators considered closing churches and missionary schools as a means to halt the disease's spread. A great deal of tact seems to have been displayed by colonial administrators on this, reassuring natives that closing churches or schools was a temporary act."[27] This is an indication that the restriction concerning the temporary closure of church meetings would not be welcoming news for many because the presence of the divine was expected to manifest to a greater degree during church meetings. When individuals meet and socialise from cultural or religious perspectives, power is generated towards the meeting of the needs of participants and a sense of belonging, care, and companionship is experienced.[28] Due to the close affinity of many Ghanaians to religion, some believe that influenza is a result of witchcraft, which religion can effectively deal with.[29]

Particular mention is made of the influenza detected in Winneba (Central Region) on 24th September 1918.[30] Apostle Peter Anim had then planned a prayer meeting in Sam's family compound at Winneba as a prelude to starting a branch of the Faith Tabernacle Church.[31] The influenza pandemic of 1918 offered the opportunity for Anim to expand or open new branches for prayer groups. This is similar to the Aladura situation in Nigeria. Hilda Afi Aleh argues that the influenza pandemic aided the spread and popularity of the ministry of Apostle

---

25 Patterson, "The Influenza Epidemic," p. 486.
26 Patterson, "The Influenza Epidemic," p. 488.
27 Evanson Zondani Sambala, "Ethics of Planning for, and Responding to, Pandemic Influenza in Sub-Saharan Africa: Qualitative Study," PhD thesis,University of Nottingham, 2014, p. 67.
28 Sambala, "Ethics of Planning," p. 88.
29 Sambala, "Ethics of Planning," p. 67.
30 Patterson, "The Influenza Epidemic," p. 489.
31 The full name of the man was Robert James Kofi Kanyi Sam. His family house is popularly called 'Sam's family Compound'. It had a spacious court in the middle that many people could use for public functions and other religious activities.

Peter Anim.[32] Aleh reported that "during the intense period of the epidemic, many victims were brought to the Faith Home [Sam's family compound] where they were miraculously healed devoid of any medication."[33] Even though the means of mediating the miraculous healings were not indicated, deducing from the beliefs of Apostle Anim, it is most likely that it was by prayer without the use of any prophylactics to aid the result. The result attracted many people to churches that emphasise prayer and healing. Aleh states that, "most of the prayer groups that sprang up in the south which later culminated into Pentecostal denominations were a response to the influenza outbreak of 1918. Also, many old Christians in the mainline churches in the south desired something deeply spiritual than what was found in their denominations."[34] This assertion by Aleh confirms Paget's proposition that during pandemic moments in some countries, religious organisations and church denominations that profess to be more spiritual are patronised by the masses. The lockdown and isolation of victims of influenza were not being observed and infected people sought solutions to their health challenges from churches without thinking that others could be infected. However, it could be argued that, because they were healed, they could not have spread the disease to members of the church. That notwithstanding, they could spread it to people they met on their way to the church or even fellow passengers. Francis Otoo Eduah argues that the exodus of victims of influenza to prayer centres and churches was due to the failure of Western medicines to adequately deal with influenza at the time.[35] This may be accurate during the peak periods of the influenza pandemic but later, Western medicines were able to control it.

In the narratives referred to above concerning how Pentecostal churches dealt with the influenza pandemic in mediating the divine for healing victims, it is obvious that: (i) restrictions for isolation of victims of the influenza were not strictly followed; (ii) the means of mediating the divine for healing of victims was by prayer and use of rainwater; (iii) information on how Pentecostals mediated the divine for healing is scarce. It seems to partly allude to the proposition of Asamoah-Gyadu that "they are waiting for the pandemic to pass and then start organising healing services. It is an ingenious way of questioning the credibility of the charismatic claims that have often been inflicted upon Christian Africa in search of breakthroughs to problems associated with evil."[36] It could also be that scholarship at the time was not interested in documenting the activities of the Pentecostals and the influenza pandemic; and (iv) the few healings that were recorded were effected through personal contact by attending

---

[32] Hilda Afi Aleh, "A Comparative Study of the Mission Histories of the Assemblies of God Church and the Church of Pentecost in Ghana," MPhil thesis,Religious Department of the University of Ghana, 2013, p. 64.

[33] Aleh, "A Comparative Study," p. 64.

[34] Aleh, "A Comparative Study," p. 104.

[35] Francis Otoo Eduah, "A History of Christian Faith Church International (CfCI), in Ghana," MPhil thesis, College of Humanities, University of Ghana, 2018, p. 28.

[36] Asamoah-Gyadu, "Dealing With a Spiritual Virus: Whither the Prophetic?"

church services in defiance of lockdown rules. The media was not engaged to minister to the victims of the influenza pandemic of 1918. The influenza pandemic and how the AICs struggled to minister to victims for healing clearly demonstrates the need for a theory to deal with religious issues during pandemics.

Charles Agyinasare: Mediating the Divine to Heal COVID-19 Victims

In this section, I discuss the media ministry of Bishop Charles Agyinasare during the first half-year of 2020. Agyinasare's background will inform how he mediated the divine presence to heal COVID-19 victims and the testimonies that ensued.

Charles Agyinasare is a beneficiary of Morris Cerullo's media ministry through the "point of contact" of television. He attended Morris Cerullo's School of Ministry in 1983 in Accra, but Cerullo did not come in person. He was represented by Alex Ness (Cerullo's ministry aid) who played a videocassette of Cerullo to the audience gathered at one location. Here is a testimony of Agyinasare, stated by Asamoah-Gyadu:

> As Dr Cerullo spoke and wept, I also wept for my powerlessness to save this sinful world. On the last day of the conference, Dr Ness anointed our ears, thumbs, and toes. When I got to my seat and knelt, I heard the voice of the Holy Spirit say, "My boy, Charles, I send you out as I sent Moses. Go, and I will put my words on your lips and take the world for me."[37]

From that day, Charles Agyinasare began to perform great miracles and attract many to his church.[38] The impartation received by Agyinasare was through multiple means: (i) through watching and listening to Cerullo on television; and (ii) anointing of oil by Ness, which was blessed by Cerullo. Agyinasare later had two media ministries: *God's Miracle Hour* on Ghana Broadcasting Television (GTV) on Saturday mornings and *Your Miracle Encounter* on TV3 on Saturday evenings.[39] On these programmes, the videotapes of Agyinasare's miracle services were being played to motivate the faith of audiences to receive miracles or come to the faith through technology.

The outbreak of the COVID-19 pandemic and its associated lockdown and restrictions have given rise to the engagement of the media space to reach members of the church in their various locations. The presence of the Holy Spirit is critical in many Christian denominations, but the ways it is mediated and acknowledged differ from one denomination to the other. For many Pentecostals or pneumatic churches, the divine presence of God must express itself in tangible

---

[37] Asamoah-Gyadu, *African Charismatics*, p. 157.
[38] Asamoah-Gyadu, *African Charismatics*, p. 157.
[39] J. Kwabena Asamoah-Gyadu, "Anointing Through the Screen: Neo-Pentecostalism and Televised Christianity in Ghana," *Studies in World Christianity* 11(1), (2005), pp. 9–28.

ways, including the healing of sick folks either instantly or through gradual means. The power to heal knows no bounds and is transmitted even through media channels.

The use of the media is not new to many Charismatic churches in Ghana. Many Pentecostal/Charismatic churches actively use the media to advertise their programmes and the charisma of the leader, which Asamoah-Gyadu referred to as a tool to expand and fulfil the global agenda of the church.[40] Therefore, the media audiences (viewers and listeners) are expected to have similar experiences (healing/miracles) that in-person audiences receive. It affords the opportunity to have distant members of the church who will later join a branch near them or visit the branch where the lead pastor (general-overseer) worships. This led to the theology of "point of contact," where audiences (viewers and listeners) can be reached through the electronic media by touching the device as directed by the pastor as a means to receive miracles.

For Pentecostals and Charismatics, radio and television are "not as instruments of technical rationality, but as means to bring individuals into physically felt contact with the transcendental."[41] In the words of Juan Sepúlveda captured by Asamoah-Gyadu, "the constitutive act of the Pentecostal movement is the offer of a direct and particularly intense encounter with God, which makes possible a profound change in the life of the person who experiences it."[42] This lived experience could take place by prayer by the member or through the prayer, mediation, and direction of the leader (pastor/prophet).[43] In the case of mediation by the pastor, hands are being laid on members (in person) who need the intervention of God through healing and other miracles.

The phrase "point of contact" is "the act of touching the radio receiver in order to facilitate both the efficacious reception and the transmission of the Holy Ghost power."[44] Arguably, the phrase was coined by Oral Roberts to "mitigate the distance from both ears of the faithful radio listener and the efficacious healing virtue of the Holy Ghost."[45] It is also used in relation to objects and substances such as water, oil, calendars, books, and handkerchiefs blessed by a man/woman of God to perform miracles.[46] The technology of radio, television, objects, and

---

[40] Asamoah-Gyadu, *African Charismatics*, pp. 99–100.

[41] Marleen De Witte, "The Electronic Touch Machine Miracle Scam: Body, Technology, and the (Dis)authentication of the Pentecostal Supernatural," in J. Stolow (ed.), *Deus in Machina: Religion, Technology, and the Things in Between* (New York: Fordham University Press, 2013), p. 62.

[42] Asamoah-Gyadu, *African Charismatics*, p. 96.

[43] Lamin Sanneh, *West African Christianity: The Religious Impact* (Maryknoll, NY: Orbis Books, 1983), pp. 179–181.

[44] Anderson Blanton, *Hittin' the Prayer Bones: Materiality of Spirit in the Pentecostal South* (Chapel Hill, NC: The University of North Carolina Press, 2015), p. 23.

[45] Blanton, *Hittin' the Prayer Bones*, p. 22.

[46] Daniel Nii Aboagye Aryeh, *Biblical, Traditional, and Theological Framework for Understanding Christian Prophetism Today* (Eugene, OR: Wipf and Stock, 2019), p. 69.

substances help the listener to connect to the anointing of God upon the life of the man/woman of God.

Agyinasare engaged in the business of "point of contact" for distant audiences to receive miracles. At the Western Region for Christ Miracle Crusade in April 2019, a cripple was healed while watching the programme on Facebook just as other cripples at the crusade were healed.[47] The cripple watched someone being healed and he was also healed. Although the cripple was not physically present at the crusade venue, he participated in the blessing through watching the programme on Facebook and tapping into the anointing of Agyinasare. Asamoah-Gyadu stated that Agyinasare would ask viewers looking for healing to place their own palms on where the TV screen projects his as he prays for them. "The belief is that as they place their open palms into his, there is a transference of 'healing anointing' to the sick through the screen."[48] Agyinasare mediated the healing power of God through prayer and "point of contact" to heal the sick.

During the period of lockdown in Ghana (16th March to 19th April 2020), many churches resorted to the use of radio, television, and social media platforms to reach their members with the gospel and church activities. Agyinasare's virtual church services were designed to have a section that mediates the power of the Holy Spirit to heal victims of COVID-19. In Pentecostal/Charismatic churches, ministration (praying for the sick, impartation, and seed sowing) is done after the preaching. Agyinasare dedicated substantial time praying for victims of COVID-19 and they received instant healing. In an interview, he confessed that it is very difficult to continuously minister to COVID-19 victims for healing through virtual church services, but God performed miracles by healing them.[49]

Throughout the lockdown and restrictions on public gatherings, Charles Agyinasare organised monthly fasting and prayers against the spread of the pandemic and healing for the victims of the COVID-19 disease. Probably Agyinasare did not want to allude to the proposition on social media (as suggested by Asamoah-Gyadu) that the clergy of the Pentecostal and Charismatic churches may be waiting to organise healing or miracle services later, after the COVID-19 pandemic had passed.[50] These services were virtual, where members were to join the service through television, radio, and social media platforms. The audiences who received miracles were expected to send messages through the social media handles to testify instantly. In one of these

[47] "Takoradi Crusade – Testimonies | Bishop Charles Agyinasare," YouTube Channel: Archbishop Charles Agyinasare, 30th April 2019 [Available at: https://www.youtube.com/watch?v=uYIbV4TB24U], [Last accessed: 17th July 2023].

[48] Asamoah-Gyadu, "Anointing Through the Screen," p. 20.

[49] Charles Agyinasare, interviewed by the author, 11th April 2021, at his office, Dzorwulu.

[50] Asamoah-Gyadu, "Dealing With a Spiritual Virus."

virtual services, a gentleman sent this testimony: "Man of God, I thank God for healing me from COVID-19. For the past two weeks, I have not been going to work. After Monday evening prayers, I had a message that I tested negative and that I should resume work on Wednesday, 1st July. I thank God for healing."[51] This testimony was received from someone who tested positive for the disease and was self-quarantined and was watching the programme live on Facebook. However, after prayers, he tested negative when the company ordered for mass testing again, since many of the staff were exposed to the disease. He tested negative and was asked to resume work. Another testimony came from a lady in Aflao, who said:

> Bishop, I had COVID-19 and was very weak such that I could not do my normal household chores. I watched the June edition of the prayer and fasting through YouTube. Just after your prayer for COVID-19 people, I began to experience some heat in my body and my strength was restored. I later went to take a second test and I was negative. God bless you, Bishop.[52]

Although these people did not send their test results to indicate positive and later negative results, it is obvious that something remarkable took place in their health status after watching Bishop Charles Agyinasare. Agyinasare believes that giving a testimony about a miracle performed by God is a means of making the miraculous healing real.[53] Hence, these people have been healed from COVID-19.

What follows is the attempt to propound a theory for healing during pandemics, which will not conflict with lockdowns and restrictions by the state.

Towards a Theory of "Space/Distance and Mediating the Divine" to Heal

John G. Wacker argues that there are four components of building a good theory: "(1) definitions of terms or variables, (2) a domain where the theory applies, (3) a set of relationships of variables, and (4) specific predictions (factual claims)."[54] In other words, "conceptual definitions, domain limitations, relationship-building, and predictions," are critical in building theories.[55] What should be the basis for a theory for "space/distance and mediating the divine"?

---

51 A testimony sent through Facebook during the programme on 2nd July 2020.

52 A testimony sent through Facebook during the programme on 3rd June 2020.

53 Charles Agyinasare, *It is Miracle Time: Experiencing God's Supernatural Working Power* Vol. 2 (Accra: Charles Agyinasare Press, 1997), p. 45.

54 John G. Wacker, "A Definition of Theory: Research Guidelines for Different Theory-Building Research Methods in Operations Management," *Journal of Operations Management* 16 (1998), pp. 361–385.

55 Wacker, "A Definition of Theory," p. 361.

Conceptual Definitions

In this study, I identify pandemic, epidemic, restrictions on public gatherings, mediation, and healing as key terms and phrases in the formulation of a theory of space/distance and mediating the divine during pandemics/epidemics. Although some scholars use epidemic and pandemic alternatively or loosely to refer to the same extent of outbreak, there is a slight difference between a pandemic and an epidemic. According to David M. Morens, Gregory K. Folkers, and Anthony S. Fauci, although epidemic and pandemic are similar terms, pandemic is the advanced form of an epidemic.[56] They explain that a pandemic has the characteristic of wider geographical coverage, fast movement of the disease, high transmission from person to person, high attack rates on humans, a minimum degree of protection by humans, and the disease must be novel, infectious, contagious, and severe.[57] These traits are equally found in epidemics but in a moderate form. The main difference between a pandemic and an epidemic is how a disease spreads and its impact on humans.[58] Pandemics and epidemics may lead to some forms of restrictions on public gatherings and the temporary suspension of church services.

Mediation refers to the mode of ministering healing to victims of a pandemic/epidemic. It could be prayer, fasting, and the use of prophylactics. The mode of mediation for healing victims of pandemic disease must critically consider and adhere to social distancing and restriction protocols.

Healing in the context of "space/distance and mediating the divine" for healing during pandemics can be either instantaneous or gradual and must be authenticated by a negative result from a certified hospital/laboratory/clinic/research centre etc. by qualified medical personnel. It is the negative result that would facilitate the release of the victim from the isolation centre, not a mere declaration of healing without medical evidence.

The Domain Where "Space/Distance and Mediating the Divine" Applies

The domain for the effective functioning of the "space/distance and mediating the divine" is Pentecostal/Charismatic contexts in Africa (or similar contexts), where faith healing is rife and there is a pandemic/epidemic situation. Contexts that share the belief in miracles during pandemics would be a fertile ground for the budding of space/distance and mediating the divine for healing.

Relationship to/with Other Theories

The theory of "Space/Distance and Mediating the Divine" is related to the belief in African Traditional Religion where shrines can be consulted to harm opponents or heal a relative from a distance without the knowledge of the

---

[56] David M. Morens, Gregory K. Folkers, and Anthony S. Fauci, "What Is a Pandemic?" *The Journal of Infectious Diseases* (2009), pp. 1018–1021. DOI: 10.1086/644537.

[57] Morens et al., "What Is a Pandemic?" pp. 1019–1020.

[58] Morens et al., "What Is a Pandemic?" p. 1020.

opponent or relative. John S. Mbiti argued that health in the African context is not solely a physical condition. Spirits and deities are consulted for diagnosis and prescriptions for cures are given at a distance, which may be known to the victim or not, but the target is the cure. Mbiti further elaborated that in situations where the victim of sickness cannot be physically taken to the shrine, or the priest/medicine man/woman cannot come to where the victim lives, rituals of healing are performed at a distance (in the absence of the victim).[59] It emanates from the belief that spirit entities cannot be limited and confined to a location perpetually.

The theory of space/distance and mediating the divine is related to healing at a distance in Greco-Roman religions and the gospels. For example, Chanina ben Dosa has performed many miracles from a distance. Rabban Gamaliel got sick of a fever and sent some noblemen to invite Chanina ben Dosa to come and heal the son. However, ben Dosa did not come but prayed for the son of Gamaliel at a distance and the child was healed.[60] Chanina ben Dosa also healed the son of Rabban Yochanan ben Zakkai from a distance. He did not honour an invitation to heal in person but put his face in between his legs and prayed. The child was healed.[61] The healing of the royal official in John 4:46-54 demonstrates the power of Jesus to heal from a distance. However, these miracles effected from a distance differ from space/distance and mediating the divine theory. The beneficiaries of the healing in the Greco-Roman religions and the gospel were not active in the healing process. What this theory rather expects is that the beneficiaries of healing through space/distance and mediating the divine are directly involved in the healing process through technology.

Specific Predictions

There is no sacrosanct theory. The space/distance and mediating the divine theory may fail where technology is not available and is limited to pandemic/epidemic situations and distance audiences (viewers and listeners of television, radio, and social media networks), which include people who are not mobile due to health challenges, where the seeker could not be present in person. If the space/distance and mediating the divine theory is upheld, it will potentially reduce religious agitation against lockdown and social distancing protocols by some Pentecostal/Charismatic churches.[62] The space/distance and mediating the

---

[59] John S. Mbiti, *Introduction to African Religion* 2nd Ed. (Oxford: Heinemann Educational Publishers, 1991), pp. 165–167.

[60] David R. Cartlidge and David L. Dungan, *Documents for the Study of the Gospels* (Philadelphia, PA: Fortress Press, 1980), p. 158.

[61] Cartlidge and Dungan, *Documents for the Study of the Gospels*, p. 158.

[62] Eva-Maria Egger, Sam Jones, Patricia Justino, Ivan Manhique, and Ricardo Santos, "Africa's Lockdown Dilemma: High Poverty and Low Trust," *United Nations Universities World Institute for Development Economic Research.* WIDER Working Paper 2020/76, June 2020.

divine theory will work where there is a Charismatic church pastor, seekers who believe in divine healing or miracles, and media technology.

Conclusion

The early African Pentecostals (AICs) ministered during the era of the influenza pandemic, but there is very limited or no information concerning how they dealt with it. In contemporary times, however, there are calls of pastors who claim to have the power to heal the sick to deploy that power to heal victims of COVID-19. Charles Agyinasare responded to this clarion call and organised virtual healing services to pray against the spread of the disease and heal victims. There were some testimonies of COVID-19 victims being healed. The basis for a theory for space/distance and mediating the divine theory is propounded. The theory has the advantage of not inviting victims of COVID-19 to congregate in a church auditorium in order to access healing but to access healing in isolation centres through the use of technology. It will give prominence to Pentecostal/ Charismatic church pastors concerning their claim of possession of the healing power of God. With the outburst of pneumatic churches during and after the influenza pandemic of 1918, it is likely that more churches will emerge during and after the COVID-19 pandemic due to prayer groups that were organised in homes during the lockdown and increased prayer time by many Christians. The space/distance and mediating the divine theory will serve as a guide to the handling of COVID-19 patients for healing.

Praising the Lord During Pandemics: A Rhetorical Critical Reading of Psalm 102 from an African Pentecostal Perspective

Mark S. Aidoo

Introduction

African Pentecostal Christianity emphasises the side of God who is a miracle-worker and who actively intervenes in the life of inquirers. It is when God meets the inquirer at the point of a need put forward that prayers of praise and thanksgiving are heard. The perception of a God who is absent, far away, or watching on as evil prevails is not widespread. This paper explores why the Pentecostal Christian needs to praise God in times of outbreaks of diseases of pandemic proportions like COVID-19, HIV/AIDS, Ebola, and yellow fever, especially when the active intervention of God is not seen, using a rhetorical reading of Psalm 102. The quest to have a meaningful life as an African Pentecostal Christian living in an underdeveloped world and facing crisis lies squarely within a relationship with the divine. Spirituality and religion thus become important resources for health and well-being, and play significant roles in thoughts, forms, and behaviours. African spirituality is founded on the belief that life is defined by God: *biribiara yɛ Onyame asɛm* (lit. "everything is God's issue"). God is the architect of everything. As such, the African does not ignore God when seeking for help or addressing holistic development physically, mentally, socially, and economically. Moreover, the African knows that, after all is done, praise and thanksgiving are vital to promoting harmonious relationships. How does Psalm 102 teach us the motivating factors that would influence the African Pentecostal Christian to praise God in times of pandemics?

The Setting of Psalm 102

The Psalms provide a framework of spirituality and help to interpret the meaning of life. They hinge on life settings, whether real or perceived, in the daily lives of the believer in God, without overlooking major life crises. For Claus Westermann, the Psalms have two distinctive categories: lament and praise. These two, he argues, are the poles that reflect life and worship. All other occasions found in the Psalms hang on these two. Life usually revolves around times when the believer laments, either communally or individually, and around times when the believer praises God declaratively or descriptively.[1] He argues:

> The division of the Psalter into lament and praise certainly means more than the fact that these two types exist. Lament and praise characterize a journey that goes over the heights and through the depths. These psalms portray the rhythm of life, the movement of every human life between joy and suffering – a rhythm like that of breathing.[2]

Walter Brueggemann, using a unique approach in his reading, understands all the Psalms as moving from theology to spirituality. He asserts that the Psalms can best be understood as a scheme of orientation – disorientation – new orientation.[3] For Brueggemann, the movement from disorientation to reorientation is not just a psychological experience or physical deliverance, although that is often the motif. It is more a spiritual one and an affirmation of hope that there is a bright future.[4]

Scholarship on the Psalms follows a framework that structures them into five books or collections: Psalms 1–41 as Book/Collection I; Psalms 42–72 as Book/Collection II; Psalms 73–89 as Book/Collection III; Psalms 90–106 as Book/Collection IV; and Psalms 107–150 as Book/Collection V. Psalm 102 is part of Collection IV and is not attributed to an individual. The superscription describes the psalm as "a prayer of an afflicted person who has grown weak and pours out a lament before the Lord." Collection IV opens, not with a Davidic psalm, but with a psalm attributed to Moses and concludes with a psalm-pair featuring Abraham (Ps. 105) and Moses (Ps. 106).

Gerald Wilson views books IV–V as the return to the land in a time when Yahweh will restore the fortunes of Israel and the responses telling Israel that Yahweh alone will be their help in the future now that the "Davidic covenant introduced in Psalm 2 had come to nothing."[5] For Wilson, Book IV, with its emphasis on Yahweh's kingship, functions as the "editorial centre" of the Psalter. It is "the 'answer' to the problem posed in Psalm 89 as to the apparent failure of the Davidic covenant with which books I–III are primarily concerned."[6] It needs to be noted that Wilson's proposals are not without conjectures; he singles out Psalm 89, leaving the rest in Book IV. Such references are almost entirely inferential. Roland Murphy observes that Wilson's arrangements "all partake of a hypothetical character; one can associate freely

---

[1] Claus Westermann, *Praise and Lament in the Psalms* (Atlanta, GA: John Knox Press, 1965).

[2] Claus Westermann, "Experience in the Church and Work of Theology," *Word and World* 10(1), (1990), p. 11.

[3] Walter Brueggemann, *The Message of the Psalms* (Minneapolis, MN: Augsburg, 1985), p. 9.

[4] Brueggemann, *The Message of the Psalms*, p. 11.

[5] Gerald H. Wilson, *The Editing of the Hebrew Psalter* (Atlanta, GA: Scholars Press, 1985), p. 213.

[6] Wilson, *The Editing of the Hebrew Psalter*, p. 215.

between one psalm and another in the context of a book. The associations hardly justify a solid context from which to draw conclusions."[7]

Psalm 102 is sandwiched between two Davidic psalms, Psalms 101 and 103. Moreover, Psalms 103 and 104 are connected as a pair by the call, "Bless the Lord, O my soul." While Psalm 103 deals with the Lord's faithfulness in dealing with sinners, Psalm 104 is about God's wisdom in creation and providence in dealing with creatures.[8] Hence, the relationship between lamentation and the call to bless the Lord is evident.

Psalm 102 is a lament for the affliction suffered from the hands of the enemies that ends in statements of praise and confidence in the Lord's ability to deliver. Walter Brueggemann, critically describing the lament, says,

> Laments are about honest dialogue with God in plain words that are raw, evocative and [...] speaking to the very core of human experience. They teach us how to speak about God in times of crisis. They affirm that alongside joy and blessing of life is "hurt, betrayal, loneliness, disease, threat, anxiety, bewilderment, anger, hatred, and anguish, and in all cases, YHWH has a role to play."[9]

Beyond these characteristics of the lament psalms, Davidson notes that, in the Christian tradition, Psalm 102 is one of the penitential psalms due to the references to "dust" and "ashes" in v. 9 and the total submission to God even amid human frailty. He says "it is the combination of such elements which makes penitence honest and keeps it from lapsing into morbidity."[10] However, there is no hint of the psalmist mentioning their sin or that sin was the cause of the sickness.[11] Such a recognition buttresses the point that there can be sickness even if one has not sinned.

Structure of Psalm 102

Psalm 102 is made up of two main parts of two movements each, with an introductory superscription narrating the problem the psalmist has gone through and their responses. In the Hebrew Bible, the superscription takes verse 1. Part one is from vv. 2-23 and part two is from vv. 23-29. In the first part, vv. 2-12 is the first movement, highlighting the complaint, while the second movement, vv. 13-23, is declarative praise, a hymnic celebration of who Yahweh is and

---

[7] Roland Murphy, "Reflections on Contextual Interpretation of the Psalms," in J. Clinton McCann (ed.), *The Shape and Shaping of the Psalter Journal for the Study of the Old Testament* Sup. 159 (Sheffield: Sheffield Academic Press, 1993), pp. 21–28.

[8] James Mays, "The Question of Context in Psalm Interpretation," in J. Clinton McCann (ed.), *The Shape and Shaping of the Psalter*, p. 19.

[9] Walter Brueggemann, *Reverberations of Faith: A Theological Handbook of Old Testament Themes* (Louisville, KY: Westminster John Knox Press, 2002).

[10] Robert Davidson, *The Vitality of Worship: A Commentary on the Book of Psalms* (Grand Rapids, MI: Eerdmans, 1998), p. 334.

[11] Derek Kidner, *Psalms 73–150*, Tyndale Old Testament Commentaries (Downers Grove, IL: InterVarsity, 1975), p. 3.

describing Yahweh's favour on Zion. The *kî* particle in v. 12 serves as a marker for closure in the first part, while the repetition of divine rejection in vv. 3 and 11 points to a structural strategy to determine the opening and closing of the first movement. Similarly, the *kî* particle in vv. 15; 17; 20 shapes the structure of the second movement, and the *kî* particle in v. 20 hints at the closure of the second movement. Although the psalm is an individual lament, it seems to include communal elements in vv. 14 to 23, especially with the use of the 3 masculine plural in vv. 15; 16; 21; 23. In the second part (vv. 24-29), the first movement, vv. 24-25, is a complaint, while the second movement, vv. 26-29, is declarative praise. While the use of *wᵉ'attāh* ("but you") opens the second movement of part one (vv. 13; 14), it serves as a mark for closure in the second movement of part two (vv. 27; 28).

There are some principal species of parallelism in the psalm. Three synonymously parallel lines can be observed:

I am --------- like a ------ desert owl//
I have become like a ------ wasteland owl (v. 7)

The name of the Lord will be ---- recounted ---- in Zion //
and his praise ---- ---- in Jerusalem (v. 22)

The children of your servants ---- will dwell //
and seeds before you ---- will be established (v. 29)

An antithetic parallel structure set in a chiastic pattern can be observed in vv. 26-27:

A – They will perish
B – but you will remain
A^1 – and all garments wear out
A^2 – like clothing that changes
B^1 – and they will change

When Sickness Leads to Isolation

The psalmist complains of being afflicted by enemies and growing weak. The enemies here can be real or imaginary; physical or spiritual; or even sickness that disturbs well-being. He is in distress (v. 3), and his days seem to come to an end (v. 4). He feels a burning sensation in the bones and his heart has been smitten like grass (v 5a; 12). He compares his loneliness to an owl in the wilderness or a wasteland (v. 7). His heart is broken (v. 5), not from emotional disappointment. Rather, it is the centre of his being, the seat of his morale,[12] under the control of

---

[12] Leslie C. Allen, *Psalms 101–150*, Word Biblical Commentary 21 (Dallas, TX: Word Publishers, 1983), p. 9.

Yahweh, that has been "blighted" (NIV), "struck down" (ESV), "stricken" (NRSV; TANAK JPS). Joseph Baumgarten and Menahem Mansoor argue that Psalm 102:5-6 is semantically parallel to a hymn found on the lower half of Plate 39 in *Osar ha-Megillot ha-Genuzot.* The significance of bodily illness of the *Hodayot* 34 gives a similar idea:

> So that I eat my bread with sighing,
> And my drink with endless tears;
> For my eyes are dimmed because of vexation,
> And my soul by the bitterness of the day.[13]

Since the heart, like the soul, characterises the wholeness and integrity of the human person, being broken shows a total lack of wholeness.

The psalmist has lost his sense of taste so he cannot eat (v. 5b). His food has become like ashes in his mouth (v. 10a) and the taste of his drink is like that mixed with tears (v. 10b). He has become lonely "like a bird alone on a roof" (v. 8b). He sees himself like grass that is withering (cf. Is. 40:6-8). He describes himself as destitute (v. 18). As Gunkel asserts, "All of these scenes transfer us to a place in the midst of life, but not in worship service, where the psalmist quarrels with his opponents, but desperate friends must comfort."[14] That is to say, his situation has cut him off from the worship setting to a situation of life where only Yahweh can bring him back to the worship space.

The psalmist is facing another major crisis of life – the hiddenness of Yahweh. Confronting Yahweh, who hides His face, could be difficult and disturbing, bearing in mind how awesome God is (Ps. 10:1; 88:14; Is. 40:27). At a time when answers are needed quickly, praying to a hidden God will not motivate hope or bring the answers as one would expect. Hence, the psalmist calls Yahweh to "turn" His ear on him and answer him quickly (v. 3). The psalmist complains: "all the days, my enemies taunt me; those who deride me make me a curse" (v. 9). In other words, the enemies have sworn not to have anything to do with him. The psalmist is not only concerned about his "lockdown," but more so about how the enemies are taunting him (cf. Ps. 22:7-9; 42:11). Although he claims to "forget to eat his food" (v. 5b), it seems probable that it is a lack of interest to eat (cf. Job 33:20-21).

The psalmist lies awake, an expression that connotes sleeplessness (v. 7 cf. Ps. 6:7; 63:7; 77:7; Is. 38:13; Job 7:3ff; 30:17). Rejection and loneliness are the causes of sleeplessness and not insomnia. Although the psalmist clearly mentions that his body is in distress (v. 5), Christenson claims the psalmist's experience is depression:

> In the language of his day, the psalmist gives a haunting portrayal of severe suffering, anguish, and despair that in today's language could be understood as

---

[13] Joseph Baumgarten and Menahem Mansoor, "Studies in the New *Hodayot* (Thanksgiving Hymns) III," *Journal of Biblical Literature* 74(3), (1955), p. 112.
[14] Hermann Gunkel, *Introduction to the Psalms: The Genres of the Religious Lyric of Israel* (Macon, GA: Georgia University Press, 1998), pp. 127–128.

> depression. In poetic terms he reports experiencing dysphoric mood, decreased self-esteem, low energy or fatigue, decreased appetite with much weight loss, loss of interest, insomnia, withdrawal or isolation, guilt issues, hopelessness and helplessness, and decreased spiritual well-being. If the writer were alive today and presented with the problems he so eloquently described in his lament, he would meet the criteria for the diagnosis of Major Depressive Disorder.[15]

Interpreting the complaint as depression makes the problem more psychological than physical, although one could lead to another. The experiences of the psalmist are similar to those infected with COVID-19. When people get infected with the COVID-19 virus, they usually lose their sense of taste and smell. While some do not show any symptoms in their bodies, others feel in their body a burning sensation. They become uneasy with fever. Their body temperature rises and they feel like they have been smitten.[16]

People affected by COVID-19 are expected to go into quarantine or self-isolation. The unclear methods of transmission and fear associated with the infection make family members, colleagues, and neighbours find it difficult to come close to those who are infected. In most places in Africa, stigma attached to the isolation centres and how the infected are shunned makes them think they are cursed. Even when they recover, some will not sit on a chair they have used.

Loneliness motivates the psalmist's appeal. He uses the metaphor of the owl and desert owl; birds which were commonly used as emblems of gloom and wretchedness. Elsewhere in Isaiah, the Lord provides water and the needs of the owl in the wilderness (Is. 43:20). In the case of the psalmist, sadness and solitude go together. Human beings plunge deeper into lonely places when they only give voice to their grief, but they encounter transformation when they have the assurance of the presence of God. Shame that is destructive will devastate them, but shame that reveals one's weakness can turn into positive spirituality.[17]

Hope in the Midst of Hopelessness

The use of the adversative *waw* in v. 13 marks a change of mood. The psalmist shifts from complaint to descriptive praise, expressing hope despite the great despair: "But you, O Lord, are enthroned forever and remembered from generation to generation" (v. 13). The marker *wĕ'attāh* "but you" leads to the recital of what Yahweh has done for Zion and the nations. Jerusalem or Zion is pictured as being in a state of ruin, yet its stones continue to be a delight in the sight of Yahweh. If this ruin can be taken as literal, then the psalm may have

---

[15] Randall M. Christenson, "Parallels Between Depression and Laments," *The Journal of Pastoral Care and Counseling* 61(4), (2007), p. 305.

[16] Centre for Disease Control and Prevention, "Symptoms of COVID-19," 22nd February 2021 [Available at: https://www.cdc.gov/coronavirus/2019-ncov/symptoms-testing/symptoms.html], [Last accessed: 17th July 2023].

[17] Mark S. Aidoo, *Shame in the Individual Lament Psalms and African Spirituality, African Theological Studies* 12 (New York: Peter Lang, 2017), pp. 201–222.

been written by those in exile who mourned over both their personal and national affliction at the destruction of Jerusalem. Although Zion has been reduced to stones and dust (cf. v. 15), the psalmist further notes that "Yahweh will rebuild Zion and appear in his glory" (v. 17). Davidson believes the description of Zion in ruins and the hope to rebuild it "would fit the late exilic or early postexilic period, when the temple in Jerusalem was still in ruins and the people either still in exile or struggling to survive in and around Jerusalem, as they face a very uncertain future."[18] The restoration of Zion echoes what the prophet Joel prophesied: "for on Mount Zion and in Jerusalem there will be deliverance, as Yahweh has said, even among the survivors whom Yahweh calls" (Joel 2:32).

The psalmist prays that Yahweh will not despise his prayer (v. 18). Yahweh is called to hear the cries for help of the one at prayer. The strategy is that he has come (v. 2). He utilises words meant to move Yahweh's heart, to provoke Yahweh to see the experiences he is going through. Yahweh should not hide His face from him (v. 2a) because that would not allow Yahweh to see how distressed he had been. The tone of the psalmist is gloomy and grave; his sad and depressed voice is enough to move Yahweh to action. Suffering can cause loneliness and make the sufferer become isolated from vital social connections.[19] The psalmist knows that Yahweh can understand the pain he is going through if he vividly describes it and explains the situation clearly.

The dark side of Yahweh is portrayed in the psalm. First, Yahweh's hidden face obstructs the opportunity to hear when the psalmist calls. Second, the problems the psalmist is going through at the hands of the enemies have been exacerbated because of Yahweh's wrath and indignation. He emphasises an aspect of the divine character that throws the people of God aside, making them lonely even to the point of death. Here is a very complex character of Yahweh, who rejects his people yet sits in heaven and looks down to hear the groans of the people (vv. 20-21). His appeal does not draw from sin in his life. In Deuteronomy, God hides His face from people who sin (cf. Deut. 31:17; 32:20). Such a view of *Deus absconditus* seems to create tension for the psalmist. Writing about Luther's view of a hidden God, Steven Paulson explains that "God also hides in order to hold humans in preparation for the time and place when they are driven to find God where God *would* be found, in mercy not wrath. God makes of the masks of creation also a grace that makes room specifically for faith."[20] As suggested by Luther, human beings experience God as both *Deus revelatus* and *Deus absconditus* as a way that the Creator God inflicts judgement and causes humans to suffer. Suffering is a way for God to remind ungrateful human beings of all the good gifts they have received from Him. In some cases,

---

18 Davidson, *The Vitality of Worship*, p. 333

19 Melissa Johnston-Barrett, "Making Spaces: Silence, Voice, and Suffering," *Word and World* 25(3), (2005), p. 330.

20 Steven Paulson, "Luther on the Hidden God," *Word and World* 19(4), (1999), p. 368. Emphasis in original.

sin has fundamental consequences for the human ability to recognise God's being and His will.[21]

Luther has explained the context of *Deus absconditus*, saying "God accomplishes his will in situations and events that may seem contradictory." He adds that a person "hides what is his own in order to conceal it, but God conceals what is his in order to reveal it."[22] John Barton is right in asserting that the dark side of God is not that "of an impassible tyrant, but the dark side of a being with warm human emotions, which include outrage at the exploitation of the weak, anger at flagrant wrongdoings, and pity for the sorrows and sufferings of humankind."[23] Allen makes a critical comment worth noting:

> The psalmist's hope lies not in his own measures of ritual self-abasement. Hope is grounded in Yahweh himself. The assurance of God's permanence is the answer to his overwhelming sense of transience. So, in praising trust he turns afresh to Yahweh, now as the eternal King, worshiped as such by countless generations of his people. But this kingship does more than impinge upon Israel's life at a cultic point: it is necessarily manifested in the time and space of their historical experience. Sight belies such faith, but faith can take the form of a hope centred in God's prophetic promises.[24]

God repeatedly points to the wonders, splendours, mysteries, and power of creation as evidence of His surpassing greatness.

The psalmist sees himself as a lonely person who has been afflicted. He sees himself like the stones and the dust of Zion (v. 15). Even the stones and dust move Yahweh to show favour. The use of the word *yĕḥonenû* (Poel imperfect 3 masculine plural) from the root *ḥnn* (grace, favour; v. 15) indicates active intensive action. The psalmist knows that it is time for Yahweh to show favour to Zion because the appointed time has come (v. 14). Here, he identifies himself with the "servants" of God (vv. 14; 29), and a prisoner who has been condemned to death (v. 21).

The psalmist accuses the Lord of afflicting his strength and cutting short his days (v. 24). He accepts the fact that he is mortal; he will perish (v. 27). The affliction itself is bad enough, but it is made worse beyond measure by the sense that God did not see or care. He does not claim to enjoy a special relationship with the Lord, "because you have lifted me and thrown me away" (v. 11b).

In spite of the affliction and rejection, the one at prayer sees Yahweh as one who is in heaven and looks down on the earth to hear the cries of the prisoners

---

[21] Sasja Emile Mathiasen Stopa, "'Seeking Refuge in God Against God': Hidden God in Lutheran Theology and the Postmodern Weakening of God," *Open Theology* 4(1), (2018), pp. 660, 661.

[22] Martin Luther, *Luther's Works*, 75 volumes, edited by Jaroslav Pelikan, Helmut T. Lehman and Christopher Boyd Brown (Philadelphia, PA: Fortress Press, 1955), p. 51.

[23] John Barton, "The Dark Side of God in the Old Testament," in Katharine Dell (ed.), *Ethical and Unethical in the Old Testament: God and Human in Dialogue*, Library of Hebrew Bible/Old Testament Studies 528 (New York: T&T Clark, 2010), p. 131.

[24] Allen, *Psalm 101–150*, pp. 14–15.

and those condemned to death (vv. 20-21). Yahweh sits enthroned forever and is remembered from generation to generation (v. 13). Yahweh remains forever (vv. 27; 28) even though the foundations of the earth and the work of His hands will perish (vv. 26-27a). Yahweh has an appointed time to show favour to Zion (v. 14), to rebuild Zion so that the glory of the Lord will appear (v. 16).

Where Hope Turns to Praise

The creation motif in the psalmist influences declarative praise, i.e. praise for who God is. God laid the foundations of the earth, and the heavens are the work of His hands (v. 26). The psalmist affirms that all created things change and perish but God does not change; He remains the same and His years do not end (v. 28). The sharp distinction between Creator and creation is drawn. All that is created remains mortal.

A key point in the psalmist's descriptive praise is the fact that those belonging to the covenant community "will live in your presence" and "will be established before you" (v. 29). This is the high point of the psalmist's faith. Although all human beings, as creatures, will die, and sickness is inevitable, "through the covenant the chosen people enjoy a sure hope; they will live and be established, sharing life with YHWH: because he lives, they may live also, safe in his caring presence."[25]

In all, the psalmist sees Yahweh as concerned about what happens on earth. Yahweh has not intervened yet but will definitely intervene at the appointed time. What the psalmist fear is that they will be cut off and will not be able to continue to praise Yahweh. The psalmist knows that all the nations fear the name of Yahweh and all kings of the earth revere the glory of the Lord (v. 16). Yahweh's credibility is that His name will be declared in Zion and praised in Jerusalem (v. 22) and even people who are yet to be born will come and praise Yahweh (v. 19b).

The descriptive praise, i.e. evocations based on the attributes of God, gives recognition to God's greatness. The psalmist uses a "double-duty preposition" in v. 28, i.e. a preposition in one line which should be understood in the next line. Literally, it can be translated as:

> But you are he //
> and your years will never end.

The reality of the psalmist's prayer is founded in humility and a genuine desire to worship and praise Yahweh. The psalmist hopes to join the community of faith in worship (v. 23).

Despite all that the psalmist is going through, there is a firm belief that their children will live and be established in the presence of the Lord (v. 29). A firm hope characterises the prayer of the afflicted. Yahweh's kingship is significant

---

[25] Allen, *Psalms 101–150*, p. 16.

in understanding that hope. His lordship over Zion and over all the nations and kingdoms gains a concrete accent: "All the kings of the earth will revere your glory" (v. 16b).

The psalmist goes on to declare something that will happen in the future – a people yet to be created will praise Yahweh (v. 19b). Their knowledge of the nature of God anchors their faith in what God will do. The verb *nibĕrā'* from the word *bārā'* used here does not imply creation out of nothing, but rather affirms God's sovereignty.[26] The people yet to be born would be the handiwork of God, created for a specific purpose to praise the Lord. The hope that generations unborn will come to praise the Lord for what He has done indicates that there will be a spectacular deliverance that will give cause for celebration. Generations to come will look back and thank God for what He did. The Hebrew *yĕhallel-yāh* (from halleluyah; v. 19), a Piel imperfect meaning "praise the Lord", emphasises the intensive call to shine, make a show, boast, and thus celebrate the favour of Yahweh.

Given, then, that the intent of the word halleluyah is to "praise the Lord" in chants and prayer, its referent must include both the low as well as the high points of life, since the actions of Yahweh will transform all, even when COVID-19 rages on. The intent is to praise Yahweh no matter what, because the one at prayer sees the commitment of the Lord to be gracious to the people of God. Even in their affliction and loneliness, the one at prayer shows a grasp of their faith and a motivation to praise Yahweh. How much more should we not lose faith and cease to praise God in times of the COVID-19 pandemic?

African Pentecostals and Transformative Praise

African Pentecostals love to sing to praise the Lord rather than to offer prayers of praise using spoken words. The theological crux of African Pentecostal worship is somehow defined in *lex orandi, lex credenda* ("the way you pray determines what you believe"). The valid sources are from experiences within the life of the church. For African Pentecostals, church services begin with praise and worship in the form of songs. The opening liturgical worship songs, usually in a slow melody, are interspersed with a few minutes of prayer. In the words of Martina Prosén, "the ritual of praise and worship functions as both *sacrificial*, giving an offering of songs and self to God, and *sacramental*, mediating the presence of God to the congregation in a special way."[27]

---

[26] Gordon Wenham, *Genesis 1–15*, Word Biblical Commentary 1 (Dallas, TX: Wood Publishers, 1987), p. 14.

[27] Martina Prosén, "Pentecostal Praise and Worship as a Mode of Theology," in *Faith in African Lived Christianity: Bridging Anthropological and Theological Perspectives*, Global Pentecostal and Charismatic Studies 35 (Leiden: Brill, 2019), p. 171. Emphasis original.

African Pentecostals sing songs of adoration in the context of praise. Such singing goes with meditation, shouting, dancing, speaking in tongues, and spiritual cries. The singing is solemn, participatory, and backed by loud instrumentation. Singing ushers one into the presence of God to meditate upon and communicate with God, receive power from the Holy Spirit, and encounter healing and deliverance with the belief that singing breaks strongholds and offers spiritual therapy. Thus, singing in Pentecostal worship is likened to prayer and is more effective than liturgical exercises.[28]

Spoken prayer, in contemporary African Pentecostal Christianity, usually aims at moving God to act. Praise is offered when speaking in tongues. The assumption is that the desires and expectations of the one at prayer, as long as the person stands in the presence of God, should be fulfilled by God because of the power of the word in the mouths of believers. The words they speak are spirit and give life (Jn. 6:63). The triumphant theology of deliverance, glory, and power anticipated in prayer, therefore, runs counter to the nature of a God who looks on or hides His face. Such prayers assume that silence is not part of God's nature; God is always quick to intervene and never too slow, since the people of God must be victorious and triumph over all forces of darkness, sickness, and misfortune. That is to say, the hiddenness of God is not given any space in contemporary African Pentecostal Christianity. It may be difficult for Pentecostals to accept that certain aspects of what we call suffering, sickness, loneliness, and anxiety are all necessary aspects of God's good creation.[29] Evil, diseases, and distress etc. do not motivate prayers of praise.

In recent times, some religious functionaries in African Pentecostal Christianity have been emphasising God's omnipotence and ability to heal all kinds of diseases. For them, the ability to pray for the sick to be healed qualifies the functionary as an anointed person of God. All diseases can be explained away through supernatural means. The pastors, evangelists, prophets, and apostles always claim their churches are the last stop for the sick. It means no matter how many churches one has visited in search of healing, coming to the religious functionary is the last point that will bring about the expected breakthrough and healing. As Baëta affirms, "Powers traditionally credited to such persons of healing, of revealing hidden things, predicting the future, cursing and blessing effectually, etc. will make a more successful showing than others."[30]

The outbreak and increase of COVID-19 since 2019, however, has raised a challenge for those who claim that all diseases can be healed by God. Again, the Lord's hidden face in times of the COVID-19 crisis challenged prayers of hope

---

[28] Mookgo S. Kgatie, "Singing as a Therapeutic Agent in Pentecostal Worship," *Verbum et Ecclesia* 40(1), (2019), p. 4.

[29] Douglas John Hall, *God and Human Suffering: An Exercise in the Theology of the Cross* (Minneapolis, MN: Augsburg, 1986), pp. 54, 55.

[30] See C.G. Baëta, *Prophetism in Ghana: A Study of Some Spiritual Churches* (London: SCM, 1962), pp. 6–7.

and praise. The lockdown contributed to the silence of worship, dimming the power of praise and worship. COVID-19 revealed lessons to the church in terms of how the people praise God and how their knowledge of the way God works is limited. It taught the church that the tendency to feel the absence of God cannot mean God is not there.

Like the psalmist who struggled with the length of time God hides His face (Ps. 13:1; 30:7), and in Isaiah's case, where the hiddenness of God led the prophet to declare that no one can fathom the Lord's nature (Is. 45:14; 15), African Pentecostals need to reconsider who God is. For Isaiah, despite complaining that their ways are hidden from the Lord, those who hope in the Lord will have their strength renewed (Is. 40:27-31). In the books of Job and Ecclesiastes, there is also a reflection on creation theology, attesting to the hidden ways of the Lord and the mysteries of God (Job 11:7-8; 28:1-28; Eccl. 3:11). The psalmist knows that, when life reaches its deepest valleys and people walk in the shadows of death, there is the Lord of creation and the lover of Zion. The Lord is hidden yet looks intently at the struggles on earth through His sovereign love and compassionate fidelity. Jesus' cross that was raised on Good Friday may show vividly in our imagination, but what happens on Holy Saturday cannot be expressed with words, yet it cannot be denied that the Lord is still with us (cf. Ps. 23:4). The gloom, emptiness, and time of waiting may add to the despair, but we know there is a Sunday when the stone that blocks the entrance will be rolled away. That is why the churches cling to the tradition of hope for a better future, even in the times of COVID-19.

African Pentecostals need to understand that prayers of praise and adoration must consider how God orders the world for our own good. It may be appropriate for intercessors to discern specifically what God wants before prayers are offered. Prayer needs to be in accord with God's plan. Sometimes, the Lord is in heaven watching what is happening. COVID-19 is not out of the sight of the Lord. If COVID-19 is going on without a cure, then it does not mean God is unaware. It does not mean God is not omnipotent, omniscient, omnipresent, and omnibenevolent. Despite life's unpredictable ups and downs, the assurance that God is watching gives a sense of hope. The fact is that God, the loving Father that He is, will do the best for His children (Jer. 29:11; Ps. 25:4-9; Prov. 3:5-6; 19:21; cf. I Tim. 2:3-4). It is through such lenses that one can understand God's actions towards the Israelites as corrective acts whenever they turn away from God, rather than punitive action.

Moreover, African Pentecostals should see prayer as providing space for the suppliant to confront God with a liturgical expression that accuses God of hiding His face and acting slowly. Contemporary Christianity portrays prayer as an active engagement of elements to become effective.[31] It must employ certain body postures and ritual action like shouting, clapping, and stamping of feet, all

---

[31] Adelakun, *Powerful Devices*.

with vigour to "feel" the power and be empowered.[32] Such a view poses a lot of challenges to those who are sick, afflicted, and depressed, because they do not have the energy to pray robustly. Laments do not normally exhibit such energy and vigour, since the intensity of the problems usually has a great impact on the body of the one at prayer. The mood in lament is intense and the one at prayer is desperate, yet the suffering does not give impetus to robustness and exuberance.

With the belief that God can allow some strange events to happen, African Pentecostals should not simply think that COVID-19 is demonic or satanic. The psalmist believed that the Lord is part of the cause of the problem, yet enters the presence of the Lord with faith and trust in the Lord, with all the heart, mind, and strength to seek answers for restoration and vindication. While it is obvious that God hides His face from us as we pray, nothing is hidden from Him. As eternal Creator, Yahweh sees all things and knows all things (Jer. 16:17; 23:24; Job 34:22; Ps. 139:7-18; Dan. 2:22). In the words of Cyril Okorocha and Francis Foulkes, "When we who are frail and sinful turn to God, feeling that our lives are short, and perhaps also distressed about the state of our country, we can realize that God is the great and mighty Creator, unchanging with the passing of time."[33]

The psalmist also offers lessons that praise should be on the lips of the believer not only when the Lord has answered a prayer, but also when suffering. Suffering should motivate prayers for help and prayers of praise. Perhaps, Christians may be crying out to the Lord and wondering if the Lord is even listening and bringing an end to COVID-19. More so, the silence of the prophets of God who always claim to know everything but cannot tell when the pandemic will be over is deafening. Even where the voice of God is not heard and no instant response is coming from the heavens, the task is to praise the Lord and sing halleluyah. African Pentecostals should continually praise the Lord, since even the generations to come are ready to praise the Lord.

Finally, the lesson is to see the tone in the prayer of the psalmist. It is that of an individual sickness, but the elements are that of the communal, towards national restoration. In times when an individual is sick, the deliverance of the whole people of God is at stake, and the move by the whole people of God to engage in praise matters. The assurance that God will restore Zion rests not only on His faithfulness, but on a prophetic promise based on the covenant that there is an appointed time when God's servants will enjoy God's presence. It is an indication that there is a time fixed in God's eternal counsels where sickness will not put all to death. The people of God will live and be established. Such hope influences eternal praise from generation to generation.

---

[32] Afe Adogame, "Dealing with Local Satanic Technology: Deliverance Rhetoric in the Mountain of Fire and Miracles Ministries," *The Journal of World Christianity* 5(1), (2012), p. 95.

[33] Cyril Okorocha and Francis Foulkes, "Psalms," in Tokundoh Adeyeyo (ed.), *Africa Bible Commentary* (Nairobi: WordAlive, 2006), p. 707.

Conclusion

The rhetorical reading of Psalm 102 has revealed how God sometimes looks on while the righteous are going through a crisis. The psalm speaks about God's eternal grace, compassion, and righteousness in contrast to the weak and transitory nature of humanity. It affirms the unchangeability of God amid change and decay in the world. It shows how God remains the same faithful and wonder-working God in the face of sickness and troubles, but at God's own time. The Lord's hidden face in times of crisis even motivates prayers of praise. In revealing how God is, the lament psalms lay an obligation on the people of God to praise God despite crises, sicknesses, pandemics, and evil.

Emphasising that Pentecostal songs of worship play the role of prayer does not give the opportunity to offer declarative praise. Spoken prayer should not always aim at moving God to act. Prayers should take into consideration how God orders the world for our own good and provide space to confront God. With the belief that the Lord sees all things and knows all things, African Pentecostals should teach the whole people of God to engage in spoken praise in addition to liturgical songs of praise. A wondering world which is struggling to keep up with the devastating effects of COVID-19 will adore the eternal God who made heaven and earth. The constant reminder is that God endures forever and the Lord's never-failing fervour to rescue the people of God is sure. No matter the fear and panic caused by COVID-19, the church's distress needs to be replaced by an increasingly confident trust that God will hear the prayer and praise of His servants.

The Old Testament, Pandemics, and Preventive Protocols

Patrick Kofi Amissah

Introduction

This chapter argues that he modern approaches to managing infectious diseases and pandemics are based on age-old biblical statutes. It can be said that some Christian leaders did not launch straight into preaching faith and hope during pandemics, but used the route of promoting the preventive protocols and ensuring that churches and individuals were adhering to hygiene, social distancing, self-isolations, and quarantine, since the preventive protocols may have been motivated by biblical law. Their approach was a way of offering hope to the community in overcoming pandemics. By analysing narratives using a biblical and theological lens, it may be understood that the protocols are not only modern measures but time-tested approaches to preventing the spread of pandemics.

In an earlier paper, I attempted to reflect on the public theological questions of the extent to which the preventive protocols used during the COVID-19 pandemic mimic their biblical antecedents and how the church's promotion of these protocols became part of the hope that the church offered at the onset of the pandemic.[1] In this paper, I reflect more generally on these same issues. The main scope of the paper, however, is on biblical stories that exemplify epidemics/pandemics and the measures used to prevent the spread. It also gives a snapshot of some responses of the church, especially as they relate to the promotion of safety protocols and from the perspective of hope.

Non-Pharmaceutical Safety Measures Against COVID-19

Coronavirus disease (COVID-19) or Severe Acute Respiratory Syndrome Coronavirus 2 (SARS-CoV-2) was first reported to the World Health Organization (WHO) on 31st December 2019. It was believed to have originated from China and was spreading rapidly among human populations on all continents around the world. At the time of the declaration, more than 118,000

[1] See Patrick Kofi Amissah, "A Public Theological Reflection on Biblical Antecedents of Protocols for Managing Pandemics," *International Journal of Public Theology* 18 (2024), pp. 1–24.

cases were in 114 countries, with 4,291 deaths. Thousands of people were also battling for life in hospitals.[2] On 30th January 2020, it was declared a Public Health Emergency of International Concern (PHEIC) by WHO and subsequently declared a pandemic on 11th March 2020. In a statement signed by Honourable Kwaku Agyeman-Manu, the Minister for Health:

> The first two cases of COVID-19 in Ghana were confirmed on 12th March 2020. This called for immediate intensive actions towards the containment of the disease across the country. Preventive measures including effective hand hygiene, respiratory hygiene as well as other Infection Prevention and Control (IPC) practices like social distancing, [and] the use of Personal Protective Equipment (PPEs) were instituted at all treatment centres and in the community.[3]

These safety protocols became the first aid measures to prevent the disease, since there was no cure. The Ghana Health Service, in a release titled "COVID-19: Ghana's Outbreak Response Management Updates," explained that the virus can spread from human contact with animals and also from human to human, especially when someone comes into contact with the infected person's secretions. The exposure factors are fluids from a cough or sneeze being transmitted through the mouth, nose or eyes via the air or contact such as a handshake. Since in the year 2020 there was no specific treatment, medical doctors relieved symptoms by prescribing a pain or fever medication, or symptoms would go away on their own, perhaps through one's own immune system defences. It was advised that people secure room humidifiers or use hot showers to help with a sore throat or cough. Also, by drinking plenty of fluids and getting enough rest and sleep, one could prevent the disease. The basic safety protocols promoted were:[4]

- Wash your hands with soap and water before touching anything including your eyes, nose and mouth.
- Cover your mouth and nose when you cough or sneeze.
- Disinfect the objects and surfaces you touch.
- If you are sick, stay home and avoid crowds and contact with others.

---

[2] World Health Organization, "WHO Director-General's Opening Remarks at the Media Briefing on COVID-19," 11th March 2020 [Available at: https://www.who.int/director-general/speeches/detail/who-director-general-s-opening-remarks-at-the-media-briefing-on-covid-19---11-march-2020], [Last accessed: 19th July 2023].

[3] Republic of Ghana Ministry of Health, "Provisional Standard Treatment Guidelines for Novel Coronavirus Infection: COVID-19 Guidelines for Ghana" [Available at: https://www.moh.gov.gh/wp-content/uploads/2016/02/COVID-19-STG-JUNE-2020-1.pdf], [Last accessed 4th April 2024].

[4] Ghana Health Service, "COVID-19: Ghana's Outbreak Response Management Updates" [Available at: https://www.ghs.gov.gh/covid19/about.php?#prevention], [Last accessed: 4th April 2024].

Similarly, on the Ministry of Finance website, the same protocols were promoted:[5]

- Wash and sanitize your hands frequently during the day and avoid shaking hands.
- Avoid touching your face, especially your eyes, nose and mouth.
- Wear your masks at all times and avoid touching your face. Remember it's an offence to go out without a mask. #maskup
- Sanitize your workspace i.e. disinfect the screens of your mobile phone, desktop, laptop, your keyboard and mouse on a regular basis.
- Observe physical distancing by maintaining physical distance of at least 2 meters always.
- Limit face to face meetings. If you definitely must meet, ensure not more than 5 persons in a meeting room and maintain physical distance of at least 2 meters.
- Delivery services - Pick up deliveries at the reception.
- Refrain from talking in the lift.
- Sanitize your hands before and after touching the lift buttons.
- Avoid crowded eating areas, observe physical distancing protocols while eating.
- Limit external visitors. All meetings with external stakeholders and third parties are to be conducted over the phone, [Z]oom, [G]oogle [M]eet etc.
- Use [a] tissue to cover your mouth when you cough and dispose of tissue immediately or [c]ough into your elbow.

Ernest Kenu, Joseph Frimpong, and Kodwo A. Koram in their publication asserted that,

> Ghana has observed a decline in the number of confirmed cases from 25th April 2020 although enhanced surveillance is still ongoing. This may be evidence that the strategies that were put in place have contributed to the control and spread of the virus in Ghana. These gains, however, need to be sustained and built on in our response efforts to end the COVID-19 pandemic in Ghana.[6]

These strategic responses adopted by Ghana had a great impact on the management of COVID-19 and offered opportunities and solutions to help combat the pandemic in Ghana.

Many Christian groups and organisations in Ghana led in the promotion of safety protocols. Leaders issued statements and guidance which were replete

---

[5] Ministry of Finance, "COVID-19 Health and Safety Tips" [Available at: https://mofep.gov.gh/mof-covid-19-updates/health-and-safety-tips], [Last accessed: 4th April 2024].

[6] Ernest Kenu, Joseph Frimpong, and Kodwo A. Koram, "Responding to the COVID-19 Pandemic in Ghana," *Ghana Medical Journal* 54(2), (June 2020), pp. 72–73. DOI: 10.4314/gmj.v54i2.1 [Available at: https://www.ncbi.nlm.nih.gov/pmc/articles/PMC7829051/], [Last accessed: 6th April 2024].

with calls to observe the preventive protocols, though these statements had messages of hope based on the Bible. For example, the leadership of the Catholic Church in Ghana,[7] the Methodist Church Ghana,[8] and the Assemblies of God Ghana[9] can be cited for promoting the protocols. While preaching messages of hope and faith, they also promoted the safety protocols. The Christian Council of Ghana, led by the General Secretary of the Christian Council, Rev. Dr Cyril Fayose, encouraged churches not to take the protocols for granted, irrespective of their beliefs about the virus, and spoke against the Christ Embassy Church in Accra for flagrantly flouting COVID-19 protocols. He referred to the Christ Embassy Church as "one bad nut spoiling the whole bunch," and urged all churches to adhere strictly to and observe all the protocols to ensure that we curbed the pandemic.[10] In an earlier forum, the General Secretary explained that the Christian Council of Ghana is not a body mandated to enforce compliance. It cannot force churches to abide by the protocol. At best, they can offer a system where churches peer review each other in adhering to the health guidelines. He said "We are going to encourage peer review, encouraging colleagues to visit other member churches to see whether they are adhering to those regulations and encourage them too. But apart from that it would be extremely difficult to police these guidelines."[11]

Plagues as Pandemics in Biblical Context

In the Hebrew Bible, the predominant word which in the noun form directly refers to an epidemic, plague, or pestilence is *deber*. The noun *nega*ʿ also in most of its appearances refers to an epidemic, plague, or pestilence. Other words that

---

[7] GhanaWeb, "Coronovirus [sic]: Catholic Church Bans Handshakes and Hugs Henceforth," 4th March 2020 [Available at: https://www.ghanaweb.com/GhanaHomePage/NewsArchive/Coronovirus-Catholic-Church-bans-handshakes-and-hugs-henceforth-884863], [Last accessed: 6th April 2024].

[8] Most Reverend Dr Paul Boafo, "COVID-19 Response from the Methodist Church Ghana," 15th March 2020 [Available at: www.facebook.com/permalink.php?id=182701041896569&story_fbid=1561], [Last accessed: 6th April 2024].

[9] Reverend Professor Paul Frimpong-Manso, "COVID-19: Cooperate with Health Officials–Assemblies of God Church," 16th March 2020 [Available at: https://www.classfmonline.com/news/general/CODVID-19-Cooperate-with-health-officials-Assemblies-of-God-Church-11849], [Last accessed: 6th April 2024].

[10] Daisy Palinwinde Jacobs, "Christian Council Takes on Christ Embassy for Flouting COVID-19 Protocols," 3rd May 2021 [Available at: https://citinewsroom.com/2021/05/christian-council-takes-on-christ-embassy-for-flouting-covid-19-protocols/], [Last accessed: 5th April 2024].

[11] Beatrice Mensah, "Christian Council of Ghana 'Cannot Enforce' New COVID-19 Guidelines," 5th June 2020 [Available at: https://www.asaaseradio.com/christian-council-of-ghana-cannot-enforce-new-covid-19-guidelines-general-secretary/], [Last accessed: 6th April 2024].

translate as affliction or blow, such as *negep*, *maggepah*, and *makkah*, could also refer to an epidemic, plague, or pestilence. In most cases, God is the subject of the actions that describe the arrival of an epidemic; nevertheless, such disasters could occur naturally and independent of human sins. Seeing plagues as God's action is in line with the Old Testament perception that God is the source of both good and evil (Is. 45:6-7). There are times when such disasters can happen as punishment for human sins. John Goldingay's and Kathleen Scott Goldingay's reference to the Lord threatening epidemics 29 times in Jeremiah and Ezekiel "as an aspect of the disaster menacing Jerusalem that they sought to prepare people for, or preferably to obviate,"[12] is appropriate here, as all of them use the noun *deber*. Goldingay and Goldingay draw attention to Solomon's prayer, which alludes to the Lord bringing an end to such disasters:

> In his prayer at the temple dedication, Solomon leaves an intriguing space and ambiguity between epidemic and divine chastisement. He entreats Yahweh to listen when people reach out to him in the context of epidemic or some other disaster... He entreats Yahweh to pardon, and to deal with each person in accordance with the state of their heart (2 Chronicles 6:28-30). Putting it this way suggests that Yahweh would know that they might need pardon, but they might not; they might just need deliverance.[13]

The first disaster of great proportion recorded in the Hebrew Bible is found in Genesis 12:10-20. Abram emigrated to Egypt, fleeing severe famine in Canaan. For fear that the Egyptians would kill him and take his beautiful wife, Sarai, Abram arranged with Sarai to say she was his sister, which she did, and that resulted in Pharaoh taking Sarai to be his wife. However, the Lord inflicted serious diseases (*nega'iym*) on Pharaoh and his household because of Sarai, so that Pharaoh had to send away Abram and his wife (12:17-20). In Genesis 20, when a similar incident happened with Abimelech and the Lord was about to strike him, Abram explains that Sarai is his father's daughter but from another mother, before she became his wife (Gen. 20:11-13). The Lord told Abimelech to return Abraham's wife to him and Abraham would pray for him. If he did not do that, Abimelech and all who belonged to him would die (Gen. 20:6-7). The purpose that the epidemic served was to rescue Pharaoh from accidental wrongdoing, rescue Sarai, rescue Abram, and thus rescue God's promise.[14] Prayer forms a key aspect of the preventive measure against the disaster.

Prior to the Israelites leaving Egypt, the ten plagues the Lord brought against Egypt may be considered a pandemic or an epidemic; only the fifth and the sixth plagues in Exodus 9:1-12 are relevant. The Lord struck all animals belonging to

---

[12] John Goldingay and Kathleen Scott Goldingay, 'Thinking with the Old Testament about the Pandemic," *Theology* 123(3), (2020): p. 193.

[13] Goldingay and Goldingay, "Thinking with the Old Testament about the Pandemic," p. 192.

[14] Goldingay and Goldingay, "Thinking with the Old Testament about the Pandemic," p. 193.

the Egyptians with a deadly pestilence (*deber*) that killed all of them (9:3). To the amazement of Pharaoh and his people, the disease could not infect the animals belonging to the Israelites. Again, the Lord sent festering boils on the Egyptians. There is no information about whether people died from the boils or not, but the severity of it, making Pharaoh's magicians unable to stand before Moses and Aaron, is indicated. These two plagues, together with all the others, were a "demonstration of the authority and power of Yahweh, but also an attempt to get Pharaoh to do the right thing in letting Israel go and thus to recognize who is the real authority in Egypt."[15] In all, the Israelites were shielded from such disasters through the Lord's own plan.

Another story of a plague or an epidemic is told in I Samuel 5 and 6. The Philistines seized the Ark of God's Covenant, which Israel took with them to war against the Philistines, hoping that the Ark, which embodies God's presence, would bring them victory. Upon capturing it, the Philistines placed the Ark in the Shrine of Dagon in Ashdod. In addition to the destruction of Dagon, the people of Ashdod began to suffer a plague of tumours that killed some of them. They passed the Ark around the other cities and a tumour struck in all the cities (I Sam. 5:12). When the Philistines finally returned the Ark to Israel, with guilt offerings, the people of Beth-Shemesh received it with joyful celebrations. Unfortunately, the descendants of Jeconiah, who were accused of not rejoicing with the people of Beth-Shemesh when they greeted the Ark of the Lord, lost 70 men to death (I Sam. 6:19). This raises the question whether the tumours that killed the Philistines had spread to Beth-Shemesh when the Ark arrived.[16] It is, however, clear in the story that, though the plague might have come to the Philistines because they captured the Ark of God's Covenant, the pestilence served to demonstrate the power and authority of God to the Philistines.

The final epidemic to consider is a consequence of David ordering his army officials to conduct a census, recorded in II Samuel 24 and I Chronicles 21. There are differences in the two accounts, but that will not be the focus of this paper. As a result of the census, God offers David a choice of three punishments: three years of famine, three months of fleeing from his enemies while they pursue him, or three days of pestilence on Israel. David chooses to fall at the hand of God, hoping to receive mercy. So, God sends a plague (*deber*) that kills 70,000 people in Israel. When God halts the destruction and orders David through the prophet Gad to build an altar and sacrifice to God, an incident in the I Chronicles 21 version is recorded that is intriguing. Ornan or Araunah (cf. II Kgs. 24) sees the angel that was causing the plague. While he continues threshing, his four children with him hide themselves. The interest here is whether they had been infected by the pestilence. If so, were they then in isolation or did they hide

---

[15] Goldingay and Goldingay, "Thinking with the Old Testament about the Pandemic," p. 194.

[16] Goldingay and Goldingay, "Thinking with the Old Testament about the Pandemic," p. 195.

themselves in the fear of the angel of destruction? Clearly, this epidemic had come upon Israel purely because of David's sin.

Significance of the Protocols

They Shall Wash... So That They May Not Die

Exodus 30: 17-21 deals with washing of hands and feet with water to ensure ceremonial cleanliness. It is to emphasise that hand washing has been a religious ceremonial ritual in the Jewish culture since then. For a community living a nomadic life in a desert, infectious diseases would have been common, and thus, aside from the religious ceremonial reason, hand and foot washing with water served as a preventive measure against any such disease. The hand and foot washing "so that they may not die" becomes very significant. Aside from the religious implication, the hand and foot washing are means of offering hope in times of an outbreak of a pandemic.

Examine, Isolate, and Pronounce Clean

Leviticus 13 revolves around the word *tsara`ath*, which is a skin disease, disorder, or abnormality. In line with the numerous academic materials that successfully argue that *tsara`ath* is not leprosy,[17] this paper maintains the Hebrew *tsara`ath* and refers to the person diagnosed with an unknown skin disease. Whereas in Numbers 12 and II Chronicles 26:19-21 *tsara`ath* is linked to punishment from God due to human sins, Leviticus 13–14 has no direct link to sin or punishment.

In Leviticus 13:1-8, after a priest examines an abnormal skin condition and is sure that the symptoms are that of *tsara`ath*, he declares the person unclean and then there is isolation (*sagar*), which means "to shut up" or "to put in prison" for up to fourteen days. The action may connote indicating an act beyond self-isolation but graduating to compulsory confinement that can only be lifted after further examinations have proved the condition to be healed or no more a suspected *tsara`ath*. After the seventh day, if there is no healing, the second seven days of isolation are applied. When the disease has not spread upon re-examination on the fourteenth day, the person is declared clean and has to wash their clothes and go back into the community. If after the fourteen-day isolation there is still *tsara`ath*, the patient is declared unclean. Leviticus 13:9-46 prescribes various levels of examination to determine the severity of the

---

[17] See A.R. Freilich, "Tzaraat Biblical Leprosy," *Journal of the American Academy of Dermatology* 6(1), (1982):, pp. 131–134; R.M. Heller, T.W Heller, and J.M. Sasson, "Mold: 'Tsara'at,' – Leviticus, and the History of a Confusion," *Perspectives in Biology and Medicine* 46(4), (2003), pp. 588–591; J. Milgrom, *Leviticus 1–16: A New Translation with Introduction and Commentary*, 1 (New York: Doubleday, 1991), pp. 774–818.

condition to decide whether the person should be declared clean or unclean, and the diagnosis had to be accurate.[18]

The mourning rites associated with the preventive measures resemble face covering, social distancing, and quarantine used in the prevention of the spread of pandemics such as the recent COVID-19. The mourning rites starts with the *tsara`ath* patient wearing torn clothes and leaving their hair unkept. After the mourning rites, the *tsara`ath* patient proceeds to the protocols of face covering, physical/social distancing, and quarantine. The first instruction is for the *tsara`ath* patient to "cover his upper lip" (*sapham*; Lev. 13:45). Since this type of covering includes the mouth, it hints at face masking to prevent the spread of the disease.

The *tsara`ath* patient then proceeds to physical or social distancing after face covering. He/she must cry "unclean, unclean" to warn and prevent people from coming close. This creates the needed physical distance that will prevent others from catching the disease. Clearly, the *tsara`ath* has unsettled the normality of the person's life,[19] and that calls for the patient distancing him/herself physically and/or socially from other, non-infected members of the community. Both the face covering and the verbal pronouncement of "unclean, unclean" show that the patient is unworthy, unclean, ashamed, and in a state of mourning (cf. Ezek. 24:17; Mic. 3:7). He/she is ritually dead in the covenant community.[20]

The quarantine outside the camp, using the idea of *yashab* ("he shall dwell"; Lev. 13:46), intensifies the sense and the pain of the isolation from the rest of the Israelite community. The first usage is in the verb form *yashab*, where the *tsara`ath* patient dwells alone. The second usage is in the masculine noun form *mowshab* (his dwelling),[21] which is located outside the camp. These two usages of "dwell," combined with *ḥuwts* ("outside"; Lev. 13:46), emphasise the rejection and banishment of the *tsara`ath* patient as unclean. In the Hebrew Bible, *ḥuwts* is used for things moved outside the camp or the city because they are either unclean or part of rites to cleanse the community. For instance, the sin offering is burnt outside the camp or the city (Lev. 4) to cleanse the covenant community of all sins and uncleanness. It is therefore clear that the *tsara`ath* patient was quarantined outside of the camp so that God's people would be ritually clean.[22] However, the unintended benefit of preventing the spread of the disease cannot be in doubt. Tidball rightly asserts that once the *tsara`ath* patient is moved outside the covenant community, he/she is not only cut off from friends

---

[18] J.E. Hartley, *Leviticus* (Dallas, TX: Word Books, 1992), p. 200.

[19] Derek Tidball, *The Message of Leviticus: Free to be Holy* (Downers Grove, IL: InterVarsity Press, 2005), p. 174.

[20] John D. Currid, *A Study Commentary on Leviticus* (Darlington, England: Evangelical Press, 2004), p. 182.

[21] Jay Sklar, *Leviticus: An Introduction and Commentary* (Downers Grove, IL: InterVarsity Press, 2014), pp. 181–184.

[22] Mary Douglas, *Leviticus as Literature* (Oxford: Oxford University Press, 2000), p. 184; Currid, *A Study Commentary on Leviticus*, p. 183; Sklar, *Leviticus*, p. 187.

and family, but also barred from drawing near to God when the covenant people gather to worship.[23] Just as being unclean stripped a person of access to the sacred,[24] the *tsara`ath* patient, who is now seen as unclean and sent outside the camp, is separated from the covenant community. Simon Skidmore sees the rite as sentencing the *tsara`ath* patient to dwell outside the camp.[25] The rotting flesh of the *tsara`ath* patient is reminiscent of a corpse and, therefore, of death.[26] This makes the *tsara`ath* patient impure, which in biblical terms "is associated with the sphere of death,"[27] perhaps depicting the distinction between the realms of life and death by connecting the boundary between the two realms.[28]

The narratives about Miriam being afflicted with *tsara`ath* and being shut outside the camp for seven days (Num. 12:1-16), Naaman's healing from his *tsara`ath* taking place outside the city (II Kgs. 5:1-18),[29] and the four men with *tsara`ath* (the four "lepers", as most translations indicate) dwelling outside the city gate of Samaria (II Kgs. 7:3-20), also give a snapshot of examination, isolation, and the pronouncement of cleanliness or uncleanliness.

To be pronounced clean means being healthy or moving from a state of death to life. It is an opportunity for one who is isolated and quarantined to become a full member of a community. Thus, though *tsara`ath* might not have been a pandemic or even an epidemic, these cleansing and preventive rites might have translated into some of the modern protocols employed to stop the spread of communicable diseases such as COVID-19.[30] As such, to be pronounced "clean" is to have hope.

Hope for a People Stricken with a Pandemic

This section reflects on the extent to which the biblical antecedents of the preventive protocols offered hope to the people of Israel. If that hope is

---

[23] Tidball, *The Message of Leviticus*, p. 175.

[24] John H. Sailhamer, *The Pentateuch as Narrative* (Grand Rapids, MI: Zondervan Publishing House, 1992), p. 335.

[25] S. Skidmore, "The Evolution of the ṣāraʿat Ritual in Leviticus 13:1-46," *Heythrop Journal* 61 (2020), p. 893.

[26] Milgrom, *Leviticus 1–16,* pp. 816–-820; Leigh M. Trevaskis, *Holiness, Ethics and Ritual in Leviticus* (Sheffield: Phoenix Press, 2011), pp. 155–156; Gordon J. Wenham, *The Book of Leviticus* (Grand Rapids: Wm. B. Eerdmans Publishing, 1979), p. 201.

[27] Milgrom, *Leviticus 1–16*, p. 816.

[28] Tikva Frymer-Kensky, "Pollution, Purification, and Purgation in Biblical Israel," in Carol L. Meyers (ed.), *The Word of the Lord Shall Go Forth: Essays in Honor of David Noel Freedman in Celebration of His Sixtieth Birthday* (Winona Lake, IN: Eisenbrauns, 1983), p. 400.

[29] P. van der Zwan, "Some Psychoanalytical Meanings of the Skin in Leviticus 13–14," *Verbum et Ecclesia* 37(1), (2016), a1590, p. 1 [Available at: http://dx.doi.org/10.4102/ve.v37i1.1590], [Last accessed: 20th July 2023].

[30] For further explanation, see Amissah, "A Public Theological Reflection on Biblical Antecedents of Protocols," pp. 17–18.

established, then the natural conclusion could be that, whether knowingly or unknowingly, when leaders of the church made the promotion of the protocols an integral part of their message during the COVID-19 pandemic, they were preaching the biblical message of life, purity, health, and hope.

Hope means that the object of fear is brought under control such that it will not be a threat to life and survival anymore. This kind of hope, which ends in overcoming the obstacles and objects of fear and panic, is never an abstract desire or fantasy. Instead, the one who has such hope experiences practical, pragmatic, and actionable situations that produce the desired goal of survival. The concept of hope has to do with security and confidence (Lev. 26:5; II Kgs. 18:19; Is. 30:15; Ezek. 34:27). In Romans, the Apostle Paul exposes how Christian hope becomes so tangible that one can boast of it, tracing a series of translations from suffering to endurance to character and to hope (Rom. 5:1-5). To Paul, the hope that comes out of this mill does not disappoint. This ties in with what the writer of the Letter to the Hebrews says about hope; that it is literally a physical structure for refuge which can secure the believer's soul, just as an anchor secures a ship (Heb. 6:13-20), alluding to Proverbs 18:10, which says: "The name of the Lord is a strong tower; the righteous run into it and are safe." It suffices to mention that hope in the Hebrew Bible had the ultimate end that God will be victorious over all His enemies and that God's people will ultimately be delivered from any form of oppression and suppression. This hope was active. There is no doubt that biblical hope culminates in the resurrection of Christ[31] and has an eschatological dimension.[32] However, throughout the biblical accounts, the challenges of daily living, in wars, oppression, poverty, plagues, and mysterious loss of lives, meant that the people's hope was channelled into actively being freed from these seemingly "out-of-control" challenges. To this end, the hope we read about in the narratives of the Bible and the hope we have today means that we expect God to intervene to end any challenge that restrains His people from thriving. During the COVID-19 pandemic, therefore, hope included bringing the spread of the virus under control. Our hope has been justified when it was brought under control. Just as the biblical rites discussed above did not only ensure physical and ceremonial cleanliness but also became sources of hope in avoiding the spread of diseases, so did the promotion of the COVID-19 preventive protocols become symbols of hope.

As pointed out earlier, although the command to wash the hands and feet was for purposes of ceremonial cleanliness, it was also instructive for physical, life-giving purposes. The reason for the command to wash was "that they may not die" (Ex. 30:20, 21). I pointed out earlier that, in the context of a nomadic people wandering in a desert, ceremonial cleanliness could also prevent contracting and

---

[31] Mitchell L. Chase, "'From Dust You Shall Arise': Resurrection Hope in the Old Testament," *The Southern Baptist Journal of Theology* 18(4), (2014), pp. 9–29.
[32] See D.A. Hubbard, "Hope in the Old Testament," *Tyndale Bulletin* 34 (1983), pp. 33–60.

spreading diseases and thus avoid an epidemic. If nothing else, that culture of hygiene provided a template for observing cleanliness that could serve both religious and health purposes. The hope that the hand washing offered was not only that the priests would not die from ceremonial uncleanliness but that both the priests and the people would not die from any epidemic that could spread among them.

A reason why isolation or banishment from the camp was prescribed was for the community to be protected from religious uncleanliness so that they could continue to enjoy the presence of a holy God. At the same time, they were protected from the physical consequences of contracting the disease that may end up leading to their own banishment or death. Thus, the isolation, distancing, face covering, and quarantine that were imposed offered hope to the rest of the community that they would not be ceremonially unclean and that they would also not bear the health risk of contracting the disease. The ritual thus served as giving life to the people so they could continue to enjoy their religious, community, and social life, without fear of pandemics.

How then does the early response of the church to the COVID-19 pandemic, especially the promotion of the preventive protocols, become part of the overall message of hope? Generally, it is believed that when church leaders add their voices to a national issue, people listen and act accordingly. We do not have statistical data on how the involvement of the church in promoting and practising the preventive protocols impacted the response of individuals. Generally, however, it is believed that where the protocols were ardently followed, the spread of COVID-19 was minimised. In promoting the safety protocols, therefore, the church has contributed to controlling the spread of the virus and thus saved many from losing their lives to COVID-19. So, if we assert that the ritual that promoted ceremonial cleanliness was a source of hope for the people of Israel to avoid the spread of any infectious diseases, then it is equally true that when the church promoted the COVID-19 preventive protocols, it was a practical means of offering hope, since the spread of the COVID-19 virus could be contained to save lives.

Conclusion

The primary aim of this discussion has been to establish the extent to which contemporary preventive protocols for managing pandemics such as COVID-19 mimic biblical antecedents. The story about God inflicting a plague on Pharaoh's household when he attempted to take Sarai, Abram's wife, for himself, and the exodus story that involves plagues that came upon the people of Egypt when Pharaoh refused to let Israel go, speak about punishments that result in widespread death. Furthermore, the Lord sending a pestilence that killed 70,000 Israelites to punish David for conducting a census and the Lord threatening to send pestilence among the people of Israel are punishments for covenant violation. These have been seen as biblical examples of hygiene, face covering, self-isolation, social distancing, and quarantine which were originally rituals for ceremonial cleanliness.

It has been established that these rituals of ceremonial cleanliness and methods used to prevent infectious diseases are what might have translated into the safety protocols that are used to prevent modern-day pandemics, such as COVID-19. The study also established that, though the early response of the church to the outbreak of the COVID-19 pandemic, especially in promoting safety and preventive protocols, might have initially sounded out of place, the biblical perspectives show that it was an integral part of the message of hope and courage that the church was expected to preach. The emphasis on hand washing, examination, isolation, and pronouncement of cleanliness were necessary to prevent death. With the general belief that church leaders have a great influence on their members and the public in many communities, it can be concluded that by adding their voices in promoting the non-pharmaceutical protocols, church leaders contributed to the control of the spread of the pandemic and thus brought hope to communities during the unprecedentedly difficult times that were experienced at the height of the COVID-19 pandemic.

Bibliography

Aaron, Daryl. *The 40 Most Influential Christians ... Who Shaped What We Believe Today*. Grand Rapids, MI: Baker, 2013.

Achebe, Chinua. *Things Fall Apart*. New York: NY: Penguin Books, 2017.

Acolatse, Esther. *For Freedom or Bondage?: A Critique of African Pastoral Practices*. Grand Rapids, MI: Eerdmans, 2014.

——. "Unravelling the Relational Myth in the Turn Toward Autonomy: Pastoral Care and Counselling with African Women." In J. Stevenson-Moessner and T. Snorton, Eds. *Women Out of Order: Risking Change and Creating Care in a Multicultural World*. Minneapolis, MN: Fortress, 2009: 218–229.

Adelakun, Abimbola A. *Powerful Devices: Prayer and the Political Praxis of Spiritual Warfare*. New Brunswick: Rutgers University Press, 2022.

——. "'Thank God for Amazon.com': Spiritual Warfare, African Theology, and Prayer Merch." *The Journal of World Christianity* 12(2) (2022): 280–302.

——. "The Healing of Maseko: Live and A-live Presences, and the Theatre of the Spiritual." *The Drama Review* 66(4) (2022): 37–55.

——. *Performing Power in Nigeria: Identity, Politics, and Pentecostalism*. Cambridge: Cambridge University Press, 2021.

Adeloye, J.O. "From the Pulpit: COVID-19 in a Time Like This." *Trinity Journal of Church and Theology* 20(3), (2020): 107–111.

Adogame, Afe. "Dealing with Local Satanic Technology: Deliverance Rhetoric in the Mountain of Fire and Miracles Ministries." *The Journal of World Christianity* 5(1), (2012): 75–101.

——. "Healing." In Moleffi Kete Asante and Ama Mazama, Eds. *Encyclopaedia of African Religion*. Volume 1. Washington DC: Sage, 2009.

Agorsah, E. Kofi. *Religion, Ritual, and African Tradition: African Foundations*. Bloomington, IN: Author House, 2010.

Agyinasare, Charles. *It Is Miracle Time: Experiencing God's Supernatural Working Power*. Volume 2. Accra: Charles Agyinasare Press, 1997.

Aidoo, Mark S. *Shame in the Individual Lament Psalms and African Spirituality*. African Theological Studies 12. New York: Peter Lang, 2017.

Akelicious Media. "Wearing Facemask About is an Embarrassment to Science." 6th May 2020. https://www.youtube.com/watch?v=VEiatmfWxvw&feature=emb_imp_woyt. [Last accessed: 1st May 2022].

Alden, Robert L. "*שפט*." In William A. Vangemeren, Ed. *New International Dictionary of Old Testament Theology and Exegesis*. Volume 3. Grand Rapids, MI: Zondervan, 1997: 1268.

Aleh, Hilda Afi. "A Comparative Study of the Mission Histories of the Assemblies of God Church and the Church of Pentecost in Ghana." Master of Philosophy thesis, Religious Department, University of Ghana, 2013.

Allen, George Cantrell. *The Didache*. London: Astolat Press, 1903.

Allen, Leslie C. *Psalms 101–150*, Word Biblical Commentary 21. Dallas, TX: Word Publishers, 1983.

Amarkwei, Charles. *Paul Tillich and His System of Paradoxical Correlation: Forging a New Way for Science and Theology Relations*. Eugene, OR: Wipf and Stock, 2020.

Amissah, Patrick Kofi. "A Public Theological Reflection on Biblical Antecedents of Protocols for Managing Pandemics." *International Journal of Public Theology* 18 (2024): 1–24.

Amundsen, D.W. "Suffering." In Sinclair B. Ferguson, David F. Wright, and J.I. Packer, Eds. *New Dictionary of Theology*. Leicester: The Bath Press, 1988.

Anderson, Allan. *African Reformation: African Initiated Christianity in the 20th Century*. Trenton, NJ: Africa World Press, 2001.

Aryeh, Daniel Nii Aboagye. "Religion and Urban Life: Space and Patronage for Prophetic Ministry in Cities in Ghana." *Alternation* Special Edition 30 (2020), 311–334. [Available at: https://doi.org/10.29086/2519-5476/2020/sp30a17], [Last accessed: 19th July 2023].

—. *Biblical, Traditional, and Theological Framework for Understanding Christian Prophetism Today*. Eugene, OR: Wipf and Stock, 2019.

Asamoah-Gyadu, J. Kwabena. *Christianity and Faith in the COVID-19 Era: Lockdown Period from Hosannah to Pentecost*. Accra: Step Publishers, 2020.

—. "Therapeutic Strategies in African Religions: Health, Herbal Medicines and Indigenous Christian Spirituality." *Studies in World Christianity* 20(1), (2014): 70–90.

—. "Anointing Through the Screen: Neo-Pentecostalism and Televised Christianity in Ghana." *Studies in World Christianity* 11(1), (2005): 9–28.

—. *African Charismatics: Current Development Within Independent Indigenous Pentecostalism in Ghana*. Leiden: Koninklijke Brill NV, 2005.

—. "Dealing With a Spiritual Virus: Whither the Prophetic?" *Religious Matters in an Entangled World*. 13th April 2020. [Available at: https://religiousmatters.nl/dealing-with-a-spiritual-virus-whither-the-prophetic/], [Last accessed: 19th July 2023].

ATLAS.ti, "Narrative analysis in Research," available at https://atlasti.com/guides/qualitative-research-guide-part-2/narrative-research [Last accessed: 9th March 2023].

Aune, D.E., T.J. Geddert, and C.E. Evans. "Apocalyptism." In C.E. Evans and S. Porter, Eds. *Dictionary of New Testament Background: A Compendium of Contemporary Biblical Scholarship*. Downers Grove, IL: InterVarsity Press, 2000: 45–58.

Baden, J.S. and C.R. Moss. "The Origin and Interpretation of ṣāraʿat in Leviticus 13–14." *Journal of Biblical Literature* 130(4), (2011): 643–662.

Baëta, Christian G. *Prophetism in Ghana: A Study of Some Spiritual Churches*. London: SCM, 1962.

Boafo, Most Reverend Dr Paul. "COVID-19 Response from the Methodist Church Ghana." 15 March 2020. [Available at: www.facebook.com/permalink.php?id=182701041896569&story_fbid=1561], [Last accessed: 6th April 2024].

Barth, Karl. *Credo: A Presentation of the Chief Problems of Dogmatics With Reference to the Apostles' Creed.* Translated by James Strathern McNab. London: Hodder & Stoughton, 1936.

Barry, John M. *The Great Influenza: The Story of the Deadliest Pandemic in History*. London: Penguin, 2005.

Barton, John. "The Dark Side of God in the Old Testament." In Katharine Dell, Ed. *Ethical and Unethical in the Old Testament: God and Human in Dialogue*. Library of Hebrew Bible/Old Testament Studies 528. New York: T&T Clark, 2010: 122–134.

Basinger, David. "Human Freedom and Divine Providence: Some New Thoughts on an Old Problem." *Religious Studies* 15(4), (1979): 491–510.

Baumgarten, Joseph and Menahem Mansoor. "Studies in the New *Hodayot* (Thanksgiving Hymns) III." *Journal of Biblical Literature* 74(3), (1955): 107–113.

Beeke, Joel R. and Mark Jones. *A Puritan Theology: Doctrine for Life*. Grand Rapids, MI: Reformation Heritage, 2012.

Blanton, Anderson. *Hittin' the Prayer Bones: Materiality of Spirit in the Pentecostal South.* Chapel Hill: The University of North Carolina Press, 2015.

Boaheng, Isaac. "Christianity and the COVID-19 Pandemic: A Pastoral and Theological Reflection from the Ghanaian Context." *Journal of Pastoral Theology* (2021): 1–14.

Bonar, Andrew A. *A Commentary on Leviticus*. Reprint. Geneva Series Commentary. Edinburgh: Banner of Truth Trust, 1983.

Bongba, Elias Kiffon. "Eschatology in Africa: The Imperative of a Transformative Social Praxis." *Svensk Teologisk Kvartalskrift* 4 (2018): 245–252.

Booth, Newell. "African Religion." In P. Beaver, Jan Bergman, and S. Langley, Eds. *A Lion Handbook of World Religions*. Herts: Lion, 1982.

Braaten, Carl. "The Kingdom of God and Life Everlasting." In Peter C. Hodgson and Robert H. King, Eds. *Christian Theology: An Introduction to Its Traditions and Tasks*. Philadelphia, PA: Fortress, 1982: 274–298.

Bregman, L. "Suffering." In J. Rodney, Ed. *Dictionary of Pastoral Care and Counselling*. Nashville, TN: Abingdon Press, 1990.

Briggs, Andrew and Michael J. Reiss. *Human Flourishing: Scientific Insight and Spiritual Wisdom in Uncertain Times*. Oxford: Oxford University Press, 2021.

Brueggemann, Walter. *The Message of the Psalms*. Minneapolis, MN: Augsburg, 1985.

——. *Reverberations of Faith: A Theological Handbook of Old Testament Themes*. Louisville, KY: Westminster John Knox Press, 2002.

Burley, Mikel. "Dislocating the Eschaton: Appraising Realized Eschatology." *Sophia* 56(3), (Sept 2017): 435–452.

Calvin, John. *Commentaries on the Four Last Books of Moses Arranged in the Form of a Harmony*. Translated by Charles Bingham. Grand Rapids, MI: Baker, 1996.

Cartlidge, David R. and David L. Dungan. *Documents for the Study of the Gospels*. Philadelphia, PA: Fortress, 1980.

Carson, D.A. "Biblical-Theological Pillars Needed to Support Faithful Christian Reflection on Suffering and Evil." *Trinity Journal* 38(1), (2017): 55–77.

Centre for Disease Control and Prevention. "Symptoms of COVID-19." CDC website. 22nd February 2021. [Available at: https://www.cdc.gov/coronavirus/2019-ncov/symptoms-testing/symptoms.html], [Last accessed: 19th July 2023].

Chadwick, Henry. *The Early Church*. London: Penguin, 1993.

Chase, Mitchell L. "'From Dust You Shall Arise:' Resurrection Hope in the Old Testament." *The Southern Baptist Journal of Theology* 18(4), (2014): 9–29.

Christenson, Randall M. "Parallels Between Depression and Laments." *The Journal of Pastoral Care and Counseling* 61(4), (2007): 299–308.

Clark, Gordon H. *The Philosophy of Science and Belief in God*. Nutley, NJ: The Craig, 1977.

Clines, D.J.A. *The Dictionary of Classical Hebrew*. Volume 8. Sheffield: Sheffield Phoenix Press, 2011.

Collins, J.J. *Encounters with Biblical Theology*. Minneapolis, MN: Fortress, 2005.

Cotterell, F.P. "Suffering." In T. Desmond Alexander, Brian S. Rosner, Graeme Goldsworthy, and D.A. Carson, Eds. *New Dictionary of Biblical Theology: Exploring the Unity Diversity of Scripture*. Leicester: InterVarsity Press, 2000.

Culver, Robert Duncan. *Systematic Theology: Biblical and Historical*. Ross-Shire: Christian Focus Publications, 2013.

Currid, John D. *A Study Commentary on Leviticus*. Darlington, England: Evangelical Press, 2004.

Cyprian. n.d. "The Treatises of Cyprian." E-Catholic 2000 website [Available at: https://www.ecatholic2000.com/fathers/untitled-197.shtml], [Last accessed: 19th July 2023].

Dalton, William J. "The First Epistle of Peter." In Raymond E. Brown, Joseph A. Fritzmyer, and Roland E. Murphy, Eds. *The New Jerome Biblical Commentary*. Englewood Cliffs, NJ: Prentice Hall, 1990: 903–908.

Daniel, Kasoma. "An Investigation of Sin and Evil in African Cosmology." *International Journal of Sociology and Anthropology* 1(8), (Dec 2009): 145–155.

Davidson, Robert. *The Vitality of Worship: A Commentary on the Book of Psalms*. Grand Rapids, MI: Eerdmans, 1998.

Davidson, R.M. "Assurance in Judgment." *Advent Review* 7 (1988): 18–20.

De Witte, Marleen. "The Electric Touch Machine Miracle Scam: Body, Technology, and the (Dis)authentication of the Pentecostal Supernatural." In J. Stolow, Ed. *Deus in Machina: Religion, Technology, and the Things in Between*. New York: Fordham University Press, 2013: 61–88.

Dein, Simon. "Covid-19 and the Apocalypse: Religious and Secular Perspectives." *Journal of Religion and Health* 60(1), (Feb 2021): 5–15.

Dodd, C.H. *The Parables of the Kingdom*. London: Nisbet, 1936.

Donders, Joseph. *Non-Bourgeois Theology: An African Experience of Jesus*. New York: Orbis, 1985.

Donnelly, Nick and Jim McManus. "Pandemic Flu: The Role of the Church." *The Furrow* 57(12), (Dec 2006): 657–663.

Dostoevsky, Fyodor. *The Brothers Karamazov*. New York: Barnes and Noble, 1995.

Douglas, Mary. *Leviticus as Literature*. Oxford: Oxford University Press, 2000.

——. "Poetic Structure in Leviticus." In D.P. Wright, N.D. Freedman, and A. Hurvitz, Eds. *Pomegranates and Golden Bells: Studies in Biblical, Jewish, and Near Eastern Ritual, Law, and Literature in Honour of Jacob Milgrom*. Winona Lake, IN: Eisenbrauns, 1995: 239–256.

Draper, Jonathan A. "A Broken Land and a Healing Community: Zulu Zionism and Healing in the Case of George Khambule (1884–1949)." *Studia Historiae Ecclesiasticae* 36(1), (2010): 1–16.

Eduah, Francis Otoo. "A History of Christian Faith Church International (CfCI), in Ghana." Master of Philosophy thesis, College of Humanities, University of Ghana, 2018.

Edwards, R.B. "Suffering." In Geoffrey W. Bromiley, Ed. *The International Standard Bible Encyclopedia*. Volume l. Grand Rapids, MI: Eerdmans, 1988.

Egger, Eva-Maria, Sam Jones, Patricia Justino, Ivan Manhique, and Ricardo Santos. "Africa's Lockdown Dilemma: High Poverty and Low Trust.' *United Nations Universities World Institute for Development Economic Research*. WIDER Working Paper 2020/76, June 2020.

Ekundayo, Lawrence B. "Taboo in the Biblical Context." *Ado Journal of Religions* 2(1), (July 2003): 40–50.

Ellis, Stephen and Gerrie ter Haar. *Worlds of Power: Religious Thought and Political Practice in Africa*. London: Hurst and Company, 2004.

Enyinnaya, John. "The Bible Meets Human Need: Reading Romans in the Light of the HIV/AIDS Pandemic." *West Africa Journal of Education* (2012): 16–32.

Ernest, Chilles. "Evil, Bad, Wickedness." In Colin Brown, Ed. *The New International Dictionary of New Testament Theology*. Grand Rapids, MI: The Paternoster Press, 1986.

Evans Jr., James H. "Eschatology, White Supremacy, and the Beloved Community." In Rebecca S. Chopp and Mark Lewis Taylor, Eds.

Reconstructing Christian Theology. Minneapolis, MN: Fortress Press, 1994: 346–373.

Fagunwa, Omololu Ebenezer. "African Pentecostalism and the 1918 Influenza Pandemic: The Supernatural Amid the Fearful and Implications for the COVID-19 Pandemic." *Christian Journal for Global Health* 7(5), (Dec 2020): 52–64.

Fatokun, S.A. "Precious Stone Society 2018." https://tacnlawna.org/precious-stone-society/ [Last accessed: 14th February 2022].

Fenn, Richard. *Time Exposure: The Personal Experience of Time in Secular Societies*. Oxford: Oxford University Press, 2001.

Flemming, Rebecca. "Galen and the Plague." In Caroline Petit, Ed. *Galen's Treatise (De indolentia) in Context: A Tale of Resiliance*. Leiden: Brill, 2019: 219–244.

Freilich, A.R. "Tzaraat Biblical Leprosy." *Journal of the American Academy of Dermatology* 6(1), (1982): 131–134.

Frimpong-Manso, Reverend Professor Paul. "COVID-19: Cooperate with Health Officials – Assemblies of God Church." 16th March 2020. [Available at: https://www.classfmonline.com/news/general/CODVID-19-Cooperate-with-health-officials-Assemblies-of-God-Church-11849], [Last accessed: 6th April 2024].

Frymer-Kensky, Tikva. "Pollution, Purification, and Purgation in Biblical Israel," in Carol L. Meyers, Ed. *The Word of the Lord Shall Go Forth: Essays in Honor of David Noel Freedman in Celebration of His Sixtieth Birthday*. Winona Lake, IN: Eisenbrauns, 1983: 399–414.

Garchar, Kim. "Sin, Sorrow and Suffering: A Roycean Response to These Deeper Tragedies of Life." *American Journal of Theology and Philosophy* 33 (2012): 57–73.

Gehman, Richard. *African Traditional Religion in the Light of the Bible*. Bukuru: African Christian Textbooks, 2013.

GhanaWeb. "Coronovirus: Catholic Church Bans Handshakes and Hugs Henceforth." [sic] *GhanaWeb*, 4th March 2020. [Available at: https://www.ghanaweb.com/GhanaHomePage/NewsArchive/Coronovirus-Catholic-Church-bans-handshakes-and-hugs-henceforth-884863], [Last accessed: 19th July 2023].

GhanaWeb. "Anglican Communion Takes Steps to Prevent Coronavirus Infections." *GhanaWeb*, 12th March 2020. [Available at: https://www.ghanaweb.com/GhanaHomePage/NewsArchive/Anglican-Communion-takes-steps-to-prevent-coronavirus-infections-892114#], [Last accessed: 19th July 2023].

GhanaWeb. "ICGC Suspends Baptism Over Coronavirus." *GhanaWeb*, 14th March 2020. [Available at: https://www.ghanaweb.com/GhanaHomePage/NewsArchive/ICGC-suspends-baptism-over-coronavirus-894463], [Last accessed: 19th July 2023].

[Last accessed Cure." *GhanaWeb,* 1st August 2020. [Available at: https://www.ghanaweb.com/GhanaHomePage/africa/Oyedepo-backs-Stella-Immanuel-says-coronavirus-has-a-cure-1023037], [Last accessed: 19th July 2023].

Goldingay, John and Kathleen Scott Goldingay. "Thinking with the Old Testament About the Pandemic." *Theology* 123(3), (2020): 191–197.

Gregory of Nazianzus. "Epistle 101." In Edward R. Hardy, Ed. *Christology of the Latter Fathers*. Library of Christian Classics, Volume 3. Philadelphia, PA: Westminster, 1954.

Gunkel, Hermann. *Introduction to the Psalms: The Genres of the Religious Lyric of Israel*. Macon, GA: Georgia University Press, 1998.

Guthrie, D. and R.P. Martin. "God." In Gerald Hawthorne, Ralph P. Martin, and Daniel G. Reid, Eds. *Dictionary of Paul and His Letters*. Leicester: InterVarsity Press, 1993.

Gyekye, Kwame. *African Cultural Values: An Introduction*. Accra: Sankofa, 1996.

Hafeman, S.J. "Suffering." In Gerald Hawthorne, Ralph P. Martin, and Daniel G. Reid, Eds. *Dictionary of Paul and His Letters*. Leicester: InterVarsity Press, 1993.

Hall, Douglas John. *God and Human Suffering: An Exercise in the Theology of the Cross*. Minneapolis, MN: Augsburg, 1986.

Hartley, J.E. *Leviticus*. Dallas, TX: Word Books, 1992.

Heller, R.M., T.W. Heller, and J.M. Sasson. "Mold: 'Tsara'at,' Leviticus, and the History of a Confusion." *Perspectives in Biology and Medicine* 46(4), (2003), 588–591.

Herrero, Montserrat, "Deconstructing Historical Expectation: Lessons from the Pandemic," *Political Theology* 21(70), (2020), 571–573.

Horgan, John. "Plague of Cyprian, 250–270 CE." *Ancient History Encyclopedia*. 13th December 2016. [Available at: https://www.ancient.eu/article/992/plague-of-cyprian-250-270-ce/], [Last accessed: 19th July 2023].

Horton, Robin. *Patterns of Thought in Africa and the West: Essays on Magic, Religion and Science*. Cambridge: Cambridge University Press, 1993.

Hubbard, D.A. "Hope in the Old Testament." *Tyndale Bulletin* 34 (1983): 33–60.

Jacobs, Daisy Palinwinde. "Christian Council Takes on Christ Embassy for Flouting COVID-19 Protocols." 3rd May 2021. [Available at: https://citinewsroom.com/ 2021/05/christian-council-takes-on-christ-embassy-for-flouting-covid-19-protocols/], [Last accessed: 5th April 2024].

James, George G.M. *Stolen Legacy: Greek Philosophy is Stolen Egyptian Philosophy*. Bensenville, IL: Lushena, 2014.

Jansen, H. "Research, Narrative, and Representation: A Post-Narrative Approach." *History and Theory* 58(1), (2019): 67–88. DOI:10.1111/hith.12100.

Johnston-Barrett, Melissa. "Making Spaces: Silence, Voice, and Suffering." *Word and World* 25(3), (2005): 328–337.

Jordan, Jeff. "Divine Love and Human Suffering." *International Journal for Philosophy of Religion* 56(2), (Oct–Dec 2004): 169–178.

Kang, Yun-Jung. "Lessons Learnt from Cases of COVID-19 Infection in South Korea." *Cambridge University Press Public Health Emergency Collection* (7th May 2020): 1–8. DOI: 10.1017/dmp.2020.141.

Kapolyo, Joe M. *The Human Condition: Christian Perspectives Through African Eyes*. Leicester: InterVarsity Press, 2005.

Kassa, Tesfaye. "Jesus Christ, Supreme Over All." In Tokunboh Adeyemo, Ed. *Africa Bible Commentary*. Nairobi: WordAlive, 2006.

Keller, Catherine. *Apocalypse Now and Then: A Feminist Guide to the End of the World*. Boston, MA: Beacon, 1996.

Kenu, Ernest, Joseph Frimpong, and Kodwo A. Koram. "Responding to the COVID-19 Pandemic in Ghana." *Ghana Medical Journal* 54(2), (June 2020), 72–73. DOI: 10.4314/gmj.v54i2.1. [Available at: https://www.ncbi.nlm.nih. gov/pmc/articles/PMC7829051/], [Last accessed: 6th April 2024].

Kgatie, Mookgo S. "Singing as a Therapeutic Agent in Pentecostal Worship." *Verbum et Ecclesia* 40(1), (2019): 1–7. [Available at: https://doi.org/10.4102/ve.v40i1.1910].

Kidner, Derek. *Psalms 73–150*. Tyndale Old Testament Commentaries. Downers Grove, IL: InterVarsity Press, 1975.

Killen, R. Allan. "Suffering." In Charles F. Pfeiffer, Howard F. Vos, and John Rea, Eds. *Wycliffe Bible Dictionary*. Peabody, MA: Hendrickson, 2008.

Kilson, Marion. *Kpele Lala: Ga Religious Songs and Symbols*. Cambridge, MA: Harvard University Press, 1971.

Kiuchi, Nobuyoshi. *Leviticus*. Apollos Old Testament Commentary 3. Nottingham, England: InterVarsity Press, 2007.

Kline, Moshe. "The Literary Structure of Leviticus." *Biblical Historian* 2(1), (2006): 11–28.

Koch, K. *The Prophets: The Assyrian Period*. Philadelphia, PA: Fortress Press, 1983.

Koehler, L. and W. Baumgartner. *Hebrew and Aramaic Lexicon of the Old Testament*. Leiden: Brill, 2001.

Koester, C. *Revelations and the End of All Things*. Grand Rapids, MI: Eerdmans, 2001.

Kolawole, Simon Adebayo. "An African Philosophy of Evil and its Implications for the Mission of the Church." PhD thesis, Nigerian Baptist Theological Seminary, Ogbomoso, 2002.

Koselleck, Reinhart and Hans-Georg Gadamer. *Zeitschichten: Studien zur Historik*. Frankfurt: Suhrkamp, 2000.

Kpobi, David N.A. *Mission in Ghana: The Ecumenical Heritage*. Accra: Asempa, 2008.

Kruss, Glenda. "Religion, Class and Culture – Indigenous Churches in South Africa, With Special Reference to Zionist Apostolic." Master of Arts thesis, Department of Religious Studies, University of Cape Town, 1985.

Kunhiyop, Samuel Waje. *African Christian Ethics*. Nairobi: WordAlive, 2008.

Kupolati, Lawrence O. "From the Pulpit: The Covid-19 Pain." *Trinity Journal of Church and Theology* 20(3), (2020): 112–115.

Kustenbauder, Matthew. "Prophetic Movements: Western Africa." In John Middleton and Joseph C. Miller, Eds. *New Encyclopedia of Africa*. Volume 4. Detroit: Thomson/Gale, 2008: 273–279.

Labahn, Michael. "The Book of Revelation: An Early Christian 'Search for Meaning' in Critical Conversation with its Jewish Heritage and Hellenistic-Roman Society." *In die Skriflig* 48(1), (March 2014): 1–9. [Available at: http://www.indieskriflig.org.za/index.php/skriflig/article/view/1833], [Last accessed: 19th July 2023].

LaCocque, André. *Daniel in His Time*. Columbia, SC: University of South Carolina Press, 1988.

Lawal, L.O. "Sin and Punishment in Yoruba Traditional Religion." *ORITA: Ibadan Journal of Religious Studies* 46 (1 & 2) (June and December 2014): 213.

Leder, Arie C. *Waiting for the Land: The Story Line of the Pentateuch*. Phillipsburg, NJ: P&R, 2010.

Lewis, P.H. "Temptation." In David J. Atkinson and David H. Field, Eds. *New Dictionary of Christian Ethics and Pastoral Theology*. Downers Grove, IL: InterVarsity Press, 1995.

Littman, R.J. and M.L. Littman. "Galen and the Antonine Plague." *The American Journal of Philosophy* 94(3), (1973): 243–255.

Luther, Martin. *Luther's Works*. Edited by Jaroslav Pelikan, Helmut T. Lehman, and Christopher Boyd Brown. 75 volumes. Philadelphia, PA: Fortress, 1955.

Luyten, Jos. "Perspective on Human Suffering in the Old Testament." In Jan Lambrecht and Raymond F. Collins, Eds. *God and Human Suffering*. Louvain: Peter's Press, 1990.

Maier, Paul L., trans. *Eusebius. The Church History*. Grand Rapids, MI: Kregel, 2007.

Manley, Jennifer. "Measles and Ancient Plagues: A Note on New Scientific Evidence." *The Classical World* 107(3), (2019): 393–397.

Mathewes, Charles. *A Theology of Public Life*. Cambridge: Cambridge University Press, 2007.

Mays, James. "The Question of Context in Psalm Interpretation." In J. Clinton McCann, Ed. *The Shape and Shaping of the Psalter*, *Journal for the Study of the Old Testament* Sup. 159. Sheffield: Sheffield Academic Press, 1993: 14–20.

Mbiti, John S. *Introduction to African Religion*. 2nd Ed. Oxford: Heinemann Educational Publishers, 1991.
McDowell, John C. "Karl Barth Having No-thing to Hope For." *Journal for Christian Theological Research* 11(2), (2006): 1–49. [Available at: http://digitalcommons.luthersem.edu/jctr/vol11/iss2006/2], [Last accessed: 19th July 2023].
McGill, Arthur C. *Suffering: A Test of Theological Method*. Philadelphia, PA: The Westminster Press, 1982.
McGrath, Alister E. *Christian Theology: An Introduction*. 2nd ed. Oxford: Blackwell, 1998.
Mensah, Beatrice. "Christian Council of Ghana 'Cannot Enforce' New COVID-19 guidelines." 5th June 2020. [Available at: https://www.asaaseradio.com/christian-council-of-ghana-cannot-enforce-new-covid-19-guidelines-general-secretary/], [Last accessed: 6th April 2024].
Migliore, Daniel. *Faith Seeking Understanding: An Introduction to Christian Theology*. Grand Rapids, MI: Eerdmans, 2004.
Milgrom, J. *Leviticus, 1–16: A New Translation with Introduction and Commentary*. Volume 1. New York: Doubleday, 1991.
Ministry of Finance. "COVID-19 Health and Safety Tips." [Available at: https://mofep.gov.gh/mof-covid-19-updates/health-and-safety-tips], [Last accessed: 4th April 2024].
Mohammadi, Bahram, Anke Hammer, Stephen F. Miedl, Daniel Wiswede, Josep Marco-Pallares, Manfred Herrmann and Thomas F. Munte. "Intertemporal Choice Behavior is Constrained by Brain Structure in Healthy Participants and Pathological Gamblers." *Brain Struct. Funct.* 221 (2016): 3157–3170. [Available at: https://doi.org/10.1007/s00429-015-1093-9].
Moltmann, Jürgen. *The Crucified God*. Minneapolis, MN: Fortress, 2015.
——. *The Coming of God: Christian Eschatology*. Translated by Margaret Kohl. London: SCM, 1996.
Morales, L. Michael. *Who Shall Ascend the Mountain of the Lord? A Biblical Theology of the Book of Leviticus*. Downers Grove, IL: Apollos, InterVarsity Press, 2015.
Morens, David M., Gregory K. Folkers, and Anthony S. Fauci. "What Is a Pandemic?" *The Journal of Infectious Diseases* 200(7), (2009): 1018–1021. DOI: 10.1086/644537.
Murphy, David. *The Doomsday Survival Handbook: Bucket Lists for Every Conceivable Apocalypse*. Naperville, IL: Sourcebooks, 2012.
Murphy, Edwina. "Death, Decay and Delight in Cyprian of Carthage." *Scrinium* 15 (2019), 79–88.
Murphy, Roland. "Reflections on Contextual Interpretation of the Psalms." In J. Clinton McCann, Ed. *The Shape and Shaping of the Psalter*. *Journal for the Study of the Old Testament* Sup. 159. Sheffield: Sheffield Academic Press, 1993: 21–28.

Neely, Alan. "Suffering." In A. Scott Moreau, Ed. *Evangelical Dictionary of World Missions*. Grand Rapids, MI: Baker, 2000.

Nelson, P.G. *God's Control over the Universe: Providence and Judgement in Relation to Modern Science*. Dunbeath, Scotland: Whittles Publishing, 2000.

News Ghana. "COVID-19 Vaccine Will Work With Nano-Chips: 5G to Control You." *News Ghana*, 1st January 2021. [Available at: https://newsghana.com.gh/covid-19-vaccine-will-work-with-nano-chips-5g-to-control-you-pastor-chris/], [Last accessed: 19th July 2023].

Noth, Martin. *Leviticus*. The Old Testament Library. Translated by J.E. Anderson. Philadelphia, PA: The Westminster Press, 1965.

O'Donovan, Wilbur. *Biblical Christianity in Modern Africa*. Waynesboro, GA: Paternoster Press, 2000.

Ogunkunle, C. "Evil Man's Apprehension of Contrary Situation." *Ado Journal of Religions* 2(2), (December 2001): 1–12.

Okorocha, Cyril and Francis Foulkes. "Psalms." In Tokunboh Adeyeyo, Ed. *Africa Bible Commentary*. Nairobi: WordAlive, 2006: 605–746.

Omenyo, Cephas N. "The Bible Says! Neo-Prophetic Hermeneutics in Africa." *Studies in World Christianity* 19(1), (April 2013): 50–70.

Omenyo, Cephas and Abamfo Atiemo. "Claiming Religious Space: The Case of Neo-Prophetism in Ghana." *Ghana Bulletin of Theology* New Series 1(1), (2006): 55–68.

Omulo, Collins. "Worsening Drought Puts 2.5m Kenyans at Risk of Starvation." *The East African*, 28th August 2019. [Available at: https://www.theeastafrican.co.ke/tea/news/east-africa/worsening-drought-puts-2-5m-kenyans-at-risk-of-starvation-1425908], [Last accessed: 19th July 2023].

Ondieki, Bosco. "Prophet Owuor Predicts Disaster if Kenyans Don't Repent." *The Standard*, 25th March 2019. [Available at: https://www.standardmedia.co.ke/ureport/article/2001318076/], [Last accessed: 19th July 2023].

Ormerod, Neil. *God and the Problems of Pain, Suffering and Evil*. Augsburg, MN: Fortress, 2015.

Oshitelu, G.A. *The African Fathers of the Early Church*. Ibadan: Sefer, 2002.

Pannenberg, Wolfhart. *Theology and the Kingdom of God*. Louisville, KY: Westminster Press, 1969.

Patterson, David K. "The Influenza Epidemic of 1918–19 in the Gold Coast." *The Journal of African History* 24(4), (1983): 485–502.

Paulson, Steven. "Luther on the Hidden God." *Word and World* 19(4), (1999): 363–371.

Phillip, Comfort W. and Walter A. Elwell, Eds. "Suffering." *Tyndale Bible Dictionary*. Carol Stream, IL: Tyndale House, 2001.

Phillips, Howard. "Why Did it Happen? Religious and Lay Explanations of the Spanish Flu Epidemic of 1918 in South Africa." *Kronos* 12 (1987): 72–92.

Plüss, Jean-Daniel. "Covid-19, the Church and the Challenge to Ecumenism." *Transformation: An International Journal of Holistic Mission Studies* (2020): 1–11.

Pritchard, Evans-E.E. *Witchcraft, Oracles, and Magic Among the Azande*. Oxford: Oxford University Press, 1937.

Prosén, Martina. "Pentecostal Praise and Worship as a Mode of Theology." In *Faith in African Lived Christianity: Bridging Anthropological and Theological Perspectives*. Global Pentecostal and Charismatic Studies 35. Leiden: Brill, 2019: 156–179.

Rad, Gerhard von. *Old Testament Theology: The Theology of Israel's Prophetic Traditions*. Volume 2. Translated by D.M.G. Stalker. Edinburgh: Harper and Row, 1965.

Rahner, Karl. "The Hermeneutics of Eschatological Assertions." In Kevin Smyth, Trans. *Theological Investigations*. Volume 4. Baltimore, MD: Helicon, 1966.

Republic of Ghana Ministry of Health. "Provisional Standard Treatment Guidelines for Novel Coronavirus Infection: COVID-19 Guidelines for Ghana." [Available at: https://www.moh.gov.gh/wp-content/uploads/2016/02/COVID-19-STG-JUNE-2020-1.pdf], [Last accessed: 4th April 2024].

Ronald, Charles. "Inside Prophet Owuor and Bishop Margaret Wnajiru's War." *HiviSasa*, 29th April 2018. Available at: https://hivisasa.com/posts/inside-prophet-owuor-bishop-margaret-wanjirus-war [Last accessed: 21st May 2021].

Sailhamer, John H. *The Pentateuch as Narrative*. Grand Rapids, MI: Zondervan, 1992.

Saint, Stephen F. "Sovereignty, Suffering and the Work of Missions." In John Piper and Justin Taylor, Eds. *Suffering and the Sovereignty of God*. Wheaton, IL: Crossway, 2006.

Sambala, Evanson Zondani. "Ethics of Planning for, and Responding to, Pandemic Influenza in Sub-Saharan Africa: Qualitative Study." PhD thesis, University of Nottingham, 2014.

Samuelson, Paul. "Proof that Properly Anticipated Prices Fluctuate Randomly." *Industrial Management Review* 6 (Spring 1965): 41–49.

Sanneh, Lamin. *West African Christianity: The Religious Impact*. Maryknoll, NY: Orbis, 1983.

Sahara Reporters. "It's Foolish to Reject COVID-19 Vaccine, Clerics Should Seek Knowledge – Pastor Ighodalo." *Sahara Reporters*, 7th April 2021. [Available at: http://saharareporters.com/2021/04/07/it%E2%80%99s-foolish-reject-covid-19-vaccine-clerics-should-seek-knowledge-%E2%80%93-pastor-ighodalo], [Last accessed: 19th July 2023].

Shea, William H. "Literary Form and Theological Function in Leviticus." In Frank B. Holbrook, Ed. *The Seventy Weeks, Leviticus, and the Nature of Prophecy*, Volume 3 of Daniel and Revelation Committee series. Washington, DC: Biblical Research Institute, 1986: 131–168.

Shea, William R. "Galileo and the Church." In David C. Lindberg and Roland L. Numbers, Eds. *God and Nature: Historical Essays on the Encounter Between Christianity and Science*. Berkeley, CA: University of California Press, 1986: 114–135.

Skidmore, S. "The Evolution of the ṣāra'at Ritual in Leviticus 13:1-46." The *Heythrop Journal* 61 (2020): 893–902.

Sklar, Jay. *Leviticus: An Introduction and Commentary*. Downers Grove, IL: InterVarsity Press, 2014

Smith, Iris M. "The Contributions of St Cyprian: Perspectives on Epidemiology and Early Christianity." *Young Historians Conference* (2014): 1–14.

Soila, Getty. "Prophet Owuor Predicts Worse Pandemic After Coronavirus (video) – GOTTA.News.' 21st March 2020. https://gotta.news/prophet-owuor [Last accessed: 15th October 2022].

Soeue, Dorothee. *Suffering*. Philadelphia, PA: Fortress, 1975.

Spiegel, Gabrielle. "The Future of the Past: History, Memory, and the Ethical Imperatives of Writing History." *Journal of the Philosophy of History* 8(2), (2014): 149–179.

Stark, Rodney. *The Rise of Christianity*. Princeton: HarperCollins, 1996.

Stone, Madeline. "East Africa's Plague of Locusts and the Bizarre Climate Science Behind It." *National Geographic Science*, 14th February 2020. [Available at: https://www.nationalgeographic.com/science/article/locust-plague-climate-science-east-africa], [Last accessed: 19th July 2023].

Stopa, Sasja Emile Mathiasen. "'Seeking Refuge in God Against God': The Hidden God in Lutheran Theology and the Postmodern Weakening of God." *Open Theology* 4(1), (2018): 658–674.

Taylor, Mark C. *Confidence Games: Money and Markets in a World Without Redemption*. Chicago, IL: University of Chicago Press, 2004.

Thaxton, Charles and Nancy Pearcey. *The Soul of Science: Christian Faith and Natural Philosophy*. Wheaton, IL: Crossway, 1994.

Thilly, Frank and Ledgar Wood. A *History of Philosophy*. New York: Holt, Rinehart & Winston, 1957.

Tidball, Derek. *The Message of Leviticus: Free To Be Holy*. Downers Grove, IL: InterVarsity Press, 2005.

Tillich, Paul. *Dynamics of Faith*. New York: HarperOne, 2009.

—. *The Philosophy of the Sciences According to Objects and Methods*. New York: Bucknell University Press, 1981.

—. *Systematic Theology, III: Life and the Spirit: History and Kingdom of God*. Chicago, IL: University of Chicago Press, 1976.

—. *Theology of Culture*. Robert C. Kimball, Ed. New York: Oxford University Press, 1959.

Timpe, Kevin and Audra Jenson. "Free Will and the Stages of Theological Anthropology." In *The Ashgate Research Companion to Theological Anthropology Edition* 1st Ed. London: Routledge, 1991.

Trevaskis, Leigh M. *Holiness, Ethics and Ritual in Leviticus*. Sheffield: Phoenix, 2011.

Troupe, Carol. *Human Suffering in Black Theology*. Sheffield: Equinox, 2011.

Ugbodada, Kareem. "Oyakhilome Reveals Frightening Story About Coronavirus and New World Order." *PMNEWS*, 5th April 2020. https://www.pmnewsnigeria.com/2020/04/05/oyakhilome-reveals-frightening-story-about-coronavirus-and-new-world-order/ [Last accessed: 15th October 2022].

Umeh, Celestine Chukwuemeka. *The Human Suffering: Concept, Nature, and Cause: Any Way Out?* Onisha: Rex Charles and Patrick, 2006.

Verby, A.D. "Evil." In Geoffrey W. Bromiley, Ed. *The International Standard Bible Standard Bible Encyclopaedia*. Volume 2. Grand Rapids, MI: Eerdmans, 1982.

Vorster, W.S. "'Genre' and the Revelation of John: A Study in Text, Context and Intertext." *Neotestamentica* 22(1), (1988): 103–123.

Wacker, John G. "A Definition of Theory: Research Guidelines for Different Theory-Building Research Methods in Operations Management." *Journal of Operations Management* 16 (1998): 361–385.

Wariboko, Nimi. *The Charismatic City and the Public Resurgence of Religion: A Pentecostal Social Ethics of Cosmopolitan Urban Life*. New York: Palgrave Macmillan, 2014.

Wariboko, Nimi. *The Principle of Excellence: A Framework for Social Ethics*. Lanham, MD: Lexington Books, 2009.

Washington, Nicole. "What is Self-Inflicted Injury?" *Medical News Today* [Available at: https://www.medicalnewstoday.com/articles/self-inflicted-injury], [Last accessed: 19th July 2023].

Weaver, John David. *In the Beginning God: Modern Science and the Christian Doctrine of Creation*. Oxford: Regent's Park College, 1994.

Wendell, Thomas. *On the Resolution of Science and Faith*. New York: Island, 1946.

Wenham, Gordon J. *Genesis 1–15*, Word Biblical Commentary 1. Dallas, TX: Wood, 1987.

—–. *The Book of Leviticus*. Grand Rapids, MI: Eerdmans, 1979.

West, Cornel. "Metaphysics." In Mircea Eliade, Ed. *The Encyclopedia of Religion*. Volume 9. New York: Collier Macmillan, 1987.

Westermann, Claus. "Experience in the Church and Work of Theology." *Word and World* 10(1), (1990): 7–13.

—–. *Praise and Lament in the Psalms*. Atlanta, GA: John Knox Press, 1965.

Western Region for Christ Miracle Crusade. "Takoradi Crusade – Testimonies | Bishop Charles Agyinasare," YouTube Channel: Archbishop Charles Agyinasare. 30th April 2019. [Available at: https://www.youtube.com/watch?v=uYIbV4TB24U], [Last accessed: 19th July 2023].

Wethmar, C. "Conceptualization of Sin in African Christian Theology." *Acta Theologica* 1 (2006): 249–248.

Wheelwright, P. *Metaphor and Reality*. Bloomington, IN: Indiana University Press, 1962.

Wilber, Ken. *A Theory of Everything: An Integral Vision for Business, Politics, Science and Spirituality*. Boston, MA: Shambhala, 2000.

Wilson, Gerald H. *The Editing of the Hebrew Psalter*. Atlanta, GA: Scholars' Press, 1985.

Wilson, Robert R. "The Hardening of Pharaoh's Heart." *The Catholic Biblical Quarterly*. 41(1), (1979): 18–36. [Available at: http://www.jstor.org/stable/43714617], [Last accessed: 19th July 2023].

World Health Organization. n.d. "Timeline: WHO's COVID-19 Response." WHO website [Available at: https://www.who.int/emergencies/diseases/novel-coronavirus-2019/interactive-timeline?gclid=CjwKCAiAp4KCBhB6EiwAxRxbpIIA2sok1TrgaFGDxUPNqnAVnOtrIg7ggUBSQgc-Ubz0ba_miMMFjxoCfpYQAvD_BwE#event-115], [Last accessed: 19th July 2023].

World Health Organization. n.d. "WHO Director-General's Opening Remarks at the Media Briefing on COVID-19." WHO website, 11th March 2020. [Available at: https://www.who.int/director-general/speeches/detail/who-director-general-s-opening-remarks-at-the-media-briefing-on-covid-19---11-march-2020], [Last accessed: 19th July 2023].

Wright, Christopher J.H. *The God I Don't Understand: Reflections on Tough Questions of Faith*. Grand Rapids, MI: Zondervan, 2008.

Wu, Katherine J. "COVID Combat Fatigue: 'I Would Come Home with Tears In My Eyes'." *New York Times*, 25th November 2020. [Available at: https://www.nytimes.com/2020/11/25/health/doctors-nurses-covid-stress.html], [Last accessed: 19th July 2023].

Wyk, I.W.C. van. "The Final Judgment in African Perspectives." *HTS Teologiese Studies/Theological Studies* 62(2), (2006): 703–729.

Yakubu, Nasiba. "Duncan-Williams Declares Thirty-Days Fasting, Prayers Against Coronavirus," My Joy Online website, 16th March 2020. [Available at: https://myjoyonline.com/coronavirus-duncan-williams-declares-30-days-fasting-prayers-against-coronavirus/], [Last accessed: 19th July 2023].

Yount, Steve. "A Century Later, Have We Learned the Lessons of the 'Spanish Flu' Pandemic of 1918?" *Denison Forum*, 6th April 2020. [Available at: https://www.denisonforum.org/columns/contributor-article/a-century-later-have-we-learned-the-lessons-of-the-spanish-flu-pandemic-of-1918/], [Last accessed: 19th July 2023].

Zwan, P. van der. "Some Psychoanalytical Meanings of the Skin in Leviticus 13–14." *Verbum et Ecclesia* 37(1), (2016), a1590: 1. [Available at: http://dx.doi.org/10.4102/ve.v37i1.1590], [Last accessed: 19th July 2023].

